from ♡

my heart

to *yours*

Part 2

more
Personal experiences
to highlight the
supremacy of Christ.

John Constantine

Unless otherwise noted, all Scripture quotations are from the Holy Bible, New King James Version. Copyright © 1982 by Thomas Nelson, Inc. All rights reserved.

Cover design by SCHOOLinSITES, LLC

Visit the author's website at www.frommyheart2yours.net.

Constantine, John R.

From My Heart to Yours – Part 2 / John Constantine

(e-book)

TABLE OF CONTENTS

PART 2

Introduction

What is this book about?

In one sentence, *From My Heart To Yours – Part 2* is a diary of sorts, a continuation of daily snapshots, glimpses, and Holy Spirit's early morning encounters with this writer, to experience Christ, *practically* and *simply*, and to KNOW HIM in His Majesty, Humility, Preeminence, Passion, and Love. It is learning daily the meaning of *walking with Him and Longing for Him Every Day*. And, *that's* my heart's desire for you as well.

At the end of the day, to have an existential sense of meaning, a *raison d'etre,* we must conclude that it's really "All about HIM".

Why this book? Honestly, it was never intended to be anything for public consumption, for its idea has been decades in the making and couldn't find even a window to take flight; either it hadn't developed mature wings of the soul or its wings unbeknownst to me were clipped prematurely. It's no volcano that erupted but was a heart that has been longing to express the basic idea found in this writing. That idea can be summed up in a word: Christ. Here is why.

I knew, in my humble view, and for no less than four decades, that something was missing, seriously missing, in evangelical churches as a whole, and I couldn't pinpoint what it was yet. I despaired trying to find the words or assemble enough thoughts to capture its substance, but like an elusive dream, a blurred image; it kept fading repeatedly staying out of focus often.

This book is a modest attempt to express regarding the unseen, to know what is readily unknowable by human means. I pleaded with the Spirit of God to know, even glimpses to quench my thirst, until I almost lost everything in life that can be quantified in dollars and cents or otherwise. Then some things began to make sense, slowly but surely. This book has seen the light at the midnight hour on most occasions, and the thoughts tucked in were a delight at first, but like the writer of old, when I swallowed them they were bitter in my gut, and gripped me more as the days went by and would not let go.

Here is what happened when I almost lost everything. On a typical summer day, the family and I got in the vehicle as we've done many times on Sunday to "go to church". But that day was soon to become as atypical as a day can be. Out of nowhere, an unknown car stopped behind us blocking our exit. I thought perhaps they were lost. So I stepped out to ask "how may I help ...", but discovered to my chagrin a hand gun was only few inches away from my face. Its bearer was anger-personified, screaming, cursing, jumping as though struck with an electric current, held the gun like a professional, demanding money and everything we had, and threats were hurled like volleys from his mouth mixed with his spit that found its landing spot on my face often. Shocked could not describe enough our state of mind, changed in seconds, unsure of the direction of life any longer. I chased him with my eyes as he made his way to my wife and son, screaming, threatening more, and looking for easy money to leave with, moving his gun from one to the other wishing it was a triple-barreled gun to point it at us all at once, thinking he was free to do so, not knowing that he was simultaneously gripped in the vice of lostness and hunger for a new day that never came.

In less than four or five minutes, he retreated to the getaway car with the gun pointed at us, threats, warnings, feeling his mission was accomplished, and we looked at him not believing we were still alive. The car disappeared as quickly as it appeared. We looked at each other, breathed a sigh of relief, and thanked God for life with a new perspective on the ease of death and taking for-granted of our day to day life and its blessing. I looked at my wife and son like never before, held them in my arms tighter than ever, cried with relief, thought of the church who were waiting for us at 5:00 P.M. to join them as we did normally for almost twenty years. I realized in a fresh way that I was gazing at a new reality like never before in my life. It was the reality of the earthly family God gave me "until death do us part", and the reality of my heavenly family that even death will not us part. Nothing else had such inherent value.

I realized that Jesus Christ came specifically to affirm these two realities, *the home and the Church,* to establish and build **both** to fulfill the journey's objectives in life and give Him glory, and in which He may dwell sovereignly forever. I also realized that what He gave mankind is *priceless*, and everything else has a price tag attached to it. I realized that He loves both, *the home* and *the Church* so much that He commanded that honor is exercised in both. One is a miniature form of the other, a laboratory in which we grow and learn great life lessons that can be exercised in the bigger family of the church. I was stunned by the fact that the world with all its smarts is very determined to *redefine* both, the family and the church, and impose its errant ways with the assumption that there is a better way. So far, the world failed miserably and the record of decades bears witness. I don't blame the world at all, but I do fault the church, and more specifically the so-called evangelical church. Here is why.

I expect the world with its systems and mindset to behave like the world, to think differently from and adversely to the church, to make every attempt at shredding the last vestige of the *Church and home*, forging a fraudulent license to what cannot be licensed, and changing, in summary, the good to bad and the bad to good, mouthing platitudes in dogged pursuit of hedonistic pleasure and loose acquisition of cheap money. Not only that, but they celebrate their accomplishments every chance they have. I don't fault them nor blame them, because they are behaving according to the very nature in which they are conceived and born.

But I do blame the evangelical establishment, and for many reasons. *First*, they claim to know the truth and flaunt the accuracy of "and the truth shall set you free", meaning summarily that the world has to become like them for the world to be "right". *Second*, they claim guardianship over accurate doctrine, and walk about making sure everyone within reach measured properly on their measuring stick of righteousness, and applauding anyone who changes his mind and joins their camp. *Third*, I have been repeatedly disturbed by the statistic that almost "three-quarters of evangelical adults have questions about their faith". *Fourth*, the disappointing statistics of drug use, divorces, and other anomalies have become *competitively the same between the church and the world*, and the differences between the two have become blurred. *Fifth*, the vast majority of evangelical members have more knowledge of correct doctrine and less acquisition of the character traits that made Jesus Christ so uniquely identifiable, not by friends only but by the enemies in His day. It was the enemies who described Him as "lover of publicans and sinners", and it was the Jews at Lazarus' tomb who saw Jesus weep and commented, "Look how much He (Jesus) loved him (Lazarus)". It was the enemies who walked away from the fallen woman whose only refuge was the Son of Man (God Incarnate) who stood taller than all in righteousness and truth and love. They knew He was correct not because of His doctrine but because of his love which they had no inkling of. *Sixth*, I was puzzled with the simple fact that Jesus did not teach anyone the agreed-upon "doctrines of the faith", ever! *But somehow people were attracted to him*, young and old, from various classes of society, the religious and the pagan, the upright and the fallen, the rejected found grace abounding in Him, and so much more about Him that brought people to sit at His feet to listen to the words of grace falling from His lips. The evangelical church for the most part has anything but grace, and is able to shower the world with all erudite verbiage except the "better way of love", and has lost the art of "him increasing" and them "decreasing", so much so that the world sees denominational names but has not heard of the distinctive "name that is above every other name". *Seventh*, the evangelical church has become excellent at delineating the doctrinal distinctive and has no clue of the Christ distinctive. Why do I say that? I say it because we are gleeful when someone "joins the church" as though they joined the ranks and can be counted as a statistic of Christendom but we leave them to the intellectual attackers to ravage their weak souls and tear their minds to the shreds of confusion and befuddlement. And the rest of us do worse, we fault them for not "going to church" enough to learn about their version of "Christianity" claiming it is the authorized version, when in fact they are yet to begin slurping the rudiments of what Christ is all about, and discover the power of the Gospel and the filling of the Spirit that enables them to have a changed resurrection-driven life and a renewed spirit every day.

I asked myself, why are the evangelical churches having such difficulty flowing with the love of Jesus Christ to the world around? Why are they holding on to the skeleton of doctrines but lacking the muscles and tendons of true Christ-like love that connects the body together? Why do **we** have difficulty flowing with the love of Christ so much that people are attracted to Him alone, and not to our program? Why have we equated our versions of Christianity to the powerful and holy name of Christ, being duped into thinking that people who come to "us" are the true Christians, not being able to define who "us" really is and what it means?

I asked myself why Jesus didn't teach doctrine in His days. Why did he not prove to the so-called enemies why His teachings were better, more "together", more profound, more lasting? Why did He not start a new school with headquarters and branches and satellite simulcasts? Why did He not publish anything? Why did He not have an army with weapons to fight? Why, Why?? And the only answers I could come up with were the fact that Jesus did not have any doctrines. In fact He *was* the embodiment of all doctrine. The doctrines were hid in Him. And to know the doctrines in the heart, people needed to come to Him and know Him and become one with Him, and know His love, and experience the power of His Spirit that flowed from Him to them. And only then, as it happened often, people were willing to leave everything and follow Him. In fact, His unequivocal assertion was that in order to qualify as a follower of His, one had to leave everything behind. Only then, He becomes their "everything", their sufficiency; and then life happens!

In our evangelical circles, we have become everything except Christ incarnate, yet again, in the flesh, in our flesh, and we experience Him so much that when we breathe we let the world know after His glorious resurrection that He is alive.

I begged to know how to express this nagging reality and stop faulting everyone else why they are not like us. We tried education, we tried dogma, we tried traditions, we tried renunciations of various types, we tried enforcement by various means, and every time we failed miserably, and doubly so for knowing the truth but claiming ownership of it, when in fact we were idolaters of a religion we created in our own images. We tried financial power, moral power, economic power, political power, strategic acumen, programmatic finesse, multiplied arrogance clothed in purple and red, or ties and white collars, or refined words and affinities, or providing humane services of health and shelter almost seducing humanity to be "Christians" and add to our numbers, not knowing, like blind leading the blind, that unless the Lord builds the house, unless the Lord guards the city, all work is done in vain. We blamed everything wrong on the savagery of the Muslims or Hindus or some other group of humanity for not allowing us to have our own utopia of religion. And like the Pharisees of old, we stood repeatedly in the doorway not going in ourselves and not allowing anyone to go in either.

To prove the wrong of our ways, God for the past two or three decades specifically has traversed many lands, moved so powerfully across the tapestry of human afflictions and suffering, has hovered through His Spirit over the obvious chaos called "humanity", and has breathed often of His Spirit, touched lives, opened eyes, found the *other sheep* of John 10, the untouchable rejects of the world and revealed Himself directly to them. As if discounting us, dismissing us, leaving us outside, He converted them to become His followers, yet again, like the early years. And now, these remnants in every nation, culture, language, and points of a compass, have come to sit at His feet at all cost and declare Him Lord.

The reason, the paramount logic of His cross, is simply that all that we do is insufficient to declare His glory. Therefore, He came to give life and make it more abundant, much more abundant. He came so that the principle of multiplication will take place again, meaning, that one grain must go into the ground and die in order to bear much fruit. In many places, the most ill-equipped in every respect are bearing the markings of His sufferings and through His stripes that they carry now many are finding healing in His wings, and are telling the world that there is forgiveness, life, acceptance, and unconditional love in Him who has been from eternity past the "joy of heaven", and now, "the joy of earth" also.

I discovered that the truth is all about Him. In fact the totality of truth is simply: Him. And unless we are able to reflect Him alone, we have failed abysmally. Perhaps we evangelicals would do well to resign our state of things, and go back to declaring Him alone as risen Lord, and the Gospel of His Kingdom has over it the banner of love, and His language is not human but divine, and His character does not know nationality or heritage but is supremely preeminent and grand that He still to this day refuses to be counted one among many, but as none beside Him.

To Him I bowed anew, and He is who my heart desired to describe with many variegated colors that only heaven can absorb. The labor pains of recent years have struggled to bring these humble thoughts, as close to reality as is expressed in the title: "From My Heart to Yours".

This document was started with no thought of publishing or making it public. It was a joy to sit during the morning quiet time and write some thoughts which seem at times fairly unrelated to one another. However, the thoughts reflected a personal journey, a discovery of the kaleidoscopic relation with the risen Lord and Savior. This exercise turned into a soul-searching exercise and, through various life experiences, became an examination of heart and soul in light of the Word of the Living God.

Major themes obviously became anchors for the writer's flow of thoughts. The Person of Jesus Christ and His centrality; The person, work, presence, and power of the Holy Spirit; and other themes that are at the core of the Christian life, such as forgiveness, faith, obedience, church life, application of God's love, and what makes the believer's walk challenging and sometimes blurred.

This document has scattered in it personal experiences over the past four years. The reason behind this thematic combination is to see the relevance of God's principles expressed in daily life. Much is written about sound doctrine. However, to me, one of the nagging issues in Christendom today is the soundness of doctrine but dead reflection of the life of Christ in everyday life. Surely, there is a bridge that is solidly founded in God's Word. Discovering aspects of that bridge is one of the objectives of this writing.

This author's premise is that doctrines are wonderful and easy to identify, and ascertain their veracity through the objective study of God's Word, but without the indwelling Holy Spirit and daily obedience, discipline, and application, such life is purely pharisaic and counter-productive in personal, family, church, and social life. *It grieves the Spirit and produces no fruit*. The fact remains that unless the grain goes into the ground and dies; it will remain alone and will bear no fruit. Rightness of doctrine is no guarantee of righteousness that's Christ born and Spirit-implemented. Beginning in faith requires faith for the rest of the journey. Only the Holy Spirit can sustain such a lifestyle, filled with the variegated beauty of Christ's character. Then I can worship in His Spirit (and my spirit) and truth. And then I can enjoy Him forever. The rest of the journey is simply diverse details making each one unique and rich.

May the Spirit who led with the flow of thoughts also grant discernment as each of us walks through the narrow gate and discovers the unique and supreme character of Jesus Christ, to whom be glory forever.

A word of thanks and dedication is in order. First, I lost two friends, Sami and Rodolphe, around the same time I almost lost my family, to the grips of death from a cancer that perniciously nagged them for two and a half years then completely devastated their bodies, and left their families behind to collect the pieces. What made them unique and alike so much was that both died young, both had two children and wives who loved them passionately, both were lovers of Christ, both bore witness to the awesome Savior they loved, both shared a living faith. Both were loved, not only by their local Christian group, but more importantly by those we label as "in the world" who kept close contact to the very end. They surrounded Sami and Rodolphe, not because of the illness but because of the love that Christ instilled in their hearts, and the friends smelled its fragrance and found it powerful and true.

To them this book is dedicated, and to the living proof they presented in a short span of time that *Christ can be real in people who are real and are willing to give up all for Him.* He bore the curse once for our sins, but will not be relying on human abilities.

A debt of gratitude also goes to those readers who took the time to read, and considered what they read a blessing to their daily life and walk with God. The debt extends also to the church of Jesus Christ in many locations with whom this author crossed paths. I dedicate this piece to the suffering church throughout the world, my brothers and sisters, in North Africa and the Middle East. More specifically I stand close to those who tasted death for the sake of Christ and died persecuted and *"this world was not worthy of them"*. To all who love His appearing, I affirm to you my love and commitment to know Him more, and to make Him known.

MEDITATIONS

GOOD HOUSE-CLEANING
From my heart to yours—

We don't have to pray for suffering and persecution. It's here. It's God's way to do His own house-cleaning, making sure that His house is *still* called the "house of prayer". Prayer is always intended to take place in His Temple, which now we are (1 Cor. 3:16). If church history, the record stands, the good news here is that under such circumstances, the largest number of new births happen and still "the Lord adds to His Church (His Kingdom) those who are truly saved (John 3:16). (Monday, July 28, 2014 at 10:46 A.M. CDT)

HOLY SPIRIT, HOLY LIVING
From my heart to yours—

Singing about holy living does not produce holy living. But holy living produces a holy hush that leads to singing glory forever. A common mistake we make while praying is that we ask Him to do for us what He instructed US to do in the power of His Spirit. The question is not Who Does What, but it is: Am I under the control of His Spirit? The old chorus says: "All is vain unless the Spirit of the Holy One comes down"

Living in the power of the Holy Spirit does not mean I become a zombie, but it means yielding my power to His, for He opens my eyes to see that my power is derived from and belongs to Him. It redefines the idea of "Living Accommodations". *(Tuesday, July 29, 2014 at 6:22 A.M. CDT)*

A SNAPSHOT OF TRUE REPENTANCE
From my heart to yours–

Feeling sorry and regret is not true repentance; nor doing penance, is. For only the conviction of the Spirit leads to change according to His will. Then He teaches me to hate the very sin I committed before Him, and abhor what disrupted the sweet communion we had. Then He teaches me to love Him anew, not because I can but because of what He did on the cross. ... Just connecting the dots... *"And He walks with me, and He talks with me; And He tells me I am His own, And the joy we share, As we tarry there, None other, has ever, known!"* (Tuesday, July 29, 2014 at 6:56 A.M. CDT)

"GOOD CHRISTIANS"
From my heart to yours–

Being a "good Christian" has a touch of deception because it gives the impression that that is good enough. Paul caught on to that when he said, *"For I know that in me dwells no good thing."* And if anyone has a question about that, just look at the world today, the so-called "movers and shakers", the money-changers, the people-traders, the ones who sent their consciences off on a twilight zone vacation, the crazed for fame and dazed by a handful of coins, and tell me that the world has not "gone to the dogs", in a manner of speaking. "Good Christian" has the airs of acceptability among people; and that's where the dilemma lies. For only what God thinks of me, at the end of the day, makes things "good enough". Taken from the yesteryears opera houses, the saying goes, "it ain't over until the fat lady sings". (Tuesday, July 29, 2014 at 7:20 A.M. CDT)

REAL FORGIVENESS
From my heart to yours—

Getting forgiven is one half of the story. *Living forgiven* is the other half. Combine the two halves, and you have the essence of the Gospel of Jesus Christ of Everyday Saints. *(Tuesday, July 29, 2014 at 7:29 A.M. CDT)*

WHAT IS THE GOSPEL?
From my heart to yours—

It is when the internal and external become one. The external is what people see, and the internal is known to God alone. It is when being forgiven and living forgiven meet. It is when God says "I did", and I say "I do". It is when I look at the cross of Christ and cease to be impressed with anything else. It is Christ and Christ alone. It is living in the realm and reality of "and God made all things new". It is God - *Past* in creation and revelation, *Present* in incarnation and sanctification, and *Future* in glorification and eternal Presence. It is the apprehending of pernicious sin on the cross, and setting the sinner free. *(Tuesday, July 29, 2014 at 7:52 A.M. CDT)*

"BIDDY" AND THE HOLY SPIRIT
From my heart to yours—

I found the common factor between the two, Biddy and the Holy Spirit. First, Biddy: That's the nickname for Gertrude Chambers, the wife of Oswald Chambers, famous for having his name on a world-renowned devotional book. It's one of more than 35 books that have his name attached to them. The fact, as I shared before, is that Oswald never wrote any of his books, but his wife, with the shorthand capabilities of more than 200 words per minute, sat at the back of the room, auditorium, chapel, or lecture hall, and took down every word that came out of her husband's mouth. Upon his death at the age of 43, yes 43, after she grieved over her love and joy, her companion and best friend, she launched a 45-year journey of compiling all of her husband's books, ON THE SOLEMN CONDITION THAT HER NAME WILL NOT APPEAR ON ANY BOOK, EVER! No one knew her husband better; she knew his heartbeat, his inflections when he spoke, his emotion and mind, his intentions and word choice. She was the most qualified to bring forth her husband's words. She said, when asked, "Just as The Lord called my husband to his ministry, God called me likewise. I just had to wait a few years." In summary, she was most capable and qualified; she knew him better than all, she wanted Jesus Christ whom her husband loved, to be glorified beyond measure. Likewise, the Holy Spirit, with all his knowledge, capabilities, insight, self-awareness of His person, He had one desire, and only one. It was, is, and will be to make known the Person, power, preeminence, character, qualities, gifts, and the very heart of our Lord and Savior Jesus Christ. Jesus said without hesitation about the Spirit, "He will glorify me because He takes of what is mine and gives it out to you." The gifts given to the church, while they are only useful when done in the power of the Spirit, when combined, they reflect the totality and full person and expression of Jesus Christ. Like Biddy, the Spirit was content with Jesus receiving all the glory, majesty, and blessing. The Spirit is always desperately needed in the church. The purpose is not to glorify the Spirit himself, but to lift up Jesus Christ. Biddy asked for one thing. The Spirit sought one goal. David said, "One thing have I sought of The Lord and that will I seek."

What is that singular desire of your heart? Is it Him? *(Tuesday, July 29, 2014 at 4:09 P.M. CDT)*

~~~

MORE LEADS TO LESS
From my heart to yours—

The American paradox says David Myers, is that we "are better paid, better fed, better housed, better educated, and healthier than ever before, and with more human rights, faster communication, and more convenient transportation than we have ever known." Alongside all of this largesse, however, are the signs of life in pain and travail. Since 1960, (the beginning of Woodstock and baby boomers), the divorce rate has doubled, teen suicide has tripled, violent crime quadrupled, the number in prison has quintupled, illegitimate children sextupled, and the number of those cohabitating has increased sevenfold. David G. Myers, *The American Paradox: Spiritual Hunger in an Age of Plenty* (New Haven, CT: Yale University Press, 2000).

This was 14 years ago. There is an alternative, and it's not religion; it's Jesus Christ and Him alone. That's why I know IT'S ALL ABOUT HIM. *(Wednesday, July 30, 2014 at 8:28 A.M. CDT)*

~~~

LONGING FOR HEAVEN
From my heart to yours—

I woke up this morning humming, mumbling words from long ago, and longing for heaven : *"There is coming a day, When no heart aches shall come, No more clouds in the sky, No more tears to dim the eye, All is peace forever more, On that happy golden shore, What a day, glorious day that will be.* Chorus -- *What a day that will be, When my Jesus I shall see, And I look upon His face, The One who saved me by His grace; When He takes me by the hand, And leads me through the Promised Land, What a day, glorious day that will be. There'll be no sorrow there, No more burdens to bear, No more sickness, no pain, No more parting over there; And forever I will be, With the One who died for me, What a day, glorious day that will be.*

He died and rose again, according to the Scriptures, so we can be reconciled back to God through Him. That's worth living for! *(Thursday, July 31, 2014 at 6:33 A.M. CDT)*

SEVEN SERIOUS DILEMMAS IN EVANGELICAL CIRCLES (SUMMARY)
From my heart to yours - (Series of 7) –

When followers of Christ overlook the following vital and powerful parts of their life, their failures are worse in nature and consequences. Making out of "evangelicalism" a mantra or hideout or savior only makes things worse, and distracts from the Person of Jesus Christ. Overlooking the power behind these items below render a life meaningless that overlooks what "The Gospel of Jesus Christ" is all about. They are: (1) Power of the Word, (2) Power of Holy Spirit, (3) Power of Prayer, (4) Power of Sin, (5) Power of Spiritual Warfare, 6-Power of Priesthood of Believers, (7) Power of True Discipleship. *(Friday, August 1, 2014 at 1:00P.M. CDT)*

SEVEN SERIOUS DILEMMAS IN EVANGELICAL CIRCLES
From my heart to yours - (1of 7) –

When followers of Christ overlook the following vital and powerful parts of their life, their failures are worse in nature and consequences. Making out of "evangelicalism" a mantra or hideout or savior only makes things worse. Overlooking the power behind these items below render a life meaningless that overlooks what "The Gospel of Jesus Christ" is all about. They are: (1) *Power of the Word.* Miracles are not a substitute; good works are not good enough. The Living Word is powerful enough to speak and put Spirit-life in a dead person in a dead world. If it is, by design, intended to shed light outside and give light within, not reading it keeps us in the dark about much of everything. Forty writers, spanning 1500 years, staying on target, and keeping the harmony and originality, demands the ever-present Spirit of the eternal God to brood over man and breathe life, then place it in man's hands to see what God is all about, and call man to a new life in Christ. Its consistent application across centuries of time, variance of culture, attacks of demonic powers, challenges of the philosophy talkers, whispers of those who devise evil to destroy it, have all failed. It passed the orality test, sign language test, all world languages, gender differences, age differences, political overtones, and devilish undertones. The only two alternatives are to apply religion by force or by biological multiplication. Yet we find that the Word of God thrives on dying, and still brings everyone to level ground at the cross of Christ. That's why we say: ITS ALL ABOUT HIM! *(Friday, August 1, 2014 at 1:02P.M. CDT)*

SEVEN SERIOUS DILEMMAS IN EVANGELICAL CIRCLES
From my heart to yours - (2 of 7) –

When followers of Christ overlook the following vital and powerful parts of their life, their failures are worse in nature and consequences. Making out of "evangelicalism" a mantra or hideout or savior only makes things worse. Overlooking the power behind these items below render a life meaningless that overlooks what "The Gospel of Jesus Christ" is all about. They are: (2) *Power of Holy Spirit*. Intuition is not strong enough. Conscience is not good enough. His Person, His Power, His Practice and His Presence radically transforms a dead man from the world, places him permanently in Christ; then puts him back in the world and keeps him holy and wholly from the evil one. The Holy Spirit is not the monopoly of Pentecostals, and is not impressed by all the rest who ignore His power. He has the monopoly on all that belongs to Christ and His Church, and intends to keep the Church moving forward with Him making everything happen that Christ intended for His Church to experience. The rest is simply "wood, hay, and stubble", and, I would add, "noise". He has the power and authority to invade, intrude infill, infuse, empower, give gifts, give words, and give grace. He desires no glory. The only attention He demands is when He points us to Christ in who "dwells the fullness of the Godhead bodily". That's why Jesus said about the Spirit, "He (the Spirit) will glorify me, for He takes of me and gives to you". The Spirit's desire is to work in the delivery room to bring newborns into the Kingdom of God, and in the hearts of the followers of Christ to conform to His image. He knows NO "closed doors", NO "high and mighty", NO "distance or dissonance", NO fractured life or dysfunction, to keep Him from effecting change, reach a soul, and radically change a life to love God and man, even the enemies. *(Friday, August 1, 2014 at 1:03 P.M. CDT)*

When followers of Christ overlook the following vital and powerful parts of their life, their failures are worse in nature and consequences. Making out of "evangelicalism" a mantra or hideout or savior only makes things worse. Overlooking the power behind these items below render a life meaningless that overlooks what "The Gospel of Jesus Christ" is all about. They are: (3) *Power of Prayer.* Personal daily practice and lifestyle of prayer keeps operating the life details from the sphere and perspective of the Presence of God. It plays the role of oxygen in the blood, and any spiritual "vitamins" even if injected into life will fall short. Prayers are intended to be a lifestyle of confession, of intercession, of adoration, of thanksgiving, of glory-giving, and of holy living. Prayer, not prayers, is what Jesus was, referring to a consistent lifestyle that was interrupted only by the Spirit's ministry to people through the Son. Prayer lifestyle focuses the whole being on God's desire in and through us. Prayer is not an emotional appeal for God to do what we want or even wish, regardless of how dignified we speak or how serious the circumstance is, but it is the more critical demand for us to live a yielded but full life, full of experiencing His Presence alone, full of observing the power of the Spirit, full of dirty hands and clean hearts not the reverse. Prayer is hard work! Maybe that's why some prefer to stand in front of people than in front of God. Further, prayer in His presence teaches us to stand flat on our faces, and to plead the blood of Jesus Christ as our only reason not to be struck dead in the Presence of an Awesome and Holy God. *(Friday, August 1, 2014 at 1:05 P.M. CDT)*

SEVEN SERIOUS DILEMMAS IN EVANGELICAL CIRCLES
From my heart to yours - (4 of 7) –

When followers of Christ overlook the following vital and powerful parts of their life, their failures are worse in nature and consequences. Making out of "evangelicalism" a mantra or hideout or savior only makes things worse. Overlooking the power behind these items below render a life meaningless that overlooks what "The Gospel of Jesus Christ" is all about. They are: (4) *Power of Sin.* It can cause serious damage to the heart, the mind, the body, the conscience, any fellowship, any relationship, any function, and for generations to come. It renders life a pile of fractured bones cracking and squeaking every time the mouth is opened. Please think about this: *how many sins did Adam commit to be cast out of God's Presence,* to lose fellowship in his spirit, to be on a path of destruction and lead a life of desolation for generations and generations to come?? ONE. But even all the power of sin could not hold back to love of God toward, for "while we were yet sinners, Christ died on our behalf." *(Friday, August 1, 2014 at 1:06P.M. CDT)*

SEVEN SERIOUS DILEMMAS IN EVANGELICAL CIRCLES
From my heart to yours - (5 of 7) –

When followers of Christ overlook the following vital and powerful parts of their life, their failures are worse in nature and consequences. Making out of "evangelicalism" a mantra or hideout or savior only makes things worse. Overlooking the power behind these items below render a life meaningless that overlooks what "The Gospel of Jesus Christ" is all about. They are: (5) *Power of Spiritual Warfare.* That's where real daily battle is. It is the frontline of every follower of Christ. Its duration is 24/7, and changes dreams to nightmares. It demands the heart's diligence, the mind's attention, a growing knowledge, a surrendered life to the Spirit of Christ, and recognizing that it is never winnable in detail or total without the Holy Spirit dominating my life start to finish. *The Spirit teaches us to choose our battles, and gives the discernment to choose our battles so we don't lose the war.* He knows, and puts us on notice, that: (1) satan is on the prowl; (2) demonic spirits are disciplined evil characters obedient to their master, and determined to wreak havoc in the church; (3) the weapons are not for decoration but for use in the Spirit's power; (4) we don't battle spiritually against people but against demonic powers beyond our ability; (5) our only way to win against them is to surrender to Him, plain and simple; (6) as his desire and intention is to glorify the Son, so our desire and intention ought to be; (7) He is with us until the very end, not the bitter end, but the Better end. (*Friday, August 1, 2014 at 1:07 P.M. CDT*)

❧

SEVEN SERIOUS DILEMMAS IN EVANGELICAL CIRCLES
From my heart to yours - (6 of 7) –

When followers of Christ overlook the following vital and powerful parts of their life, their failures are worse in nature and consequences. Making out of "evangelicalism" a mantra or hideout or savior only makes things worse. Overlooking the power behind these items below render a life meaningless that overlooks what "The Gospel of Jesus Christ" is all about. They are: (6) *Power of The Priesthood of All Believers.* Priests in the OT were intended to be intermediaries between God and man, to present to God on behalf of the people, to be servants of God among His people, to work diligently throughout their days, to remain pure and sanctified before they are able to serve, to know they are under judgment when they seek personal gains, and to be found faithful in all their doing. In the OT, everything they did on behalf of the people was *symbolic*, awaiting the coming of Christ. However, since the death and resurrection of Jesus Christ, as in the OT, Jesus became our Eternal High priest, and all those who are His followers have become priests serving Him in His Church. Holding on in the NT to OT pattern is enticing because it appeals to: (1) rank, (2) power, (3) control, (4) corruption, (5) tradition, (6) diversion, and (7) ceasing to be salt in a tasteless world and light in darkness. The Priesthood of Every Believer enables him/her (1) to intercede on behalf of anyone before God and plead Jesus' eternal sacrifice, (2) to serve God not people, (3) to remain pure and sanctified, (4) to serve the nothings in the world's eyes (orphans and widows) to reflect the true nature of Christ's love, (5) to seek no personal gains, (6) to be clean instruments in the hands of the Holy Spirit, and (7) to keep front and center nothing but the glory of Jesus Christ in real-time. All believers are priests. Having "ranks" as priests places undue burden and creates two classes in the church: clergy and laity. This divides people into two classes: Performers and Spectators. The Performers are the go-between, and the spectators use revolving doors and are numbed by religious talk and lulled into spiritual coma. *(Friday, August 1, 2014 at 1:08 P.M. CDT)*

SEVEN SERIOUS DILEMMAS IN EVANGELICAL CIRCLES
From my heart to yours - (7 of 7) –

When followers of Christ overlook the following vital and powerful parts of their life, their failures are worse in nature and consequences. Making out of "evangelicalism" a mantra or hideout or savior only makes things worse. Overlooking the power behind these items below render a life meaningless that overlooks what "The Gospel of Jesus Christ" is all about. They are: (7) *Power of True Discipleship*. If evangelism was so critical, why did the "Great Commission" not include the term "evangelism"? Why did Jesus not say: "Go and Evangelize, and Disciple, and Baptize, and Teach"? The reason is simple. Discipleship contains evangelism as the first event that takes place in the life of a dead person. But Evangelism alone can keep a person alive as much as a newborn can survive after birth and is asked to survive on the sidewalk of life. Evangelism demands faith - not in religion or tradition but in Christ. Discipleship demands obedience - not to people or hierarchy, but to the Spirit of Christ who brings the Word to life, and keeps the follower in the faith (see Rom 1 and 16). Evangelism cannot be separated, isolated, substituted, or minimized. Real discipleship is not a program or book, not seminar or workshop, but it is the combination of Life in the power of the Spirit and daily Sustaining Obedience that transforms life to be fully dominated by the Spirit. *(Friday, August 1, 2014 at 1:09 P.M. CDT)*

PRAYER AND FAITH, INDISPENSABLE POWER
From my heart to yours–

In one of his letters to Hudson Taylor, George Muller wrote: "I have in my own experience found it of the utmost moment to make the care about my own soul the chief business of my life. Now in your case, the temptation is, to be overpowered by the immense quantity of work to be done, and not be minding sufficiently your own soul. But this would only lead to loss. No amount of work can make up for the neglect of meditation in the Holy Scriptures and for the neglect of prayer. Moreover it is not the amount of work we do, at which our Heavenly Father looks, but the Spirit in which we do His work." George Muller, known as a man of faith and prayer, directly cared for 10,000 orphans in his life without asking for money. He was well known for providing an education to the children under his care, to the point where he was accused of "raising the poor above their natural station in life". He also established 117 schools which offered Christian education to over 120,000 children, many of them being orphans. Hudson Taylor went to China at 22, and served 51 years. He established the China Inland Mission (CIM). CIM was responsible for bringing over 800 missionaries to the country who began 125 schools, established more than 300 stations of work with more than 500 local helpers in all eighteen provinces. God can raise people like Muller and Taylor who speak Arabic, with clean hands and pure hearts. I'm praying to that end! *(Saturday, August 2, 2014 at 12:58 P.M. CDT)*

CHRISTIAN IDOLATRY
From my heart to yours–

There is the impression that when I become a Christian, I cease to worship idols that sneak into my life. May I suggest that we consider the following idols as likely and sometimes successful candidates: (1) When I make my allegiance to Jesus Christ submit to my allegiance to anything or anyone else, (2) When I give the deep-seated affection of my heart toward anything or anyone else superior to my wholehearted affection to my Lord and Savior, (3) When I allow anything to detour my life in the slightest away from pursuing Knowing Him and loving Him, (4) I'm stepping into the territory of idol-worship; I'm setting myself up for falling into diverse temptations; I'm exploring gray areas in my own wisdom and will; and I'm walking away from experiencing His Holy Presence in my life.

I've always wondered why 72% of evangelical adults have serious questions about their faith! I've always wondered why the Scriptures say, "*Examine yourselves if you are in the faith*"! "*Dear children, keep yourselves from idols.*" (1 John 5:21 NIV) May we always worship Him in Spirit and Truth. *(Sunday, August 3, 2014 at 7:00 A.M. CDT)*

WHICH - ER — R— U — IN?
From my heart to yours–

There is a growing trend these days of people rushing to the Emergency Room (ER) for the least discomfort they encounter in life, real or perceived, mainly for two reasons: one, because someone will be there day or night; and, two, because someone else will always pay the bill. Similarly, I find that increasingly common in religious circles. A church-goer who frequents his church a good bit reminded his pastor of that when he encountered a serious problem in his life. His comment to the pastor was, "That's why we have you here". Otherwise, the pastor confided in me saying, "This man hasn't changed one bit in his maturity level outside his comfort zone. No involvement in church life; no change in character or attitudes; no increase in his love for the Lord; no service given of any sort; Nothing!" That's sad! The other "ER" that I would recommend is another *Engine Room* (ER). Tucked away from view or access or public curiosity on a huge ship is an Engine Room (ER). It's (1) ugly, dirty, hard work, and goes unnoticed. (2) To get there, one has to go down. (3) Without it, the ship is never complete and cannot go anywhere, regardless of how massive, elaborate, accommodating, feature-full, or populated it is. The travelers will be very frustrated. Also, (4) this ER must be capable of moving the ship every time to its many intended destinations. Not only that, but (5) no captain in his right might would want to command a ship without an Engine Room (ER) in it. The Engine Room in the life of a Jesus Follower is a "Prayer Life". Jesus said, *"But when you pray, go into your room, close the door and pray to your Father, who is unseen. Then your Father, who sees what is done in secret, will reward you."* Which ER is busy in your life? Do you need a captain or a doctor? *(Thursday, August 7, 2014 at 9:43 A.M. CDT)*

THE WHOLE ENCHILADA (1 OF 2)

From my heart to yours–

As important as the task of salvation was, Jesus, the Son of man, found obedience to the Father of greater significance. He also knew that accomplishment of redemption and obedience to the Father required the full presence of the Holy Spirit in His life to make it happen; so much so, that He not only experienced the presence, power, and work of the Spirit, but He also knew that true obedience required daily complete surrender of Self (on his part) in all that makes him unique for the sake of living "to do the will of him that sent me". His life mission, his life's purpose, was to do the Father's will. The Father's will was not one of many items on his plate. It was, in fact, the whole enchilada. *(Tuesday, August 12, 2014 at 1:23 A.M. CDT)*

THE WHOLE ENCHILADA (2 OF 2)
From my heart to yours—

Jesus never said, "*I have a vision for the world*". But, he did say, "I have come to do the will of him who sent me." "Being", to him, was more important than "doing". A world of difference! He could not accomplish any part of the redemption plan without the permanent presence of the Holy Spirit in his earthly life. In fact, the "presence" of the Spirit was not enough. The Spirit took up residence in him, and took over with dominance of him, and willingly he surrendered his whole being to the Spirit in order to accomplish the will of the Father. Likewise, we, in our earthly journey, can "DO"" the will of the Father if we "BE" like Jesus in his journey. Three requirements: Obedience, Surrender, Singleness of heart. None of these ingredients can even begin to happen without the Spirit taking over our life, and molding us in the image of Jesus Christ. The rest is simply details. What makes us different rests in the details of our individual lives. What makes us alike? His likeness expressed in us. What is the common denominator? The Holy Spirit. What is the outcome? The glory of Christ. What is that masterpiece? Union in Christ, Communion in the Spirit, and all the love of the Father, every day, forever. I call that: Amazing Love! Jesus prayed (John 17): "*Father...for their sake, I ask...All that is mine is yours...All that is yours, is mine...And I am glorified in them...Let them be one as we are...For their sake, I sanctify myself...As you, Father, are in me and I in you, I ask that they be one in us...that the world may believe.*" *(Tuesday, August 12, 2014 at 1:24 A.M. CDT)*

JESUS NEVER DID, BUT WE DO
From my heart to yours—

Today it hit me hard as I was quietly driving to meet a dear brother; I almost ran off the road and missed my exit. Jesus *never ever* gave any advice to anyone; yet we do just that all the time, giving advice, or run somewhere seeking advice. I wondered, I mused over that, and then decided to remain silent in my grief because I determined it was better. Here's why: If I don't give Jesus to people (speaking Him, living Him, reflecting Him), I have nothing, *nothing* that has life in and of itself, because He IS life; He Alone IS life. Then I read: *"In him was life, and that life was the light of all mankind."* (John 1:4) All accurate theology is precisely and completely dead. All "good practices and works" have no life in and of themselves. At best, these are a Band-Aid to my injured pride when I heard Him say that I have to deny myself. And I find myself running to and fro looking for fig leaves, again. He said, *"I AM the Truth, the Way, even the Life"*. All else is "death" flipped over on the grill of human existence, smothered in flavored sauce. His Spirit, on the other hand, gives His life to see His glory and become His follower ... For Life. *(Thursday, August 14, 2014 at 12:48 P.M. CDT)*

SEIZE THE MOMENT
From my heart to yours—

When you are with someone in person, and they entreat you saying, "Will you pray for me?" Instead of replying, "Yes, I WILL pray about that", say, "Can I pray for you NOW?" That's what they are really asking if they mean it; they just don't want to be imposing. Oh, don't worry about people passing by surprised, or giving "that look". They all do much worse things in public :) SEIZE THE MOMENT, especially if you're in a Mideast country. Even the Muslims respect someone praying. PRAYER! That's what true ministry is all about. The Where, When, How, How long, and all other questions depend on the WHY. And you and I will never know the WHY until and unless we pray. The leading in real ministry always comes from the Spirit of Christ. Although Jesus, while on earth, was "the Father of All Compassion", He never expended one minute listening to 'people' as his motivator, but to the Father in heaven. The dilemma in ministry that lacks a prayer lifestyle is this: "How do I know always in whose power I'm moving and serving?" Sight is no gauge! *(Thursday, August 21, 2014 at 9:29 A.M. CDT)*

A CHRISTIAN CHARACTER IN THE IMAGE OF CHRIST- PART 1 - (1 OF 3)
From my heart to yours—

"...to be conformed to the image of His Son" (Rom 8) Some Surface Observations:

(1) Change is required,

(2) Change is to be expected,

(3) Change must be global,

(4) Change is personal,

(5) Change is done by someone else,

(6) Change requires complete surrender,

(7) Change requires complete obedience,

(8) Change brings an expected end,

(9) Change brings a new beginning,

(10) Change has a model,

(11) Change is the design of the Holy Spirit,

(12) Change is always for the better,

(13) Change preserves uniqueness,

(14) Change is NOT according to: (a) my desires, (b) my preferences, (c) without suffering, (d) without cost, (e) without discovering, (f) according to earthly models, (g) according to traditional preferences.

However, Change IS according to the desire and by the complete power of the very Living Spirit of the Living God, and in keeping with the consistent and perfect image of Jesus Christ His Son on whom ALL the Father's eternal love has been showered, and through whom ALL that is in heaven has been given to us in order for us to worship Him in Spirit and Truth, and glorify His Holy Name. *(Saturday, August 23, 2014 at 6:17 A.M. CDT)*

A CHRISTIAN CHARACTER IN THE IMAGE OF CHRIST- PART 2 - (2 OF 3)
From my heart to yours–

"...to be conformed to the image of His Son" (Rom 8) IF CHANGE DOES NOT HAPPEN, God Help, because we have chosen:

(1) to be rebels, even in the church or pulpit,

(2) to be created in our or someone else's image,

(3) to suffer the consequences,

(4) to depend on incapable resources leading us through uncharted waters without any compass except of my own making,

(5) to claim as mine what is definitely not mine,

(6) to experience sheer idiocy of going where no one has gone before and never getting there, and,

(7) to miss out on ALL that God in Christ has in store for me. *(Saturday, August 23, 2014 at 6:19 A.M. CDT)*

A CHRISTIAN CHARACTER IN THE IMAGE OF CHRIST- PART 3 - (3 OF 3)
From my heart to yours–

"...to be conformed to the image of His Son" (Rom 8) IF CHANGE DOES HAPPEN:

(1) I learn to walk with Him

(2) I experience His changing power

(3) I discover the essence of true change with a purpose

(4) I will be placed in a useful role

(5) I will be able to see others change

(6) I will experience His Presence, His glory, His anointing, His grace, His goodness and mercy, His absolute and eternal love He gave me in Christ Jesus my Lord.

......and this is only the beginning! *(Saturday, August 23, 2014 at 6:21 A.M. CDT)*

VALUE OF ONE
From my heart to yours–

When ALL die for one, NONE has any value; but when ONE dies for all, that shows the true value of *everyone*. His name is Jesus, and He made that possible through His cross. *(Saturday, August 23, 2014 at 7:48 A.M. CDT)*

AFFORDABLE SERVICES
From my heart to yours–

Today I am heading to DTW (in Detroit) then ATL (Atlanta) then CDG (Paris) airports. I already miss my two families, but Going in peace, and in the Spirit. Satan is such a nuisance. I hugged my

Honey and Son, but strangely more than ever before I felt that's where I wanted to stay, missing them deeply already. I walked toward the plane and my mind went completely blank about the subjects I was to present in Detroit. Then before takeoff I checked my email once more, and got a spam email with the Subject line saying: "Affordable Burial Insurance- Have Peace of Mind". Mental anguish, I wanted to stop the plane and exit, felt very useless, remembered what happened, and just wanted to go home. Then a sense of quiet deep within, and I was still. I leaned back in my seat and closed my eyes". As the plane took off, Joshua came to mind and God said, *"Don't be afraid, I'm with you."* I smiled and drifted off to sleep, remembering the words of a song: *"I love you Lord; And I lift my voice! To worship you, Oh my soul, Rejoice!"* (Sunday, August 24, 2014 at 1:10 P.M. CDT)

SATAN'S INTENTIONS
From my heart to yours–

Without doubt, we live in a world of rampant ambiguity, many doubts, and global instability. To be sure, we are wired to handle a certain level of these ambiguities with our intuitive capacity to think, create, and navigate through life. Sometimes, we fail; but all in all, we are expected to manage...up to a certain point. To counter that, I'm learning to be clear and precise in my decisions, commitments, thoughts, affections, actions, and words. I discovered anew that satan and his cohorts also have a very high level of similar commitment, and is very clear and ruthless about his intentions: to steal, to kill, and to destroy. *Father, I'm all yours, and into your hands I surrender all. Keep me as long as you think I'm useful, and*

grant that I experience your grace daily, and see your glory.
(Sunday, August 24, 2014 at 5:58 P.M. CDT)

JOURNEY SUPPLIED
From my heart to yours—

So, I'm going on this trip and God has already gone before us, even before boarding the plane in the departure city. I can't wait to tell you as soon as we settle down. I walked through security, through the gate check, to the 747 plane and can't wipe the grin off my face and can't stop shaking my head side to side in absolute amazement. We're leaving in about 20-30 minutes. It's not just amazing that we got a free upgrade for that flight, and six feet of leg room, and top level in the 747, but how God worked out all details, not only for this trip but He already answered a prayer that's been going on for six months. It was only icing on the heavenly cake. He's my Abba!
(Sunday, August 24, 2014 at 7:31 P.M. CDT)

ENCOUNTER AT THE COUNTER
From my heart to yours—

Part of what I said in a post previously: "It's not just amazing that we got a free upgrade, and six feet of leg room, and top level of the 747, but how God worked out all details, not only for this trip already but He already answered a prayer that's been going on for six months. It was only icing on the heavenly cake. He's my Abba, and yours!" Here's what happened: Steve, my persistent praying friend from Colorado, was already in Atlanta airport eight hours. He went to the counter and asked to have two seats for us next to each other. The agent couldn't divulge any confidential information and Steve didn't know what to say, but was glad when he saw me. I arrived later that evening and walked up to the desk only to hear from Steve what happened and that they wouldn't do anything until I arrived. But the young travel agent had a sheepish grin on his face.

Agent: Dr. Constantine, it's good to finally meet you in person :)
John: Excuse me?
Steve: What?! Dr. Constantine?? You must be a celebrity ha-ha
John: Yeah right! And who might you be, kind Sir?
Agent: I do this work here part time, but my real work is with a satellite station and I've been doing all the video editing of your messages and presentations with pastor Raif :)
John: Oh really now!
Agent: Yes, Sir, and I really love my work.
John: and you like your work?
Agent: Love it.
John: I've been praying for over six months with a friend of mine in Birmingham to find someone who did that and also knew Arabic.
Agent: I would love to help.
John: Jack S. is president of BBC school.
Agent: Yeah.
Steve was following the conversation absolutely stunned...
Steve: I *told* you John I'm going to love this trip and it already started :)

Then, we heard over the PA system: "All First class passengers are welcome to board at this time". ...and we sat down at 150 feet above ground grinning at each other and no need for words. *Oh Father in heaven, how wonderful is your name in all the earth*! (*Monday, August 25, 2014 at 8:58 P.M. CDT*)

GOD'S NOW (1 OF 2)
From my heart to yours–

God's "Now" makes eternity possible, plausible, viable, meaningful, and actionable. God lives in the Now - Always. The only reason He entertains the concepts of "past" and "future" is because of us, and the simple fact that He loves us, and doesn't mind making accommodations for our sake. However, He doesn't wish for us to be in the driver's seat hopping between the windshield view and the rear view mirror, once looking way ahead, and then looking way back into our past. The reason is that He prefers that we live in His Now, and walk with Him day by day. He answers our prayers also in His Now. That's why He's never late, never rushed, always moved by, not our needs, but His glory and endless love. Many times, just like kids who don't get what they want WHEN they want, we say to Him, "You don't LOVE me anymore." The next post (2 of 2) will illustrate how. *(Friday, August 29, 2014 at 9:14 P.M. CDT)*

GOD'S NOW (2 OF 2)
From my heart to yours

After leaving the Mediterranean Pond area last April, the plan with my Sudanese friend Nasser was to talk again soon after that and plan next visit. I made several attempts to contact him, but it never happened, for *four* months. I was getting frustrated, and felt abandoned. So, without worrying any further, decided to wait and see. I plan this trip to Morocco (with new friends) and to S. Sudan with Malees (a S. Sudanese friend I haven't seen in 15 years). While in Morocco, I get an email from Malees in S. Sudan saying he won't be able to pick us up at airport, and I need to rent a car (that's $100/day). Now, I hate driving in Beirut. However, driving in S. Sudan challenges all my existential reason for being, physical endurance, and mental acumen (which is getting less and less by the day)... Not to mention that in S. Sudan there are NO traffic lights hardly (not needed), and the one I noticed was blinking at me in sheer exasperation and sense of worthlessness, NO street signs, and cars/motorcycles go *freely* in both directions in the same lanes, not to mention on sidewalks too. So, I decide in Morocco, I'm going to try walking when I get to Sudan ha-ha. The next day, *one day* before leaving Morocco for S. Sudan, I get an email from my long lost friend Nasser. It was short and sweet. "Pastor John hello how are you, I'm in Cairo call me on (this number) if you need me. How is everybody? Nasser". So I called - after repenting for all the thoughts that rushed through my mind and words I had lined up to say to him....(of course! speaking the truth in love :) Nasser: "ah, yes how are you john? Yes I'm in Cairo. Are you still going to S. Sudan soon?" (Sic). John: "Ah yes, I will be there tomorrow. I guess I won't see you there." Nasser: "If you like me to, I will go back to Juba but we can talk in the U.S. when you go back." John: did you collect the information regarding the projects we needed to talk about? Nasser: "yes. Are you meeting someone else in S. Sudan?" John: "yes, I'm meeting Malees. You know him?" Nasser: "no but I left my car there in S. Sudan and I can ask my friend S. to pick you up at airport if you need him and take you wherever you need." John: "really?" Nasser: "yes, I will call him and he can meet u at airport". He couldn't see, but I had the *biggest silliest* grin on my face. Thank you, Jesus. While I give up on you often like a child, you always have a smile on your face, whispering to wait. *(Friday, August 29, 2014 at 10:02 P.M. CDT)*

SYNCHRONY
From my heart to yours

God's "NOW" and my "NOW" don't translate to mean the same. That's why His thoughts and ways are not mine, and my thoughts and ways are not His. And that's why He chooses to show His love to me on time, always. He also desires for me to grow up constantly and discover, not His ways and thoughts, but His immense love that took Him to the cross. To know Him! *(Friday, August 29, 2014 at 10:06 P.M. CDT)*

DIFFICULTIES WITH PRAYING PARTNERS
From my heart to yours

One problem I'm having on my trip with Stephen, my praying partner, is that I don't know when he is talking to me and when he's talking to God. He starts to say something, or we might be in the *middle* of a conversation. Then I look up and his eyes are closed or his face looking up and he's talking to God. Then he looks at me and thanks me profusely for allowing him to come along on this trip. And he came *at his expense*. Oh my God, how awesome and wonderful is your name!!! If you're reading this, I ask you: Do you have a prayer partner who hounds God on your behalf? *(Saturday, August 30, 2014 at 1:29 A.M. CDT)*

HIS THOUGHTS AND MINE
From my heart to yours

His thoughts are always better. Here's why: (1) His thoughts include that He knew me from afar and loves me (2) His thoughts are ways for the good of those who love Him and for His glory (3) His thoughts don't need planning, just execution. (4) He has all resources; He allows me access, not to His resources, but to Himself. (5) I may not know about people very much, but I know what His intentions are about me. And that's another reason why I love Him so. *(Saturday, August 30, 2014 at 1:38 A.M. CDT)*

JUST A WORD OF THANKS!
From my heart to yours–

Now, it's 1:00 A.M. Not a night owl because I went to sleep at 8:30 the previous evening. Very exhausted after speaking 9:30-2:30; lunch at 2:30; then 3:30-5:30. To be sure, part of the time was interactive, and the people were very transparent. They discovered how much it hurts to be transparent, but therapeutic as well. Time went by as God's Spirit spoke to hearts. All were pastors, steep in tribal traditions and associated conflicts. Naturally, these traditions came into the church. Their call to serve was evident, but their hearts were lonely. The content revolved around the power of prayer, power of the Holy Spirit, and His power to overcome limitations. It was obvious, God was speaking, because their words reflected their internal tribal struggles and personal heart anguish and their desire to be set free. Jesus said, *"The Spirit of God is upon me...and anointed me to proclaim the good news...to bind up the brokenhearted ... to proclaim freedom to the captives"*. May all our Kingdom work be fruitful to His glory. Yes, Stephen, my praying partner, was praying in the back. At times, I glanced and his face looking up was like the face of the angel praying and worship; other times his eyes well-up as he prayed for the people. We talked about a few topics but the Spirit kept bringing us back to communion with the Father, and of course back to the high priest of the new covenant. As I shared with Stephen the prayer requests each one wrote on a piece of paper they gave me, he selectively would take a few whom the Spirit prompted him about, and he prayed for them right there and then. Oh my, how sweet to always BE in the Presence, to HAVE access through the veil, and to know that what distinguishes us is that we have a God who walks among us, brings us into One, and who answers our prayers! THANK YOU SO MUCH FOR YOUR PRAYER. *(Saturday, August 30, 2014 at 5:20 P.M. CDT)*

WHAT PEOPLE SEE
From my heart to yours—

A Funny incident: I stopped at customs security checkpoint in Casablanca, walked through the metal detector, agent meets me on the other side with a Big smile, like meeting a long lost friend and says, "You look like a Lebanese, your face is Lebanese, your smile is Lebanese." Then he looks at Steve and says, "And your friend is NOT Lebanese :)". I said, "Really now! and how did you know?" He said "I've been here for 17 years and I can tell people :). And he leaned over and hugged me and wished me a "Bon voyage". I said, "Merci beaucoup". He said, "See! I told you you're Lebanese!" ha-ha. I mumbled "Oh God Help!" :). He said, "Pardon!?" (French accent). I said, "I'm very glad to meet you". Steve turns to me in shock and asks, "Do you know him?" "Of course not", I replied :) How can people look at us and can tell we belong to Him, just from looking?! But seriously, very nice and courteous people! Vive le Maroc! *(Saturday, August 30, 2014 at 5:36 P.M. CDT)*

IS IT THAT DIFFICULT?
From my heart to yours—

In an article that appeared Aug 31, 2014, entitled: "NASA Will Reformat Mars Rover's Flash Memory From 125 Million Miles Away", Robert Sorokanich, of Gawker Media wrote, "NASA's Opportunity rover is still trundling across the surface of Mars, more than 11 years after its 90 day mission began. But its software is getting bogged down, so NASA's doing a full system backup, memory wipe, and reboot." And I thought: So why is it so difficult to accept the fact that God can start all over with a human heart that's been so bogged down in sin and shame? Then I remembered that it is a "no-brainer" to accept that God shouldn't have a problem recreating man "in the image of His Son" since he made man in his image to begin with, but NASA just happened to stumble on this slimy robot that slithered its way to Mars and they got all excited about. Oops! Did I say that backwards?!!! *(Saturday, August 30, 2014 at 7:54 P.M. CDT)*

I'm learning that living in poverty is NOT synonymous with living in misery. Even Jesus, who was rich, made himself poor for our sake so that we might be made rich through Him. *(Sunday, August 31, 2014 at 12:45 A.M. CDT)*

WORSHIP TIME
From my heart to yours–

After Sunday worship that started at 8:30 A.M., ended 12:00 noon. Guests came to front and introduced themselves; crowd welcomed them with singing, clapping, and "zaghareed" :). The choir sang with clapping and dancing. Then one lady ventured out toward the front, lifting and waving her Bible, singing with "zaghareed"; twirling with the quartet in harmony. They welcomed her into their circle, rejoicing together; then they prayed with passion. No telling which dialect was used; everyone managed in understanding. The facility is used sometimes by different tribes (just for people from the tribe itself filling the place), and other times several tribes come together. Spoke from John 13:1-17 about what Jesus knew, his steady focus knowing that Judas was never on the same wavelength, his immense love toward the Father, His persistent love toward the disciples, his complete love that kept flowing until the very end, the firm but gentle exchange with Peter, the power of love that never fails. Sweet time, Sweet Spirit, Sweet fellowship, Sweet communion in the Body. *(Sunday, August 31, 2014 at 9:37 A.M. CDT)*

OPEN DOORS
From my heart to yours

When God opens doors, no one can close them, but He expects us to go through them unconditionally. If we choose not to go, He won't punish us, but He will simply find someone else. Why? Because it's all about Him at the end of the day, not about me. And the awesomeness is expressed by an invitation to join Him and see His love and glory. *(Monday, September 1, 2014 at 2:30 P.M. CDT)*

EAGER TO LISTEN
From my heart to yours

One of the powerful highlights of this journey is the many, many occasions where people were silent with desire to hear more about the "love of God manifested in Jesus Christ". It was captivating, it was healing like salve, and it was gentle and inviting. Many decided during the conversation to lay their weapons down when the Holy Spirit stunned them by the powerful message of Christ's love. An engineer from Zimbabwe, a businessman from Sweden, a restaurant server in Juba. And to top it all, one of the guards at the compound where we stayed, almost jovially said, "We finally find a white man from America who loves us". The strange thing is that we were simply taking pictures of them and us. I can acquire many earthly skills from here and there to promote the cause of Christ. But I have to "know" the wonderful love of Christ that will not let me go in order to speak it to someone I don't know. It is not words; but rather fire that comes to life. I learned that all my "Christian skills" are ineffective as to cause life to happen until HIS LOVE is communicated through me. And only the Holy Spirit can do that, nothing else. A line from an old song says: *"Amazing love, how can it be; That thou my God hath died for me."* *(Monday, September 1, 2014 at 2:45 P.M. CDT)*

WRAPPING UP
From my heart to yours

So we sat at the breakfast table, and I asked my praying partner friend, Steve "If you could redo the whole trip from beginning to end, what would you change?" He replied without hesitation, "Nothing. But, the better question is: 'what has this trip changed in me?' And I will tell you what it has changed in me: I need to be more like Jesus, I have seen that what people are looking for is not what I know but who I know, I need to be intentional in my life, and I need to listen more to the Holy Spirit of God." Then, without advance notice, he began to pray. What grabbed my attention, from his tone and inflections and continuity of thought, was that I thought he was still talking to me, but when I looked at him; my dear friend was talking to the One that mattered. My sweet Lord, what a joy to walk in your Presence regardless of the details! *(Tuesday, September 2, 2014 at 1:22 A.M. CDT)*

Quick Update: Just landed in Atlanta. Will head to Birmingham in an hour. God has been SO good, and can't wait to share with you. All that I need is prayer. I can summarize the trip by saying that your prayers carried me through this trip on eagle's wings. It's not fluff and emotion because what happened could not be explained except that God orchestrated it; and to Him we give glory and praise. *(Wednesday, September 3, 2014 at 2:58 P.M. CDT)*

SHAME, SHAME
From my heart to yours—

Shame has degrees but is certainly universal. It does not discriminate on any basis. Its stain has come upon all; and, *nothing* can take the stain of shame except a relationship in which there is total unconditional acceptance. And *that* took place at the cross of Calvary. His name is Jesus! And that's another reason why I love Him so. *(Wednesday, September 3, 2014 at 3:35 P.M. CDT)*

FORGETTING ALL THINGS
From my heart to yours—

At the end of the day, three things really matter in the economy of God (meaning, what He desires to accomplish). They are: (1) Faithfulness (2) Availability (3) Obedience The rest is details: where, how, when, how long, how much, how far, what circumstances, hurdles, challenges, etc. To Him, I seem to forget, all things are possible. That means He knows no hurdles, no challenges, no human infirmities. His grace is sufficient. Believe me, it is! Oswald Chambers prayed: "Lord, don't let me stay on earth one day beyond my usefulness to you". May that be your prayer and mine. *(Wednesday, September 3, 2014 at 5:36 P.M. CDT)*

PROPER PERSPECTIVE FOR SERVICE
From my heart to yours–

After three friends returned from Yemen, one texted me saying "Pastor John, just wanted you to know that we're back in town and would love to get together and update you." I replied with text saying, "Welcome back, would love to get together." Then I texted again and asked, "First impressions?" He replied, "They are beautiful people. I loved everything." And I thought, "Yemenis? What?" Then, I smiled, because I knew he's got fire within. *"The love of Christ constrains me"*. Here is why: (1) It's the proper motivator, (2) It's the proper starting point, (3) It's the proper resource, (4) It's the proper motivator of others for service, (5) It's the proper destination of service. It's all about Him! When my friend said, "they are beautiful people", I thought: He did well. Thank you Lord, because truly it is your work, it is your love, it is your church, it is your heart, it is your amazing grace that makes your desire happens. May your will truly BE on earth as it is in heaven. *(Thursday, September 4, 2014 at 3:57 A.M. CDT)*

FIRE WITHIN
From my heart to yours–

What could not keep the Son in heaven was *fire within*. Do you have fire in your heart? Heartburns need to be treated. But Fire in the heart cannot be quenched, cannot be controlled, cannot be self-initiated, need not be advertised, and cannot be marketed. It's *fire*. It burns within, and burns without. It melts a hardened heart. It melts selfish desires. It melts stubborn habits. It energizes the soul properly. It shapes character in time. Yet, it cannot be told what to do. *Fire has a mind of its own.* It goes where it pleases. And it burns everything in its path. *All fires destroy except the fire of Christ's love.* It brings dead bones to life. It brings about life where it goes. It constrains. It cleanses inside. It moves with determination. It accomplishes His purpose because it has His Name on its brand. Its fire is from the altar, preparing the heart to worship. Its fire is from the Holy Spirit, preparing a person to serve. Its fire is from heaven, declaring the Name that is above every other name. It is the fire of the love of Christ, not a question of its direction. But I know that I love Him because He first loved me. Do you have His fire within? *(Thursday, September 4, 2014 at 4:12 A.M. CDT)*

WHAT DO YOU SEE?
From my heart to yours–

The needs of people are so vast and shocking. Seeing them and knowing them is indeed overwhelming, but doesn't motivate to accomplish God's purposes. However, His holy love crushes the servant's heart, and then shapes it according to His heart to accomplish His purposes. Then, the servant doesn't see *needs* but sees *people*, and extends to them the same love that molded his heart and character in the first place. *(Thursday, September 4, 2014 at 4:52 A.M. CDT)*

Tomorrow and until Monday, (9/5 - 9/8), I will be in Toronto at MEBC "College and Career" conference. Theme: "The mind of Christ: (a lifestyle of decision making) for His glory" Session 1: Obedience is the twin sister of faith; Session 2: Christianity according to the flesh Session; Session 3: Practical: Does God have a specific will for my life? Session 4: Practical: How do I make the right decisions? Session 5: Actionable steps: What next? Where do I go from here? Your prayers are appreciated very much for His Presence, His Power, His Spirit, for His People, and for God to give me grace when I open my mouth. *(Thursday, September 4, 2014 at 7:14 A.M. CDT)*

ANSWERS IN LITTLE PACKAGES
From my heart to yours—

Onella Y., a girl for whom the parents prayed and God answered. She was born a bit early, but doctors are pleased with growth. We prayed again and thanked God for His faithfulness and care at every detail. She's a joy to hold and look forward with great anticipation to what God will do throughout her life. Needless to say, she's cute as a button. As for her parents, they are assured in their heart that "He who began a good work will complete it to His glory." I love you, Akad and Elizabeth! *(Monday, September 8, 2014 at 5:17 P.M. CDT)*

A GOD APPOINTMENT
From my heart to yours—

He said, "I'm Joe". I said, "I'm John". He said, "My grandfather is Yousef L.". I said, "I taught your grandfather and grandmother English in Lebanon back in 1975". Joe and I met in Canada. Talk about laughter and hugs!!!!!! I think I was more excited because I remembered how sweet, gentle, transparent, God-loving, and just a good friend his granddad was! I can still hear him laughing, especially when he was persecuted for the sake of Christ. He taught me to love people as we distributed Bibles and they cursed us, for the sake of Christ. My prayer for you, Joe, is that you have a double measure of your grandfather's spirit! *(Monday, September 8, 2014 at 5:32 P.M. CDT)*

~

Being on the cross with Christ puts a follower in the cross-hairs of satan. PRAY so you don't fall in temptation and your heart never entertains coming down from the cross. Jesus prayed. *(Thursday, September 11, 2014 at 6:11 A.M. CDT)*

~

BEING FAITHFUL
From my heart to yours—

Serving Christ faithfully was never intended for the follower to see what he/she can do, but to see what CHRIST can do through him/her. Having the brand of Christ on me makes it illegal to carry someone else's too. If I die with Him, He is alive for others in me. *(Thursday, September 11, 2014 at 6:20 A.M. CDT)*

~

TWIN SISTERS
From my heart to yours—

Obedience is the twin sister of faith. Obedience without faith is slavery. Faith without obedience is meaningless. Faith plus Obedience is Worship. For then I see His face, and touch the hem of His garment. *(Thursday, September 11, 2014 at 6:22 A.M. CDT)*

~

LOOKING UNTO JESUS
From my heart to yours—

Since the early church, following Christ faithfully has a price attached to it. It always comes without discount of the cross. *(Thursday, September 11, 2014 at 6:23 A.M. CDT)*

Loving Christ purely grows with time, but is intended for eternity. *(Thursday, September 11, 2014 at 6:25 A.M. CDT)*

"For in all things, He must have all preeminence" (Col. 1). He died in time and on time, so I can live for eternity. How can I not love Him?! How can I not adore Him?! How can I not worship Him?! His name is Jesus Christ. *(Thursday, September 11, 2014 at 6:28 A.M. CDT)*

He gave up ALL for me. That's a fact! (Phil 2) Is it too much to give up ALL for Him? That's the question. For me, it is settled. *(Thursday, September 11, 2014 at 6:30 A.M. CDT)*

HOW IMPRESSED WAS JESUS
From my heart to yours–

Jesus was not impressed by what impressed his disciples, did not value what they valued, and was not troubled by what troubled them. And all of that was not because he was the Son of God walking on earth but because he was the Son of Man who walked in the Presence of the Father and was always led by the Spirit of the God. That same Spirit kept Him and taught him to be in the presence of the heavenly father all his days. He calls us to do likewise. *(Thursday, September 11, 2014 at 6:50 A.M. CDT)*

Transformation was first exemplified by Jesus who emptied himself and learned obedience by the consuming power of the Holy Spirit. Then He gave us that same eternal Spirit to dwell in us to obey and to empty ourselves and be transformed for His sake. *(Thursday, September 11, 2014 at 6:54 A.M. CDT)*

OBEDIENCE IS BETTER
From my heart to yours—

Obedience breeds holy living, and pleads the name of the only One who obeyed unto death. Holy obedience begins in the heart, invisible, unreachable, until it emanates towards the outer shell of our existence and becomes visible. Then others see Him who was in us all along. *(Thursday, September 11, 2014 at 6:56 A.M. CDT)*

GENTLE PERSISTENCE
From my heart to yours—

True obedience is completely the persistent work of the Holy Spirit in us. That's why, as long as we are alive, He is at work. And as He is always at work, we ought to be as well. To obey is not external but is simply responding in complete faith and surrender to his work in us. *(Thursday, September 11, 2014 at 6:58 A.M. CDT)*

NOW ABIDES THREE
From my heart to yours—

Transformation has three major elements: faith, love, hope. Faith anticipates the Spirit's work. Love surrenders to the Spirit's work. Hope yearns for the day when we shall see our beloved Lord and Savior. Therefore, it breeds more faith, hope, and love. But when we are with him in glory, and see his face as the disciples did, faith and hope bow outside the door, and love goes in in total purity and surrender, ready to worship in holiness and splendor. *(Thursday, September 11, 2014 at 7:01 A.M. CDT)*

OBEDIENCE AND TRANSFORMATION
From my heart to yours—

The ultimate purpose of our personal transformation is so that we may be useful members of the Kingdom of God in this world, and give glory to our Father in heaven. We will then be like salt and light. Transformation was the summary of the life of Jesus Christ on earth. It ought to be ours too. *(Thursday, September 11, 2014 at 7:05 A.M. CDT)*

THE PLANE AND THE CROSS
From my heart to yours—

I was sitting in the airport and saw a United Airlines plane, and thought of the Cross of Christ that united us. And I thought: Both have a Captain, Both have a destination, Both have a Price, Both have many passengers, Both have a Brand, Both have a Point of Origin. BUT, this is where the similarities stop, because: For one you pay, but the other is Paid In Full; one has few passengers, but the other has passengers from every tribe, tongue and nation; one has United on the outside, But the other we're United on the inside; one runs out of fuel in time, But the other is powered for eternity; one has "customer service department" for complaints, But the other has grateful passengers for all the kindnesses and mercies and so full of grace; one they tell you "I love you" for marketing purposes, But on the other the Captain opened His arms and said, "Welcome Home!" His name is Jesus Christ! *(Saturday, September 13, 2014 at 2:57 P.M. CDT)*

GOD'S TIMING
From my heart to yours—

Dr. David and I have been trying to make this trip to the area happen for almost three years. For obvious reasons, it never happened. Then sometime in August, David called me from JFK on his way to the field and said, "Brother John, let's make it happen in September if at all possible." I prayed because the person I needed to talk to has been unable to call me back for couple of months. But then that same morning, I got a text, and all the pieces fell in place. Then Bonnie, his assistant, shows up too, and *what a blessing it has been*. .....and this is only the first day of the trip. I'm really looking forward to see what God will be up to this time. *(Sunday, September 14, 2014 at 3:44 P.M. CDT)*

~∽~

THE INSIGNIFICANT ONE
From my heart to yours–

"*As he was talking with them, Goliath, the Philistine champion from Gath, stepped out from his lines and shouted his usual defiance, and David heard it. Whenever the Israelites saw the man, they all fled from him in great fear.*" (1 Samuel 17:23-24 NIV) Dr. David looked at me while we were in Heathrow airport waiting, and said, "Brother John, I want to share something that has really touched my heart. I was reading the story of Goliath facing Saul and his army (in 1 Samuel 17). He hurled insults and dared them at least 80 times (morning and evening for forty days). They were obviously afraid and wishing they could just run away." Then, Dr. David said, The Lord focused my attention on that little phrase at the end of verse 24 that changed the whole picture. It says, "*...and David heard it*". Then my friend obviously touched deep in his heart, turned toward me and said, "Brother John, *one* person heard it, and that was ALL it took. The whole picture changed. Can you imagine what can happen if one person hears and with the Lord by his side takes action? Can you imagine if *one* person in Lebanon 'hears'? Or Syria, or Jordan or Egypt, or North Africa, or the Gulf? My, My, My!!!" Suddenly I had this longing, a longing for holy fire, fresh and new! Just imagine what might happen if only 300,000 in one day, throughout the Middle East, come to Christ!!! May I be bold and say, Just imagine if 500,000 or 2 million lift up their hearts and call upon the Name of The Lord!!! At the end of Genesis 4 it says, *"At that time people began to call on the name of the Lord."* And it shall be that *"Whosoever shall call upon the Name of The Lord shall be saved".* I thought to myself how UN-qualified David was: too young, untrained, unable by Saul's standards, mocked even by his siblings, beautiful but that didn't help, a shepherd, *so* insignificant by all standards, but David had *fire,* and David loved God with his whole heart. So, my friends, here's the contrast: Everyone else heard and were sore afraid. But David heard it too. I urge you not to be impressed or swayed by the numbers of people or multitudes of excuses why "you can't", or the so-called "challenges", or be deterred by fear or excuses or distractions on the inside, or what I call the "soft and reasonable intentions that get nowhere", thoughts of "planning your future" or "career first, then God" or why you can't. The fact *is* that "with God ALL things are possible". Peter said, *"God must be obeyed first".* ...and David heard it. *(Sunday, September 14, 2014 at 11:30 P.M. CDT)*

~⸫~

CATCHING UP ON READING
From my heart to yours–

Some books I'm currently reading are: *Living As Salt and Light* (by Derek Prince) - *The Insanity of Obedience* (by Nik Ripkin) - *The*

Insanity of God (by Nik Ripkin) - *Problem of Christian Leadership* (by John Stott) - *Revolution of Character* (by Dallas Willard, et al) - *Fresh Wind, Fresh Fire* (by Jim Cymbala) - *The Mother of God* (by Tim Keller). Challenging to the mind and heart to action. They are *Kindle*-downloadable. Read anything by Dallas Willard, John Stott and Tim Keller. Mike Mason authored *The Gospel According to Job*. It's a masterpiece. Almost all others have addressed the theme of pain and patience as an antidote. Mason, however, points out that Job's book is not about patience—an end in itself-- as its main theme. Interested yet?

What is completely "inspired by God" in these books are all the direct Scripture quotes only. Everything else they say describes their journey of faith, and you will find encouraging and uplifting, and calling you to action in *your* journey of faith. Looking to Him!
(Monday, September 15, 2014 at 7:33 A.M. CDT)

CHRIST'S MANDATE OF "SERVING TOGETHER"
From my heart to yours–

It is nothing less than heartbreaking that *church* people who call themselves believers and true followers of Christ (especially Arabic-speakers) and are involved in ministry, have a very limited view, if any, on the concept of "*one another*" found throughout the New Testament. In many quarters, it is completely foreign despite the culturally-driven lip service we offer when pressed. I add my voice to the many who are calling for *change* to the status quo. Here is how: (1) Beg the Spirit of God to help you to STOP thinking it (the 'it' refers to "working singular", "not trusting", "always questioning motives", "thinking you can't", "I'm a self-made man type", and such ideas), STOP, Because "as a man thinks in his heart, so is he".

The other reason is that there is *"a better way"* (last verse of 1 Cor. 12). (2) Before you remotely consider taking external action toward others, take internal action toward self, because that is where everything incubates and starts. Here's how to accomplish that? (a) Recognize it as part of the culture in which we grew up, and (b) drop what is destructive and aimed at protecting self. *Be Vulnerable.* Jesus did. A paraphrase of Rom 3:23 is "All persons in all cultures have sinned and come short of the glory of God". No Culture has what it takes to be "Please Him", for *"without faith it's impossible to please him"*. Jesus is the fountainhead of all true faith. Do you trust Him? Confess it (what you recognize in #1) as sin because it doesn't advance the cause of Christ, and if you and I don't get rid of it, we are counter-productive in the Kingdom of God. (b) Ask for internal healing in your heart, spiritual healing, of broken and shattered dreams and broken promises and dysfunctional lives that trained us in the art of "Giving Excuses". (c) STOP giving excuses, and (d) *Be* intentional and specific in your steps. Why? Because, *"the steps of a righteous man are ordered from The Lord"*. Other steps bring no glory to Him. (e) Identify by the Holy Spirit the cause(s) in your heart, such as (i) devastating fear, (ii) corrupting pride, (iii) desire to control, (iv) experience of rejection that you transfer to others, (v) sense of false ownership. There may be other causes. (f) Whatever the Holy Spirit points out, acknowledge, NO EXCUSES, and confess, and ask for forgiveness, and hate that sin with holy passion. (g) Take action in the opposite direction. Here is how: (i) Instead of "fear", Love with a pure heart, the kind of love that not only led our Master to the cross, but also crucified you with Him (*"With Christ I have been crucified"*, right?) (ii) Instead of "pride", Yield and prefer one another more than yourself; Submit, Listen, accept another laborer's input as-is. Pride brought the "hovering cherub" down, and it will bring you and me down too. (h) Instead of "desire to control", *Share and Be Transparent* (non-existent in Arabic culture) (i) Instead of "being rejected", Thank God that you have been ACCEPTED AS YOU ARE in Christ, and ask the Spirit of Christ to show you how to Accept others, especially if they disagree with you. (j) Instead of a "sense of ownership", share the gains and distribute the wins and burdens. If everything is done "*In His Name*", that means He Owns everything. You are simply a steward who is on his way out. (k) Equip others to take your place, and rejoice with gratitude that He, Christ, is making it happen through His Spirit. Life is too short. (l) Learn to forgive intentionally, because otherwise, you are not forgiven yet (as He taught us in the "Lord's Prayer"). And true forgiveness begins with your shattered heart and with rejecting all accusations from satan, who is the "accuser of the brethren". (m) Ask yourself a New Testament Church question: "How do I need to change (yes, You too), in order for someone else close to me to be successful, and growing, and effective, and advancing, and serving, and experiencing all the "spiritual blessings in the heavenlies"?

⌒⌒⌒

BETTER TO BE TOGETHER
From my heart to yours–

Again, it is crucial to have *change*. Here is WHY: The Holy Spirit of our beloved Savior is on the move, hovering over the chaos of the Middle East, and breathing the breath of a new life in places where individual recipients haven't even heard of Him. In every country, without exception, He is at work, and bringing people unto Himself out of darkness into light, from death to life, from brokenness to wholeness, and from hell to heaven. It *is His desire* that all should be saved. It is His desire that we love one another. Someone told me once about another believer, "I DO love him, but I don't trust him." *That simply doesn't work.* IF we don't realize that we are "*members of one another*", we are contributing to the fragmentation of the Body, pure and simple, and Christ will NOT bless any effort that doesn't have His Spirit A-Z. What do you say? Isn't it time? Please *pray* to that end. I know for me, I don't want to be part of the Laodicean vomit, or Balaam's stubbornness or seduction of money and fame. Do you? If not, what are you doing about it? It is *not* about denomination name or domination fame; but it is about Him, JESUS CHRIST, that in all things He might have the Preeminence. If I don't change first, I mean really *change*; I will never see the change in others and be given the chance to bow in worship to Him who changes not. Whether satan or Christ, it's about worship! *(Monday, September 15, 2014 at 10:19 A.M. CDT)*

PICK ONE
From my heart to yours

I've been wondering lately why Jesus never turned down anyone especially those who have been turned down by everyone else! And if you say, "Well, it's because He's Jesus, the Savior of the world", my response is, "didn't He call us to *Be Him* while on earth?"!!! Didn't he even stop the crowds to attend to one, only one? To find out why, my challenge to you is this: make a new list of friends, at least one from each category, whose names you will never find on FB. The categories are: a drug addict, a homeless person, a prostitute, an orphan, a widow, a blind man, a jail bird,...you know! This crowd! Here's my take on Him when it comes to these people who are "less fortunate": Jesus saw in them a gem, roughed up and worthless, and He decided to put together a new formula. It is this: (1) He became rejected so ALL will be accepted by the Father because of the Father's love for the Son (2) He became homeless, (Son of Man has nowhere to lay His head), so that ALL can come home (3) He became blind (Isa 42) so that all will see His face and behold His glory (4) He became worthless in the eyes of all so ALL can find out how much worth they have through Him in the Father's eyes (5) He was known as "lover of publicans and sinners" so that they find in Him all the love they yearned for all their life and never found it. (6) He became the father to the fatherless, the lover of the worthless, the living water to the thirsty, the manna for the homeless, and life to raise the dead. His name is Jesus Christ. And He saw in the eyes of the blind and the rest what sent him to the cross. No wonder they gladly come these days from afar and receive Him with their whole being. My, My, My!!! Not much has changed. Even the Greeks in his days came and said, "*We want to see Jesus.*" And His disciples had no idea what to do. They formed a committee (Philip and Andrew), and scrambled to find an answer in the manual, and didn't realize that the *Eternal Manual* was among them, and they didn't know. That's sad! No, even destitute people are not looking for handouts and programs. They are looking for Jesus. Do we take them to Him? *(Monday, September 15, 2014 at 2:20 P.M. CDT)*

~~~

THE GOOD FEAR
From my heart to yours–

It is always experienced and little expressed, because there's no need, It is what the eyes of the heart behold, and are content, It flavors the character beyond compare and enriches the heart, It is the hush of the Spirit for the Lord is Present, It is what drives me toward Him when I sin, because I know He forgives, It is what keeps me clean because His blood flows, It is what keeps my conscience pure, because I've been redeemed, It is what renders satan ineffective, because I'm justified in His eyes, It is what keeps me with Him, because His love is everlasting, It is what leads me to love Him, because He never fails me, It is what keeps the fire burning within, because it's from His altar, It is what calms my soul when storm rage, because He's my captain, It is what keeps me from sinning, because He means so much to me, It is what hovers over me, and I live in peace, It is what gives me wisdom to know Him, and Him alone, It is - "the fear of the Lord". *(Tuesday, September 16, 2014 at 1:44 A.M. CDT)*

KEY WORDS LIKE "NOW"
From my heart to yours–

(1) Fighting with GOD always leads us to surrender. And *that's* when we win. Why do we win? It's because He fought the battle in our place, and He won on the cross. Then He invites us to come to Him, on the cross, and be attached to Him eternally so that He may live the new life in the power of God's Holy Spirit through us. (2) Fighting with *others* always leads us to frustration. That's when we will *never know* who won. And even if we win, someone always loses. And that's worse, because that establishes firmly our self-righteousness because we would win only in our own eyes. Why we will never know? Because each becomes the judge in his own eyes, and there is no ultimate verdict. (3) Fighting with SELF always leads us to stagnation and ultimate collapse of heart and soul. And

that's when we will surely *lose*. Why do we lose? Because, like the dog chasing its own tail, first it's a game, then it's the same, then we run into walls of our own making that frustrate us endlessly, then bleed us until we die. And we lose, most times hearing internal mumblings, and at times hearing few vain words from others across the life-death divide that are only murmurs and clichés said about others too that make them "feel good about themselves" as they continue to run into walls of their own making. With God, one comes to the end of self and wins. With others, one comes to no end and spins. With self, one comes to a sure dead end. "There is, therefore, No condemnation NOW to them who are in Christ Jesus." (Romans 8). *(Tuesday, September 16, 2014 at 11:42 P.M. CDT)*

THE CHANGING FACE OF THE CHURCH (1 OF 4)
From my heart to yours—

One thing for sure about the Church of Jesus Christ of Everyday Saints. It is more vibrant than ever, spread throughout the globe more than ever, and with fire deep within to "proclaim the acceptable year of The Lord". To put things in perspective, (1) only 200 years ago the global population was one billion; now it is pushing seven billion. (2) Large groups of people are being transplanted across the globe by forces outside their control: nature, politics, and social change. (3) While 24-26% of the world has computers, those who have smart phones are pushing 80%, and at present (4) those who have all types of cellphones are more than the number of persons who dwell on planet earth. (5) the ability of spreading the Gospel of the Kingdom of our Lord is at an all-time high, and (6) there is no reason for anyone to think anymore that there are those who cannot not hear the Good News that Jesus

Christ came, died, and rose again, according to the Scriptures. I call that: GOOD NEWS by itself. Here is why: (Please go to part 2 of 4). *(Wednesday, September 17, 2014 at 10:22 P.M. CDT)*

THE CHANGING FACE OF THE CHURCH (2 OF 4)
From my heart to yours–

The One who said, "I will build my Church and the gates of hell will not prevail against it" is more intensely focused on what was planned in the mind of God from eternity past, and He is seeing it through to the very end. His eternal love expressed itself, manifested full of grace, totally undeserved, but made possible through His cross. The truth of the matter is that He is the only one working, and choosing those whom He fills with His Spirit to execute His purpose. And He has invited us to come along to watch His majesty at work. The truth of the matter, with all human efforts, is that it still takes a spiritual crisis in the heart brought about by the Holy Spirit to bring one from darkness to light and from death to life. This exponential growth, by human standards, requires revving up all efforts with the cliché "All hands on deck". But numbers were never impressive when God moves. The amazing thing about Him is that, as always, He delivers everything in time, on His calendar, in His power, in His Spirit's power, and in complete harmony within all that makes up His character as God. (Please go to part 3 of 4). *(Wednesday, September 17, 2014 at 10:22 P.M. CDT)*

THE CHANGING FACE OF THE CHURCH (3 OF 4)
From my heart to yours–

The "look and feel" of the Church is changing. Here is how:

(1) More people movements are taking place than ever before, and by the tens of thousands. All within reach of the Gospel.

(2) More turmoil exists than ever, and while no one on earth knows what's going on, God remains in control. He remains changeless and sovereign.

(3) The faces of those scattered around the world proclaiming the Good News to every creature are from places we never thought they would come from. The Far East and countries south of the equator have already sent tens of thousands fanning them where the need is highest: across the Middle East and North Africa, with one purpose in mind: Taking the Good News of the Kingdom to Every Person.

(4) Millions were looking in all the wrong place are now leaving their religion with hearts yearning and seeking answers that can *only* be found in the Person of Jesus Christ; NOT religion, NOT denomination, NOT cults, NOT dead traditions, NOT philosophies, NOT so-called "holy places", but ONE PERSON who loved them with an everlasting love and gave His life a sacrifice.

(5) More people, now more in the west than ever, want to know and get answers to existential questions. They are done with "religion".

(6) The "American Dream" is increasingly becoming a pipe dream and their sweet slumber is becoming a nagging nightmare. More people are in debt. Corruption is running rampant and in all the high places where the masses placed their trust.

(7) Evil in its many faces is becoming more pernicious and corrupting, and all hell is breaking loose on many fronts that matter: the home breaking apart, the established church, so-called "civilized societies", academic institutions of all levels, and governments...

All have shut God out singing "I did it my way". But the day is coming when God expresses the power of the final word and will say, "Then, have it your way, All the way". (Please go to part 4 of 4). *(Wednesday, September 17, 2014 at 10:23 P.M. CDT)*

⌁

THE CHANGING FACE OF THE CHURCH (4 OF 4)
From my heart to yours–

(8) Even nature is "groaning" with volcanoes, tsunamis, hurricanes, fires, earthquakes and such events. (9) Wars and rumors of wars are like the sands of the desert, everywhere. Restlessness abounds reflecting the restlessness in the human heart. (10) False teachers singing the lullabies of easy beliefs and prosperity gospel are leading many by the droves. (11) There are so many of the "little people", who have been marginalized, disenfranchised, duped and dropped from the map of human consciousness, who are coming "as they are" in their filthy rags, homeless, hopeless, drugged, and dis enchanting with the pleasures of the world, are coming to the One who has "healing in His wings". His name is Jesus Christ. And He is the same, yesterday, today, and forever. He came to give life, peace, hope, joy, and forgiveness through His shed blood, calling as many as hear to come, all the thirsty to come, all the hungry to come, and take from the tree of life. One good news remains. HE IS COMING AGAIN! "*He who is holy, let him go on being holy. He who is evil, let him go on being evil.*" The great divide is fixed forever, and there is no crossing-over outside the cross. *(Wednesday, September 17, 2014 at 10:23 P.M. CDT)*

WHEN IS PRAYER TIME?
From my heart to yours–

It's called, "Prayer Time". Dr. David, asked, "Can we pray for you?" One lady lifted her arms toward heaven and cried out, "Thank you Jesus for saving me". Then she looked at the doctor and said, "Yes, but when you're done praying, I want to pray for *you*". And OH did she *pray*!!! What an awesome God we have. She said, "Lord thank you for bringing me out of my country and I got hungry and slept on the streets but, Lord, I found YOU, and that was worth it all". Isn't He Wonderful?! *(Thursday, September 18, 2014 at 3:57 P.M. CDT)*

SNIPPETS FROM THE TRENCHES
From my heart to yours–

This grandmother, in one of the clinic visits, leaned close to the doctor after she received treatment, and held his head close. It was time to kiss the doctor :) Very precious in His sight. *(Thursday, September 18, 2014 at 4:03 P.M. CDT)*

We met a short pleasant-looking young lady who came from a Muslim background, and said that Jesus appeared to her. Upon request, she prayed for us, in the mighty and matchless Name that's above every other name. It's Jesus, and there is None like Him. *(Thursday, September 18, 2014 at 4:05 P.M. CDT)*

I looked at Beirut, a city of many complexities by the sea of many sorrows. But there is a Blessed Hope coming. *(Thursday, September 18, 2014 at 4:08 P.M. CDT)*

She said she never knew what a father is. From the wheelchair, she smiled, grateful, and tender because of many heartaches...until she found Jesus Christ. *(Friday, September 19, 2014 at 9:58 A.M. CDT)*

He caught my attention. Frozen gaze. Mostafa has one thing his mind. It is all the images of decapitation he saw. Now he walks around the house, says "Baba Baba" ("Baba" is Arabic for "Dad") and runs his hand across his throat scared to his core of his little heart. We prayed to the One who has access to Mustafa's heart and soul that He may quiet the rage and fear within. Please pray with us too. *(Friday, September 19, 2014 at 10:19 A.M. CDT)*

~~~~

LIKE SHEEP WITHOUT SHEPHERD
From my heart to yours–

A snapshot of what it's like in Erbil: (from Middle East Eye news agency) "People are everywhere - confused-looking kids eating crumbly stale bread, worried mothers wiping their children's faces or fanning them in the heat. A few sit in silence, looking stunned. Men crouch in the shade with their families, or carry rubbish to an overfilled dumpster in the middle of the churchyard. It's tidy, but there are too many people, too many thin mattresses stretched on the ground, too many bags stacked up with small children crouched nearby in the scrap of shade provided." You can find more. Sheep without a shepherd! I know, the Good Shepherd cares. *(Saturday, September 20, 2014 at 12:25 A.M. CDT)*

UNHCR Public Information Officer in Erbil told Middle East Eye, "Now those Christians are among an estimated 1.2 million Iraqis on the move." The game is changing, stakes are high, dreams are shattered, hearts are beyond broken, pithy words are found lacking character, evil is running rampant, leaders are in hiding, children are dying, resources are drying up, eyes have no more tears to flow, and satan is navigating his destructive schemes from the shadows. But, in the shadow of the cross are hiding thousands upon thousands who came to be washed by the blood of the Lamb that was slain, because they heard that there is healing in His wings and believed. The last good news is: "The King is Coming". :) His name is Jesus Christ! What a day that will be! *(Saturday, September 20, 2014 at 12:36 A.M. CDT)*

❧

As I read about freedom and life in Christ, it's amazing how no lines are drawn. (Saturday, September 20, 2014 at 5:06 P.M. CDT)

❧

Now THAT's Good News
From my heart to yours—

The GOOD NEWS is: There are no rejects at the cross. All are welcome! He was despised so that we will always be honored and loved in His Presence. He was separated from the Father so we will never be separated again, Forever! He was bruised so we may be healed. He was spat upon so that the least one may be kissed at heaven's door. He shed His blood for me, so that I may be washed clean! His name is: Jesus Christ and He's my Lord! *(Saturday, September 20, 2014 at 5:17 P.M. CDT)*

❧

More Snippets From The Frontline
From my heart to yours—

Too much is going on, and I had to hide. I found myself humming: *"My Jesus I love thee, I know thou art mine; For thee, all the follies of sin I resign; My gracious redeemer, my Savior art thou; If ever I loved thee, my Jesus 'tis now!"* *(Saturday, September 20, 2014 at 5:19 P.M. CDT)*

She said, I lost my husband and everything and my son is all I have. The heavenly Father said, "I have lost my Son, so you can have everything." *(Sunday, September 21, 2014 at 4:33 A.M. CDT)*

Had to stop by the Raousheh Rock at sunset. The beauty is deceptive because one sign that draped the rock expressed concern over the suicides taking place at the rate of one every 3 days. *(Sunday, September 21, 2014 at 12:03 P.M. CDT)*

Very special couple with a story to tell. They became followers of Jesus Christ, were serving with discipleship groups and about 30 handicapped persons, in country of origin. God brought them together from opposite sides of the track, and had been answering their many prayers to overcome insurmountable hurdles, and are learning the power of surrender and prayer. They've been married .... 19 days :). *(Monday, September 22, 2014 at 4:55 A.M. CDT)*

PROMPTING OF THE SPIRIT
From my heart to yours–

So, as we were planning some details for the week, it became obvious that there were quite a few things to do and the week was not enough. Then Sister Shams spoke up unexpectedly (as we were leaving) and said, "If it's ok, I can do translation for the doctor as much as needed, and interact with the patients he will be seeing!!!!!" Unplanned, Unexpected, but The One who "thrusts workers into the field" tapped her spirit to take part in a much needed ministry reaching out to displaced persons. She offered gladly, and we were very grateful. God bless you, Shams! Please, pray for this week. Tomorrow will be full starting at 8:00 A.M. The awesomeness of God is that He desires all His children to work in the Kingdom, and there is plenty of room. *(Monday, September 22, 2014 at 1:33 P.M. CDT)*

⌁

TALKING AND WALKING
From my heart to yours—

Anyone can talk about Jesus, and not even be a follower of His. But to live Jesus, to think Jesus, to behave Jesus, and to speak Jesus, THAT can only and always be done by the full indwelling person and power of the Holy Spirit. No book, No seminar, No mission trip, No physical location, No ministry, No "years of experience! No status, No country, No holy land, No holy man, No workshop, No CDs, No pulpit, No pastor, No One, Nada! can take the place of the Holy Spirit Himself, who is God and bring it to pass. It takes a crisis; it takes unconditional surrender; it takes giving up everything in order to be like Him, just as much as He gave up everything as well to be just like us. Like the song says, "All is vain unless the Spirit, Of the Holy One comes down; "Brethren pray, and holy manna will be showered all around". *(Monday, September 22, 2014 at 2:43 P.M. CDT)*

⌁

AT WHAT PRICE
From my heart to yours—

Now it's 5:45 A.M. Erbil time. I woke up shaken to the core of my being, as with a cow prod, by the thought that there are actually innocent people who have been kidnapped by evil people, and were abused and used, and are really sold and traded (like worn-out garments or vegetables), alone and lonely, having nothing but the shirt on their back, looking searching for food, shelter, and finding little or nothing. These people spend their days in utter shame and horror being handed from one man to another. The comment made was that they were taken (snatched) from their families and have become the "rightful property of evil kidnappers" for a while before they are sold again, and again. Finally suicide awaits them in the shadows of their minds and broken soul. And I cried because that's exactly what satan has done, and every single survivor lives in utter shame, trying to make sense out of their existence, failing again and again, and then they commit suicide in utter despair in one form or another. Satan came to "steal, to kill, to destroy". That's what these girls and abused women do when their families take them back (oh wait, but there are no "families" any longer because their flesh and blood rejected them now having difficulty to survive with that in addition to their own shame and misery), so much so that they in fact commit suicide being devastated by another host of abuse – (physical, mental, emotional, psychological, social, and mainly spiritual without them knowing), and cease to be humans who were designed to worship with our whole being. Care to buy one, I was asked. Anyone shopping for abuse and pleasure products? The scars are easy to inflict but way too much to bear! Somehow, we humans have been so warped in our collective soul that it ceased to be what it was intended to be altogether. Jesus Christ said "the Spirit of The Lord has anointed me ..... to set the captive free". He purchased us back unto Himself to be vessels of honor rather than shame. He swapped life, taking us from the shadows of death to hide us in the shadow of His cross, taking our shame and sorrow, taking our grief and our torment, taking our death and the state of being constantly stunned by sin again and again. Oh my sweet and loving Jesus and God who took my place of shame to set me free!!! The song says: "*How can I say Thanks for the things you have done for me;*

Things so undeserved, yet you came to prove your love for me; The voices of a million angels could not express my gratitude; All that I am or ever hope to be, I owe all to Thee." In deep gratitude I bow to worship you, Lord, this morning! I adore you and thank you for emptying yourself to fill me and us (all who love you with a pure heart, all who come to you by faith, with your eternal self). May Your Name be worshipped and glorified today by many, to know you and your eternal love that only you are able to pour, Who never decreases by measure and never have need or want. You brought us to you, Father, through the cross of your Son to know you, to love you, to see your glory, to take any sandals off our feet and know we are home. Lord, my prayer today is to give gifts of service to your Church to reflect to anyone they meet your true nature, to walk you here on earth, to speak your words, to look as if your eyes look, and to truly be what you designed us to be from the start, but now even *better, because of the cross.* May your Spirit descend on your Church in all the Middle East countries, bringing revival of repentance, brokenness, hope and salvation to many. I love you, Lord! *(Monday, September 22, 2014 at 10:30 P.M. CDT)*

PRESENTATION THINKING
From my heart to yours–

I offer a suggestion to all who are involved in one way or another in the promotion of or making any presentation or offering a sermon or lecture or putting on a conference on "leadership" to consider complementing their content on leadership with its other half and proper counterpart, namely, that of "Being A TRUE Follower". To "lead" intrinsically and inherently and seductively and subconsciously appeals to certain characteristics in humans (such as pride, self, aggressiveness, taking charge, directing, delegating, and all the rest), such that one can self-destruct easily in the long run, and now with greater consciousness of the matter, if they fail to learn (may I say, *first*, too) the art of being a True follower. The primary intent in leadership talk is to bring a person to consider Jesus Christ as the supreme model. Otherwise, we would be caught in improving people so that people will emulate other people in the way they think, dress, talk, walk, smile, and with all the clichés that bring nausea to the heart and soul. While we can talk the talk and present theories on the matter, I'm not sure we, in our human capacity and talent, have what it takes to transition people effectively from theory to practice in the art of "following in true Christ-like obedience". So people somehow get the deceptive impression that once one finishes the seminar or conference, and bought the material peddled by its authors, they are well on their way to being a great leader, when in fact none will guarantee in writing that if one follows their words he/she will certainly be a leader. But Christ did just that! And He put it in writing too. I understand, and I dare presume even, that talking about "Being A True Follower" does not have the *seminar* appeal as "Being A True Leader". We assume that all are reasonably acceptable followers, and now all we need are "a few good men". Has anyone looked in the mirror as a first step?? I respectfully say, "Not So Fast". Here's why: (1) We assume the best in people when we haven't done due diligence and presentation about the true makeup of people. (2) There is so much "under the hood" that is clunking with people and we assume it's easy to deal with. (3) "Leadership"-talk always appeals more to vainness, not realizing that in fact brokenness is the path to usefulness and leadership, not a good shine on an old shoe.

Or, was Christ wrong about it in Philippians 2? (4) Unless we speak Jesus Christ, the only true and complete representation of true leadership, we sell people short on the subject, less than what it was intended to be, and we will only get the $99.95 seminar special. (5) The Jesus principle still, in my estimation, remains best: He who wants to be first, should be last. He, who wants to gain, must lose. He, who wants to gain heaven, must lose everything on earth. He, who wants to rest, must tire. He, who wants to survive, must die first. Serving in obscurity is what He favors because that's the only way for Him to "have the Preeminence". Isn't that what leadership was intended for in the first place? His name is Jesus Christ, and that's yet another reason why I love Him so. *(Monday, September 22, 2014 at 11:29 P.M. CDT)*

INTERCESSORY PRAYER
From my heart to yours–

Prayer is much appreciated. - Demand is many folds beyond overwhelming - People are becoming mere numbers quickly and like shadows, moving about in numbing silence - Kids will always be kids. Consensus is that if you can get the kids to smile, the adults will too - "Standing in the gap" has been redefined - Satan is attacking viciously - The Holy Spirit is bringing people into the Kingdom, snatching them out of real hell. Intercession is appreciated. *(Tuesday, September 23, 2014 at 1:59 P.M. CDT)*

EVEN MORE SNIPPETS
From my heart to yours—

A little boy of eight, after a day in the camp, insisted on giving me a kiss. I couldn't turn him down. It felt like a kiss from the holy lips of God. *(Tuesday, September 23, 2014 at 3:22 P.M. CDT)*

Of a woman who never knew a father, I'm trying to capture the expression and find its meaning. I'm not sure it's sadness of pain or failing to make sense of what's going on but unable. I asked her if I can have a picture with her. She smiled and nodded, but with a touch of "thank you for noticing me still deserving to be loved again". *(Tuesday, September 23, 2014 at 3:25 P.M. CDT)*

My sweet friend who couldn't wait to have his picture with me. He ran and grabbed me, almost tackled me backwards, and knocked me off balance a bit. The very thought of someone even touching such a precious soul is heart-breaking. *(Tuesday, September 23, 2014 at 3:27 P.M. CDT)*

He had to wipe a tear before the picture. May have felt worthless, but I saw myself in him before I met the Master who came near and loved me. *(Tuesday, September 23, 2014 at 3:31 P.M. CDT)*

MISERY IN FULL VIEW
From my heart to yours—

Each has his/space on the ground, plenty of room to stretch the aching legs, trees for shade, make-shift residence, items stored in plastic or wrapped in paper, and time, all the time in the world. If I begin to think that improving the human condition is all that life is about, I should get really busy, right? Then to seduce my mind into a comfort zone of my own making, I began to think: "how sad and unfortunate", "I have achieved and am better", "I've done my duty and need to move on", "oh, who is that?", "it's so sad they don't have all the cable channels", or maybe the religious pious me says, "I'm glad God will take care of them" (whatever that means), and I move back to my comfort zone, and forget. But deep inside my soul, yes, deeper than that, I have a nagging pain that doesn't quit, seeing how massive and horrible misery and shame are, and I can't do a thing about it to restore the original condition. Then I look in the mirror and close my eyes. *(Tuesday, September 23, 2014 at 9:56 P.M. CDT)*

COMFORT ZONES
From my heart to yours–

I tried to gaze into his eyes, but couldn't, not for very long. I tried to find the connection "in our humanity" (as some say), and found very little. I tried to love him, and found that to be difficult, because my first thought was, "oh, what will happen to my clothes?!!" Then I could begin to understand how much God loved me on the cross and wrapped his arms around me and did not let go. *(Tuesday, September 23, 2014 at 10:02 P.M. CDT)*

THE BELOVED SON
From my heart to yours

What amazes me about Christ is not that He just brought me back to God, but that He attached Himself to me when I believed, and He would not let go. As He died, I died. As He lives, I live....forever. The woman, who wiped his feet with her hair, after she gave all she owned in life and was worthwhile, experienced the return of His fragrance back on her. That's what worship is all about. That's the love that will not let me go. That's the love the world is searching for. That's the mission of everyone who believes and lives, as Christ did, in complete surrender. So, He invites us always (you and me), not to just do good religious stuff, but to worship. How can do anything for Him who has done everything?? That's what it's all about. And satan knows it even. Think about it, and you will find that it's like a nagging toothache; it will never just go away until you do something about it. *(Tuesday, September 23, 2014 at 10:22 P.M. CDT)*

COZY SERVICE NEVER
From my heart to yours—

I have concluded that there is no such thing as loving God or serving Him in any form, or worshipping Him in the least, from the coziness of my comfort zone. He constantly disturbs all who follow Him to be sure they bring Him empty hands (nothing), that He may fill them continually with Himself. *(Tuesday, September 23, 2014 at 10:43 P.M. CDT)*

EXTRA SNIPPETS FROM THE FRONTLINE
From my heart to yours—

Please meet Yara. Very sweet girl who loves to smile; interactive, alert, delight to talk to. She said she wanted to kiss me before she left. I just had to let her do just that :). She giggled as she walked away :). She said, "Bye Amo" (Amo is Arabic for generic "uncle"). Then she smiled. What a joy to see innocence. *(Wednesday, September 24, 2014 at 11:15 A.M. CDT)*

I spent the day with the children at camp as the doctor was caring for them. The song says: *"Jesus loves the little children"*. I can see why. *(Wednesday, September 24, 2014 at 11:43 A.M. CDT)*

She couldn't believe that I asked her if I can have a picture with her. Just like a little girl that was missed in the carousel of time. *(Wednesday, September 24, 2014 at 11:47 A.M. CDT)*

❧

SUFFERING PLENTY
From my heart to yours–

Put your seatbelt on now. Unfortunately, this is a very true story. As you read, please see if you can formulate in your mind what might be the "theology of suffering". Meanwhile, time might be better spent by asking transparently the Spirit of the Holy One to speak to your heart. This woman to my left lost her husband, and that was hard enough. Then the extremists kidnapped her 3-year old baby girl few days ago. That brought a bitter end to her own existence and now remains alone shutting out the world, even in a room of 300, she doesn't want to talk or eat, and is utterly crushed. It was rare that she would agree to speak to anyone. She allowed me. I spoke to her; embraced and prayed with her while she stayed gazing toward the floor. She rested her head on my chest and cried bitter tears and in silence. I kissed her head and froze for a moment to soak in the moment with God. Time stood still, but somehow her anguish made its way to my heart as her eyes welled up in silence. I promised her that many will pray for her. I'm finding that in an evil world, the only antidote to evil is the love of Christ, expressed in the cross, and is communicated through each one of us who call ourselves "followers of Christ". Please, let's not squabble, shooting religious, artificially-dignified, theological bullets that are dry, cold, and dead, while the world is hurting and bleeding. Religiosity is no cover for inability to show and communicate the love of Christ to the "undeserving". May we always remember that at one time we all were "undeserving" but He made us worthy. Love to All, John. *(Wednesday, September 24, 2014 at 1:25 P.M. CDT)*

WORK WHILE IT IS DAY
From my heart to yours–

At the end of a busy day, in the makeshift hall, formerly used for wedding celebrations, but now occupied by 150 families who slept there, many came together toward the front. Many others decided to stay in their carved-out spaces on the floor and listened from a distance. Of course, the children wanted to come closer than all. Took few minutes to share with them about the love of God poured out toward us through Christ, about their conditions that will change one day, about their stresses, losses, and frustrations, about hope, faith and love, about their children who cannot express but doesn't mean they are numb; that parents can succeed without knowing it because in the frequent gentle embracing of their children there is therapy and release of tension and in the cuddling of their little ones they can understand more completely what it means to be truly vulnerable; just because they are going through their own crisis and can growl as they please, doesn't mean their children with squeaky voices who can't raise their voices and don't have the ugly vocabulary adults learned, can't also be given the chance to spread their wings and fly one day into the face of the sun. The adults will have created a new and better generation for sure. But, ah, the sad part is that adults may have forgotten the language of children who can love endlessly, and have acquired useless skills toward a loving heart; that by loving their kids, they experience the love of Him who said "Don't keep children from coming to me because of such is the kingdom of heaven." The team members were recognized, those who traveled and the locals who pressed us and wanted to take part, and gladly stayed with us for 12 hours yesterday despite obvious signs of fatigue in their eyes. Then we thanked them for giving us the opportunity to serve them because it's "All about Him". Of course, I had to have my moment with the kids. Then we prayed; I told them that I will lead in prayer first, they can listen as I pray alone. Then we can all share together in the Lord's Prayer out loud. However, as I started praying, they started repeating out loud every phrase I said. I paused; I wasn't expecting it; I choked, but thanked God in a split second for the wide open door He gave us all to enter His holy place and lift our hearts and eyes toward Him, then continued with my prayer. The kids prayed and repeated the phrases louder than the adults (surprised?), then concluded with what the Master taught. Interestingly, one little boy kept walking quietly out with us after we packed our bags and then down the marble stairs then across the street to the waiting van. I glanced and noticed him. He looked up and said, "Amo, ana bahibbak (I love u)". I was busy loading the vehicle and getting one more piece of meds to an older man. I asked the little 10-year old, "what?" He repeated what he said "Ana ba-hibbak" (Arabic for *I love you)*, then he added, "moumkin aboosak? (Arabic for *Can I kiss you?*)" I said, "You want to?" He said in Arabic "Ah" (meaning *Yes*). I leaned toward him, hugged him and gave him my cheek to kiss. To him, it was a heartfelt "thank you". To me, that was a kiss from the lips of God. What a moment of intersection between the free human will (of a little boy) and the sovereign grace of God! What a wonderful Savior we have! Isn't He really Wonderful? What honor, what joy, what privilege He gives us to serve Him! His name is Jesus

Christ, and that's yet another reason why I love Him so. *(Wednesday, September 24, 2014 at 11:10 P.M. CDT)*

INSIGNIFICANCE REVIEWED
From my heart to yours–

The value of my Insignificance lies not in what or how hard I try for Christ, but in what I'm sure He alone can accomplish. The "icing on the cake" is not that He accomplishes it, but in that He invites me to watch Him and worship Him every day of my life. And I look at what He completed and say, "How marvelous is your name, Oh Lord, in all the earth." Then it will be night; then a new day begins... ...forever. *(Thursday, September 25, 2014 at 4:43 P.M. CDT)*

Now it's 12:45 A.M. Friday morning. Agenda, subject to change: (1) We leave at 8:30 A.M. to meet one family for breakfast, (2) Make three stops at special camps, (3) Head to Erbil Airport at 2:00 P.M. on our way home. There is so much work to be done, but there are enough hours in the day to only do the work of Him who sent us. In God's economy, there *are* enough hours to complete His work because it is HIM who sent us and works through us. *(Thursday, September 25, 2014 at 4:52 P.M. CDT)*

DIVINE INTERRUPTIONS
From my heart to yours–

The plan on earth was to have breakfast and go. Food was good, but God had more work to do. They heard the doctor was in the house, and they brought their son. The father's heart was broken, mumbled few words but anguish filled his heart. His son has brain tumor needing surgery. The grandfather was like a caged lion. He said (about the father), "he's my only son", then pointed to his grandson and said, "And he's the only son too". The Father's work is done when He says so. Our job is to remain: - Faithful - Available – Obedient. *(Friday, September 26, 2014 at 3:19 A.M. CDT)*

GLIMPSES OF HOPE(LESSNESS)
From my heart to yours–

A refugee woman crouched on the ground. She wouldn't even acknowledge my existence or presence even, because she lost her entire altogether. I asked, and found out she lost everything, and walked for two days. Destination: Unknown. I couldn't think of how to get her there. *(Saturday, September 27, 2014 at 1:20 A.M. CDT)*

One of the tribe's leaders complained that people come, people click their cameras, people make promises, but people don't live up to their promises. Said he was very happy to meet Christians because they love, they care, they stay with him and check up on him. Said, Christians have hope and he wants that. *(Saturday, September 27, 2014 at 1:24 A.M. CDT)*

Haunting Images, Daunting Task, Awesome God. He is so, because he brings hope, faith, and love and keeps bringing people to Himself. Here are some of these images: *(Saturday, September 27, 2014 at 2:03 A.M. CDT)*

FORM AND SUBSTANCE
From my heart to yours–

"Form" matters to all religions except Christianity. However, Jesus Christ did not come to give another religion and form, but He came to give life. He came to give a reason for the "why not". *(Saturday, September 27, 2014 at 3:08 A.M. CDT)*

KINGDOM WORK
From my heart to yours—

I'm discovering that my usefulness to the Holy Spirit in Kingdom work is not tied to what I learned in school nor to what others say I can do, but what the Holy Spirit instills in my heart day by day, for He expects obedience not know-how, availability not feasibility, faithfulness not hard work. He is prepared to cut me to pieces (like Jacob), take away every last crutch in my earthly existence, and recreate me anew in the image of Christ, as only He can, in order to accomplish His purpose through me. And the whole time, I know that He loves me, because he never leaves my side. *(Sunday, September 28, 2014 at 7:32 P.M. CDT)*

ORGANIC LIVING
From my heart to yours—

I'm discovering that the Holy Spirit, uncompromisingly, insists on hovering over the Church alone to create, not employees or structure for human understanding and edification, but a royal priesthood, very peculiar people, all His, without price tag, dressed in holiness and destined to glorify Him who laid His life willingly for her. This is only the beginning; and *If* I think otherwise, I'm the consummate fool par excellence. *(Sunday, September 28, 2014 at 9:53 P.M. CDT)*

ALL FACES ARE THE SAME
From my heart to yours–

Many said the Yazidis fear satan, and don't wish anyone to say something bad about him. I asked the Yazidi tribesman "May I pray with you?" The reply, with hands raised toward heaven, "I wish you would, because we need it more than you know." *(Sunday, September 28, 2014 at 9:18 P.M. CDT)*

EXISTENTIAL QUEST
From my heart to yours–

I'm discovering in the midst of human misery that He doesn't exist for me/us, but in fact I exist for Him. He is not a relief agency even though He said "Come unto me all you who are heavy-laden and I will give you rest". The agency of the Holy Spirit on the other hand releases me to be useful, and all along I'm experiencing His amazing grace making Christ the sum total of my story. I'm discovering that when earth ceases to have any value in my eyes, He opens my eyes to see Him like never before, and I take my shoes off and worship. And that's a daily journey. "One thing I have asked of the Lord..." *(Sunday, September 28, 2014 at 9:53 P.M. CDT)*

WHO CARES
From my heart to yours–

William Leslie served in the dense jungles of the Congo for 17 years, and concluded that he was a failure. He returned home and died after few years. Then 84 years later, others went and discovered a network of churches planted as a consequence of his faithful service.

One location had built a massive structure that seated over 1000 people who gathered to worship. A "nobody" who is serving faithfully is always a "somebody" with God. The reason is not the person, but it's God. For God does not send the equipped, but He equips the sent. For us, we could possibly call it: "Faith". But for God, He faithfully calls it: "Possible". *(Monday, September 29, 2014 at 9:54 P.M. CDT)*

~~~

TOUCHING LIVES
From my heart to yours–

Touching people's lives is not because we know Biblical doctrines and principles, as important as those are, but it's always the work of the Holy Spirit who weaves through the tapestry of God's love and reaches out to touch the heart of people for whom Christ died and rose again. Being "led by the Spirit" (Romans 8:14) is when we step into the realm of the Holy Spirit's flowing through us toward others. It's not about me, but it's about Him, Always! *(Monday, September 29, 2014 at 10:05 P.M. CDT)*

~~~

PLEASING HIM ALONE
From my heart to yours–

Being "led by the Spirit" distinguishes the spectator from the musician in the symphony called: "Ministry". For no orchestra performs for people but for the Maestro. When he smiles, they know they did well. Words are optional. May we never think for one moment that He relinquished any part of governance or execution to a man-made organizational outfit or a local church that's not filled by Him who fills all, being mindful the Church is the organism that has life in and of itself. Any organization never does. Aaron was anointed in his holy garment for service unto God. That never meant that his children inherited the garment and same anointing. They had to be anointed separately, and only to serve in the Tabernacle where God was present. Walking by faith happens when I raise my foot to walk, and the Holy Spirit places it where He pleases, and I know it. "The steps of a righteous man are ordered from the Lord". *(Monday, September 29, 2014 at 10:19 P.M. CDT)*

SIMPLE QUESTION
From my heart to yours—

To serve Him properly, I either forget who I am or I forget who He is. The rest is mere details. "He must increase and I must decrease." - John Baptist

Living for Christ is the character connection to Him. It's my life in Him through the Holy Spirit. Living Christ is character connection to people. It's His life in me through the same Holy Spirit. Two sides of the same coin. Single-sided coin is counterfeit. *(Monday, September 29, 2014 at 10:29 P.M. CDT)*

LOVING GOD COMPLETELY
From my heart to yours—

Loving God with all of my heart and mind and soul can only be accomplished by the full power and presence of the Holy Spirit in my life. He declines any negotiations on account of the high cost paid at Calvary. Since His motivation was love, He inquires about mine, and offers me something better. That's another reason why I can't settle for less than His love. *(Tuesday, September 30, 2014 at 6:53 A.M. CDT)*

JESUS SPEAKING TO PEOPLE
From my heart to yours–

An Incomplete insight into the mind of Jesus - when He spoke with PEOPLE: Jesus was simply different. No one knew exactly what to do with Him, how to speak to Him, how to approach Him, or the reason why He did what He did. Yet when He tried to explain, few understood what He meant, and usually they were not the ones you'd expect. He didn't walk like the big guys, or the religiously dignified, or the well-to-do, or the overly sophisticated. He respected all, but had few choice words for certain ones, No, not the "little guys". He didn't side with the underdog "just because"; He didn't go overboard with anything. He was always punctual, specific with His words, and always loved the unlovely and lifted the unworthy. What kind of a man was He? Here are few insights that peek into Him who "humbled Himself unto death of the cross":

(1) He normally reached out to people "where they were", and guided them like a shepherd to "where they ought to be". Whether in thought, deed, or word, He tirelessly took time to be the model for servant leadership. His secret did not lie in "how he led", but in "how he followed and obeyed". For obedience does not appear in leadership but in true follower-ship. That's my Lord.

(2) He knew where he was going, how He was getting there, and what His exit strategy was. Interestingly, He knew all that not because He was the "Son of God" but because He was God in the flesh who absolutely and totally, in details and in total, was governed by the very Spirit of God who hovered over the deep and brought beauty out of ashes. In Jesus' case, the Spirit brought beauty to ashes so that we might receive His beauty on us forever.

How did He accomplish that? He obeyed until the seed died, and brought forth much fruit.

(3) He was intentional to define the problem, and to provide the solution. It's not beneficial to define the problem alone. Anyone can possibly do that, but Jesus provided solutions. How did He accomplish that? He was 100% in tune with the Father's will, and 100% blind to the world (Isaiah 42). He gained wisdom and discernment every day of His life until he was transformed into the bearer of our pain and sin so that crushed Him and we were set free. He changed for our sake so that we can become the best through Him. That's my Lord!

(4) Jesus explained what He meant by what He said. Reason being that He assumed the responsibility to arrive with the other person, together, at the solution He had in mind. And when the other person "didn't get it", Jesus had complete faith that the same Spirit, in time, will guide us "into all the truth". That's called "Anointing of the Spirit" (Isaiah 61).

(5) Jesus always began with a heart full of love, whoever the other is and whatever they bring to Him. He always took the initiative from within, led by the Spirit, and moved into the realm of the other person. His love for the other person intended to understand the other person's dilemma, and accept them "before" the solution is put into effect. For to receive and accept the other person "after" the problem is solved makes His love conditional. That was not who He really was.

(6) Jesus' way always offered something "Better". We ought to as well. He always desired the "Better", and Paul knew it too (1 Corinthians 12).

(7) Jesus always exercised self-control that was controlled by the Holy Spirit in Him, not by His own ability. Human efforts never suffice. His way is always better. *(Thursday, October 2, 2014 at 5:11 P.M. CDT)*

BY DESIGN
From my heart to yours–

Any plane, by design, was intended to fly. Humans, by design, were intended to be forever. What keeps the plane in the air is not good weather or favorable temperatures, not the shape or size, and not the outside colors or even the compartment space. The food is not exactly first class either. For most passengers it's just peanuts anyway. What really keeps the plane in the air are invisible governing principles of physics and a lot of engine fire. Likewise the true follower of Christ, all he/she need are governing unchangeable principles and lots of fire within. I'm speaking of the fire of the Holy Spirit. Do you have the Jesus principle in your heart? Do you have the Spirit's fire within, or are you basically gone with the wind? *(Friday, October 3, 2014 at 1:16 A.M. CDT)*

THE JESUS PRINCIPLE
From my heart to yours–

Contrary to popular Christian views, Jesus Christ *is* all we need for the foundation of and continuation in the Faith. That is why:

(1) He *came* so that we *can* never be alone again, EVER!;

(2) He *gave* what He received so that we can *give* too what we receive from Him ;

(3) He *made* us His own so that we *can* have an identity in Him;

(4) He *died* so that he *can* bring death to death and we can speak life to others;

(5) He *loved* completely so that we *can* love Him completely;

(6) He *trusted* fully in the Father so that we *can* trust Him completely;

(7) He *yielded* to the Holy Spirit so that we *can* surrender to the very same Spirit all the days of our life... ...and be with the Lord forever!

"I can do all things through Christ..." right? *(Friday, October 3, 2014 at 9:10 A.M. CDT)*

SPEAKING WITH THE FATHER
From my heart to yours–

An Incomplete insight into the mind of Jesus - when He spoke with the Father:

(1) Unlike us, He always spoke with His Father out of deep desire and longing;

(2) Unlike us, He always spoke with the Father filled with Faith;

(3) Unlike us, He always spoke with the Father filled with with gratitude;

(4) Unlike us, He always spoke with the Father knowing that ALL He needs is found in the Father;

(5) Unlike us, He spoke with the Father interceding on our behalf as our high priest;

(6) Unlike us, He always spoke with the Father and to no one else;

(7) Unlike us, He always expressed the Father to us for he had nothing of himself. The reason I repeated "unlike us" is because He *really* IS Unlike-Us.

So, that's WHY the Holy Spirit desires and intends to transform us on the inside every day to BE like Him; And, that's HOW Jesus Christ can flow through us to others all the time. This is the only way Jesus can be communicated transparently throughout the world; and that's why His beautiful Bride, the Church, comes from all over the world. *(Friday, October 3, 2014 at 9:39 A.M. CDT)*

IMPERFECT DISCIPLES
From my heart to yours—

Here is an incomplete insight into the mind of Jesus when He chose His DISCIPLES. Usually when we make selections of any type, we choose the best of what we see. But, not so Jesus! Please note the following:

(1) He chose the unqualified to accomplish the impossible Lesson: don't look for the qualified or dignified, but look for the ones available;

(2) He never gave up on them, a good sign of leadership Lesson: if as a leader all I talk about is problems, I have forfeited my role and didn't know it;

(3) He never stuffed their mind with doctrine as standard for following him, but He spoke life and truth to them always in love Lesson: doctrine for doctrine's sake is always a dead end. But Christ leads his followers through proper doctrine back to himself;

(4) He knew who He was to them, and accepted the fact that they didn't know Lesson: don't go by what the eyes see or the ears hear;

(5) He always pointed them to what was beyond their human capacity to comprehend Lesson: nothing wrong with appealing to the mind, but life in Christ is beyond a mental exercise;

(6) He always loved them, from beginning to end, completely

Lesson: love is where things begin, and stay, and continue to the end. Anything less will never accomplish much;

(7) They were frustrated with Him, afraid of Him, puzzled about Him, and they finally fled from Him; but they knew that He had what they were looking for.

Lesson: Are we willing to walk with Him alone and be content?
(Friday, October 3, 2014 at 11:41 P.M. CDT)

DOOMED, YET LOVED
From my heart to yours–

An Incomplete insight into the mind of Jesus - when He spoke with FALLEN PEOPLE: I'm defining "Fallen People" specifically as any person who, after living many years in a given society, did not "live up to the expectations of others, and has fallen from their graces so far that he/she has been judged as 'rejected', as 'unqualified', as 'undeserving' to live a 'normal' life any longer in such society." They're all over the place, from India and China to the Middle East, even in America. Africa and South America are not exempted. Jesus Christ was especially and specifically attracted to such individuals. Some of the reasons are:

(1) The claim is that "God so loved the world". No one is excluded. And Jesus came also for the FALLEN specifically bringing hope, healing, and unconditional love. As the Incarnate Son of God, Jesus became man so that, as a human being, E-v-e-r-y L-a-s-t O-n-e of them who met Jesus knew they were accepted by at least One. No one understands like Jesus.

(2) Suddenly, there is a shift. The unqualified became qualified; the undeserving, now deserving; the rejected, now accepted; the nameless, now can have a name; the ugly, now beautiful; the shamed, now can lift up their head. Do you know such people?

(3) Amazingly, everyone who was "FALLEN" came to Jesus because they knew there was something special, different, about Him -- that He was their last chance before committing existential suicide, that precisely He was NOT fallen and He was NOT "like all the rest". "Jesus - There is something about that Name".

(4) To compound the blow, even when they looked in the proverbial mirror, the "Fallen" looked at and accept themselves now as "Fallen" too, and believed what people said. Their days have become eternal nights, and no light at the end of the tunnel. Jesus said, "I am the light of the world." Jesus said to His followers, "You (plural) are the light (singular) of the world." He did not say to His followers "You are LIGHTS" to highlight their "uniqueness and individuality". This is not the place or time for that. There can be, and needs to be, only ONE light. That ONE light is Jesus. His followers, who are all over the world, and now through the Holy Spirit, can now be light in Christ's stead.

(5) Each of the fallen persons in one way or another attached themselves to Him. The thief on the cross said "Lord, remember me when you...." Then there was the adulterous woman, and the woman who brought the alabaster box and broke it at his feet, and Zacchaeus, and the blind, and the paralytic, and Mary, and the man who was doomed to live among the tombs, and on and on. These days, they live in corporate offices, but are fallen, and no one knows it...until they look in the mirror.

(6) Also, remember Tamar, Rahab, Ruth, and Solomon who was born "from the one who belonged to Uriah" - what rejects! All shamed by family, by race, by class, and by power, from the streets to the palace, they found their connection to Jesus. You see, for Jesus to reach to people before His earthly life, there has to be a connection. And vicariously, they were all connected - to Him.

(7) Even the most blessed and virtuous woman, Mary who gave Him birth, found her connection to Him and called Him her savior. The ground is leveled now. "All have sinned and come short."

Now, here's the awesome part. The Scripture says: "We are ambassadors FOR Christ." and also, "Christ died FOR us." The word "FOR" means specifically "one in the place of another". While Jesus was on earth, the Holy Spirit governed his life so much that He was able to live such holy life pleasing to God. Every true follower of Jesus is someone who, like Him, is governed by the Holy Spirit and, like Him, is able to live this Spirit-filled life, so much so that people will see Jesus, again. *(Saturday, October 4, 2014 at 6:44 A.M. CDT)*

"TO BE IN CHRIST" AND "TO ABIDE IN CHRIST"
From my heart to yours—

(1) "To BE IN" is an organic union with Christ; "To ABIDE IN" is to daily communion with Christ

(2) "To BE IN" happens once (like birth), that is, He breathes life into me; "To ABIDE IN" happens every day (like breathing), that is, He breathes life through me to others.

(3) "To BE IN" is the Holy Spirit's work during our second birth event (John 3:8); "TO ABIDE IN" is the Holy Spirit's work for the rest of my life until I die.

(4) "To BE IN" took place universally on the cross and eternally sealed at the resurrection; "TO ABIDE IN" took place specifically and personally when I consciously was made aware by the Holy Spirit of my personal need of Christ and asked Him to save me, thus appropriating what He did on the cross to me personally.

(5) "To BE IN" uniquely distinguishes Christianity from all others; "TO ABIDE IN" has the experiential element that keeps Christianity unique.

(6) "To BE IN" is what Christ offers anyone who wishes to follow Him; "TO ABIDE IN" is what Christ demands of anyone who follows Him.

(7) "To BE IN" means death to the world; "TO ABIDE IN" means life to Christ.

(8) "To BE IN" is positional, like being born into a family; "TO ABIDE IN" is practical, meaning, experiencing everything that the family experiences.

(9) "TO BE IN" brings me to Christ for identity; "TO ABIDE IN" brings Christ to me for community.

(10) "TO BE IN", aims at a new way of life IN ME; "TO ABIDE IN" aims at instilling a life of worship in me.

(11) "TO BE IN" Christ is when I learned that He loves me so much; "TO ABIDE IN" Christ is when I learn to love Him so much as He loved me.

(12) "TO BE IN" is to discover that I'm forgiven, I'm clean' I'm guilt-free; "TO ABIDE IN" is to discover every day that I am STILL forgiven, clean, and guilt-free.

(13) "TO BE IN" is expected to begin life; "TO ABIDE IN" is expected to stay alive. Put differently, there is no such thing as faith without obedience.

Allow me to say it slightly differently: THERE IS NO SUCH THING AS FAITH WITHOUT OBEDIENCE. Faith without obedience is meaningless. Obedience without faith is legalism.

Both fail to please Him separately. It's satan's way of making things easy and say "Just believe, and you'll be fine", giving the label of "Christian" as a badge, having the "form of godliness" but no power, and causing Christians to falter all their life. Faith is easy; even satan believes but few know he also trembles. But, obedience costs, always. Jesus being our only example, He obeyed through suffering (Hebrews 5:8) and was perfected by death. Obedience brings us to the end of self and to the beginning of life in the Spirit. Now, this is where satan bows out. And that's why he was kicked out in the first place. Does it not seem strange that satan wants us to keep our eyes on each other, comparing ourselves with one another, thus confusing us every day, and does not want us to look to Him - to Jesus Christ - everyday, on Him who died for us and rose again?! It's a nasty trick, and we know it. I pray that this settles the heart of some - into Him, and prompts others to move on as they abide in Him. It's not about me; it's all about Him! *(Monday, October 6, 2014 at 7:22 A.M. CDT)*

SHOCK TREATMENT
From my heart to yours–

A "Defibrillator" is "An electrical device used to counteract fibrillation of the heart muscle". That is, when the muscles begin to act not in coordination and stop conducting the impulse of the heart, the defibrillator tries to "restore normal heartbeat by applying a brief electric shock (to the chest)." We've seen that many times, I'm sure. If "defibrillator" is too technical, use "shocker" instead. It's the same thing. I woke up this morning with a Spirit's defibrillator applied to my heart. It's called: "God's *HOLINESS*". The Scripture says that "without holiness it is impossible to see God." Without it, I cannot see Him. I'm in the dark in my existence, in my actions, in my thinking, in my direction in life, in my purpose, in my relations, in my "sphere of influence". I cannot see Him and experience His presence and power, His pleasure and the touch of His hand in my life. Do you want to see God in your life, keep reading. "Holiness" is not a person, but it is a *dye*, applied daily by the Holy Spirit to the heart of the follower of Christ who *died* once and lives forever. Holiness is the only character trait that is demanded. Jesus said, without hesitation, condition, or promise, that the follower *must* be "holy". He did not say I MUST be educated or illiterate, handsome or ugly, rich or poor, organized or cluttered, introvert or extrovert, from one nation or another, seminarian or vegetarian, humanitarian or Unitarian, ordained or detained, committee chair or minister everywhere, on TV or below the radar, weak or strong, Arab or Jew, eloquent or stammering, deacon or beacon, loud-mouthed or "church mouse", visible or invisible, near or far, religious or heathen, good or evil, tall or short, man or woman, active in church or sleep in church, minister or attendee, spectator, motivator, or moderator, at any time, now or later. But He *did* say and required of every follower saying "Be ye holy as I am holy". Holiness never happens without fire. It's a shocker! It burns! I would rather live quietly a holy life all my life, then He uses me once and I die, rather than be on the New York Best Seller list, or occupy the best pulpit, or travel all over the world, or sit with kings and queens. If we are to be useful to Him whenever and wherever and however He is pleased, we are to be "holy", *always*; before, during, and after our years of usefulness. What He is really saying is that you and I can never be "holy" without the Holy Spirit, start to finish, without Him who is "holy" working in us *always*. For His words are still true: "Without me, you can do nothing". Maybe that's one reason why He said, *"Complete your salvation with fear and trembling"*. I urge you, one and all, don't be impressed by the big names, big pulpits, big writers, big money, big whatever. For the minute anything detract us from the cross of Christ, we lost the war and we haven't even begun a single skirmish yet. In other words, if there is no Holy character and Life, then, *forget it*! You and I are wasting our breath in claiming to belong to Him or doing anything in His Holy Name. He's not running a popularity contest, and he's not running for president, especially that He is the "King of kings, and Lord of lords". His name is "Holy", and He is jealous to protect His name. Maybe that's why when the scribes wrote the manuscripts, and arrived at that holy name, each time, they showered, prayed, changed the reed they used, and very carefully and in gold ink wrote those four letters of God. Whatever we think of Him, one thing for sure: He is a Holy God. This morning this thought shocked me back to the reality in which He desires for me to live. May He reign in your heart and mine, without question or doubt, every day. Paul said, "May it never be that I should boast except in the cross of Christ and Him crucified." It's about Him, All about Him, Really about Him. *(Wednesday, October 8, 2014 at 6:56 A.M. CDT)*

WHEN GOD MOVES
From my heart to yours–

The awesomeness of Jesus Christ is not that we can be holy, but that as sinners, filthy and dead, he met us at the cross where He settled our debt, gave us life, and His Holy Spirit dwells in us to make us and to keep us holy. Isaiah was made holy with fire from the altar (chapter 6). Jacob was broken before he was able to see God. Peter was crushed before he was made useful. Paul was knocked off his high horse before he was useful. And the list goes on and on. Are you on the list? It's all about Him! *(Wednesday, October 8, 2014 at 7:12 A.M. CDT)*

ONE-SIDED COMMITMENT IS "NOT ENOUGH"
From my heart to yours–

Jesus prayed in agony saying, "Father, if it be *your* will, take this cup away from Me; nevertheless not My will, but Yours, be done." (Luke 22) Questions: (1) Was it not enough to say, "But Your will be done"? (2) Why was it necessary for Him to say also, "not my will"? (3) Does not the first include (or safely assume) the second automatically? The answer is a resounding: NO. Here is why:

(1) Some people think that by saying "if God wills" " اذا بيريد الله " او "متل ما الله بيريد " , they give the impression that they are ok with God's will too. Not necessarily, because, should things really start going from bad to worse, They start stressing out, then get frustrated beyond measure, then start directing that toward God, then start verbalizing their anger into a numbing state of despair. Right?

(2) By tolerating God's seemingly gradual loss of control of life's situation(s), some people like to give the impression that it's "patience", which is "good". But it's really not.

(3) What they are not saying is that their patience, which they're about to lose, is directed toward God, but they are still hoping deep inside that He would "fix" things so the pain stops.

(4) We treat doctors the same way. If I'm not happy with one, I simply find another. With God, we're stuck!

(5) To say "let it be your will" is acknowledging His sovereignty. Not enough!

(6) To say "Not my will" affirms my complete surrender. NOW we're talking! To keep my will and take His too is pure selfish. No?

(7) It's easy to say the first, but it does not declare my conviction yet.

(8) It is much more difficult to say the second, because it's not words to say but brokenness to experience.

(9) The good news is that in my brokenness I can experience, not only His sovereignty and power, but also His nearness, His presence, His Spirit's power. Isn't that what we really want?

(10) It is not a question of brokenness then, but it's a question of identity - Mine. Stated differently, if I really belong to Him, I do not belong to myself at all, anymore. He has given me His identity when He died in the flesh on my behalf.

Now, I live in the flesh on His behalf by faith and in the power of the Holy Spirit, the same Spirit who controlled Him while on earth so that people will not see me, but Him. He succeeded. Therefore, I can too, right? Do we not say, "I can do all things through Christ who strengthens me?" "*I have been crucified with Christ; it is no longer I who live, but Christ lives in me; and the life which I now live in the flesh I live by faith in the Son of God, who loved me and gave Himself up for me."* (Galatians 2) *(Wednesday, October 8, 2014 at 11:04 P.M. CDT)*

~~~~~~

PURE IS PERFECT
From my heart to yours—

To be saved from the wrath of God is good news. But to be made pure is even better news. That's been made possible through Jesus Christ. The first, He took its full impact upon Himself. The second, (being pure), He put upon me. The first, He took because He became sin for my sake. The second, I took because I was made acceptable before God. The first, I was hiding from, but He faced on the cross. The second, I was always looking for, but couldn't find until He found me and loved me. The first executed death but the second transacted life and peace. *Hallelujah, what a Savior!* *(Thursday, October 9, 2014 at 6:36 A.M. CDT)*

~~~~~~

ON BEING IMPRESSED
From my heart to yours—

My thought this morning as I woke up was to urge you to NOT be impressed by what Jesus Christ was not impressed with, and certainly anything any of us does. That's why when the 70 returned very impressed, He said, I'll tell you what you can be impressed with....that your names are written in the Lamb's Book of life. How much did we contribute to that one? Nyet, Nada, Rien de tout :) What always impressed Him and drove Him passionately toward was the Heavenly Father. His response was loving the Father with absolute dedication of heart, mind, and soul. And He was able to accomplish that by means of the Spirit that controlled and filled

Him. He invites every true follower to do likewise toward Him (Jesus) because we come through Him to the Father, showered by His love, and can say "Our Father". And we too can accomplish that by means of the same Spirit and can love Him absolutely with all our heart, mind, and soul "and we shall dwell in the house of the Lord forever". *(Friday, October 10, 2014 at 11:51 A.M. CDT)*

GIFTS ARE MEANT TO BE GIVEN
From my heart to yours—

In thinking about the Holy Spirit, I'm learning the following: (1) He chooses the gift and matches it with the recipient that He chooses, not for me to use it, but for Him to use me. My only objective is to be sure I'm clean in His sight. His only objective is to glorify always and 100% of the time none other than the Lord Jesus Christ who died and rose again. (2) He guides day by day, step by step, and thought by thought, so that everything is done according to His will and desire. Now, imagine a group of people experiencing just that! (3) My only purpose in life, if I'm a true follower of Christ, is to be pure, sanctified, confessed up, totally submissive to Him, reflecting His fruit practically in my life, belonging totally to Him, totally surrendered, all of Him and none of me, and daily intentional to please only Him. (4) Just because there is a local group who call themselves a "church" and act so dignified, doesn't mean He's obligated to that group. The sad thing, I suspect, is that He has moved on somewhere else, and they go on with their program not noticing (like Samson) that the Spirit has departed. (5) He gives a gift only as long as it's needed. It's the gift, not the recipient that really matters. Once I attempt to do things "my way" He will not hesitate to move me out of the way. That's why the three warnings are: (a) Don't grieve, (b) Don't resist, and, (c) Don't quench the Spirit. *(Monday, October 13, 2014 at 4:32 P.M. CDT)*

DESIGNED NOT MALIGNED
From my heart to yours–

I always wondered who came up with the idea of the Boeing jet, and who created it. Now, with minimal research, I know; it's Joe Sutter, "the legendary creator of Boeing". And every part of his Boeing creation has a name (not a number). And every part has a function. And the whole structure has a purpose. And even a metal/fiberglass/plastic/or other material, when put together, makes the whole look beautiful. And I always was under the impression that bits and pieces, nuts and bolts, here and there, and other metallic plastic concoctions just kinda, sorta .... Uh ... Happened! :) Although some people insist on slimy origins, or prefer going to the nearest zoo to see suspected ancestors, I'm inclined to think that there is a more honorable beginning; and maybe, just maybe, there was a Creator after all. Oops, I think Darwin just rolled over in his grave. *(Tuesday, October 14, 2014 at 11:26 A.M. CDT)*

NO CAN DO
From my heart to yours–

There are definitely some things the Holy Spirit is NOT interested in. (1) He is not interested in ONLY distributing gifts, (2) He is not interested in me doing ministry work, (3) He is not interested in doing what I ask, (4) He is not interested in wasting any resources, (5) He is not interested in "doing what he can". What the Holy Spirit *is* interested in, is: (1) He is interested in using the one he gives, (2) He is interested in His plan for the Church, (3) He is interested in owning whom he uses, (4) He is interested in holy people doing holy things, and, (5) He is interested in transforming us into the image of Christ. *(Tuesday, October 14, 2014 at 3:01 P.M. CDT)*

ALL OF HIM
From my heart to yours—

The Capability of the Holy Spirit: In summary, (1) As administrator, he takes what is in Christ and makes available to whomever He chooses to glorify Christ 100% of the time without exception; (2) As all God, He achieves his eternal goals that he purposed before the world was formed; and, (3) As to his nature, He makes the work of Christ effective, in the lost to come to the cross and live, and in the believer to come to the cross and be crucified so Christ can live through him and be glorified. In a little more detail, (1) As the administrator of Christ's Church on earth, He seeks to accomplish his tasks that he chooses for the completion of the Church in beauty, in number, in mission, and in the centrality of Jesus Christ in its life. (2) As All God in power, in knowledge, and in presence, He does not expect humans to comprehend or grasp, and He does not seek popularity or primacy. He, nonetheless, moves in human history driven by the makeup of His person and personality to achieve His eternal objectives, about which He, the Spirit, is in complete harmony and unison and passion that always existed in the Triune God from eternity. (3) As to His nature, He does not expect any human to stop him or delay his actions. His supreme objective when it comes to interaction with mankind is to take what Jesus Christ offers, and give to us. To the sinner, the Holy Spirit takes the redemptive work of Christ on the cross and convicts man of his unrighteousness and his need of salvation. To the believer, the Holy Spirit crucifies the follower with Christ on the cross so that he lives no more but Christ lives through him to be glorified forever. *(Tuesday, October 14, 2014 at 7:31 P.M. CDT)*

HOLY INTERACTION
From my heart to yours—

How does the Holy Spirit interact with followers of Christ *individually?* (1) The Holy Spirit always takes the initiative, the first step towards a person (2) The Holy Spirit says just enough to make his intentions known very clearly (3) The Holy Spirit walks with that person day by day, in simple and specific steps (4) The Holy Spirit declares to such person the kind of specific holy life He desires (5) The Holy Spirit trains such person to live a daily schedule of disciplined life (6) The Holy Spirit captures the person's heart regarding the holiness of God to walk all his life with worship as his sole desire, for without holiness no one can see God (7) The Holy Spirit leads effectively in a life of complete trust, surrender, and waiting on God, living a life of faith, the faith without which no one can please God. *(Tuesday, October 14, 2014 at 7:45 P.M. CDT)*

THE HOLY SPIRIT - SOME DO'S AND SOME DON'TS
From my heart to yours—

(1) Do expect the Holy Spirit to be gentle, but don't misinterpret that. (2) Do expect the Holy Spirit to lead you into all truth, and don't expect people to do that. (3) Do expect the Holy Spirit to glorify Christ alone, and don't try to "reach and take" of that glory. (4) Do expect the Holy Spirit to change your life, always, and don't develop "an attitude" about it. (5) Do expect the Holy Spirit to teach

you the mind of Christ to live like Christ, but don't take the practice and make it a rule but take the rule and make it a practice. (6) Do pray, sing, serve, live, (and everything else as follower of Christ) in the power of the Spirit, and don't try to do anything at all in your own power. (7) Do expect the Holy Spirit to reveal your sin and convict you regularly in order to lead you back to worship, fellowship and communion. Don't grieve or resist or quench the Spirit in retaliation and blame someone else. (8) Do expect the Holy Spirit to show you the beauty of Christ so your heart gets attached to Christ. (9) Do learn to be transparent with the Holy Spirit; He knows your heart already. Don't lie (remember Ananias and Sapphira). Don't even think about it. (10) Do worship Christ in truth and Spirit. Don't come before Him with dirty hands to offer sacrifice of thanksgiving. *(Tuesday, October 14, 2014 at 7:59 P.M. CDT)*

Fiery Tongues, Holy Tongues
From my heart to yours–

I'm not sure the Holy Spirit wants to give the gift of speaking in tongues if we have difficulty controlling the one we got. I'm not sure He wants to give the gift of speaking in tongues to declare the Gospel of Jesus Christ if we don't use the one we have to do that. While some fuss over tongues, relying on the Pentecost event, I must ask: why did the tongues appear over the 120 and not over the 3000 to confirm? Instead, they "continued in the Apostles' teaching, fellowship, Lord's Supper, and Prayers". The Church grew naturally. As we often do, we focus on the wrong thing. *(Tuesday, October 14, 2014 at 8:52 P.M. CDT)*

REUNION -
From my heart to yours—

Twenty-five years ago, Drs. Nader and Safaa lived in our city and we had great fellowship with them. Their son Daniel was two years old. Today, I visited with them in their home in Cairo. The reunion was *wonderful* (I'm trying to control my *excitement* HA-HA. Some amazing things we noticed: (1) We picked up where we left off in conversation, mindset, attitude, love, fellowship, and so many memories. (2) We heard what has been accomplished during the 25 years (3) We loved talking about God's mercies and many kindnesses (4) We realized that the minor change: the hair turned white, kids have grown, evil increased in the world, new challenges, and God's Spirit is on the move more than ever. Good Doctors, it was really good to see you! *A Foretaste of Heaven!* *(Friday, October 17, 2014 at 12:22 P.M. CDT)*

NO EXCUSES LEFT
From my heart to yours—

"Two chairs and a cup of coffee", were used by God to bring at least 500 known people to know Christ as Savior. The story, later. I would encourage and ask that you look for your own "chair and coffee cup". Each of us who loves Christ and His Church has these items sitting somewhere. *(Sunday, October 19, 2014 at 7:42 P.M. CDT)*

WHAT DO YOU HAVE
From my heart to yours—

When Jesus was about to feed the multitudes, the disciples were in management shock - shock as to crowd management, food management, team management, resource management, and self-management. But all along, Jesus "knew what he was going to do". Then he asked, "WHAT DO YOU HAVE with you?" Jesus doesn't think "management". He thinks, "Father, let them see your glory, and that you sent me". When we look in the ministry mirror, what do we see? Here's the story of Abu-Issam, the story of the chair and the cup of coffee: Abu-Issam passed away recently, and rested from all his toils on earth. But in his younger years, as a non-believer, he served his country for 30 years loyally. But God was about to change that royally. A pastor was at the border crossing when he was stopped and searched, only for the guard to find out that "his papers" were missing something. The guard dragged him out of the car like a criminal to his boss. His boss was Abu-Issam. This is where the story starts taking its sovereign turns. Abu-Issam saw how the guard was treating the pastor, "a man of the cloth", and he reprimanded the guard. Then he personally drove the pastor's car to his house after he examined "the papers", and determined that they just needed a minor correction. While in the car, Abu-Issam asked the pastor why he was at the border. The pastor told him he was on his way to a worship meeting and was taking some food along. The pastor seized the moment and shared the Gospel message with Abu-Issam. Within 48 hours, the Holy Spirit touched Abu-Issam's heart so deeply, and he was converted as he reflected on his conversation with the pastor. Being so overwhelmed by all that happened in his heart, Abu-Issam soon retired, and dedicated the remainder of his life to share the story of Jesus his Savior. The village soon found out how "Abu-Issam" was in life and conversation that they came to trust, respect, and love his gentle treatment of everyone who heard or met him. Abu-Issam began to have physical problems with age.

Diabetes took its toll on his health - Cholesterol, heart, blood pressure, etc. He finally could barely move. Yet, every morning he would wake up at 3:30 A.M. and as "the call to prayer" is announced from the mosque, Abu-Issam began to pray until 7:00 for the people walking by his door going to pray. At 7:00 A.M., his kids helped him with his chair to put it outside his front doorsteps, and he prayed that the Lord would give him "just one person" each day to share the message of faith, hope, and love. Every day, Abu-Issam called the first person he saw walking by him, and invited them to have a seat in the other chair close by. Being a respected man, people invariably came to him and sat in the chair. As they had a cup of coffee together, Abu-Issam shared with them about Jesus who saved him. In his earlier days, Abu-Issam managed to walk up and down the street, meeting people, and as long as he walked the streets during the fighting nearby, people felt at peace and came out of their homes without fear to do their daily chores and shopping quickly. His family helped him go outside his doorsteps, sit in the chair daily, and have his cup of coffee with people. God always gave him someone to talk to about becoming a follower of Christ. During his last handful of days, Abu-Issam was bedridden. He did not sit outside. He did not walk the streets. People did not feel at peace to go do their shopping. After three days, they came to his house asking about Abu-Issam. His daughter told the people that he was not feeling well at all. Abu-Issam heard, and with great effort he said that he is doing fine, and asked his children to help him get out of the house. As he walked the street, people feared no more, and came out to do their daily chores. They loved Abu-Issam and cherished even the sight of the fragile figure that hobbled outside to sit in that chair every day. At his funeral, his children who also were committed followers of Christ attempted to distribute copies of the New Testament to the more than 500 people who attended. They were unable to convince anyone to accept. The reason was that their father had already done so to every one of the people who attended his funeral. More than 500 people became followers of Jesus Christ, one at a time; sipping coffee and listening to Abu-Issam speak Jesus to them. They loved Abu-Issam, and soon they too became lovers and followers of Christ. In spite of his many physical challenges in his later years, Abu-Issam was SO overwhelmed by Christ and what He did for him that he completely surrendered, followed, and shared Christ's love with everyone until he died. Do you have "a chair and a cup of coffee" around the house? Or, are you waiting to be qualified so you can impress people? Paul said, "For the love of Christ constrains me." It's really ALL about Him! (The story still motivates all his children to serve selflessly. As his daughter told it to me yesterday, she said, "every time I think I don't have what I need to serve the Lord, I remember my dad." *(Sunday, October 19, 2014 at 9:38 P.M. CDT)*

PURE INNOCENCE
From my heart to yours–

Pure innocence, Pure sweetness, Pure joy to meet. The future is looking good. I always wondered why Jesus said, "Let the children keep on coming to me and don't forbid them." Sometimes I think He wants us to go back to where we started, and learn to live again. *(Monday, October 20, 2014 at 8:34 A.M. CDT)*

FEELING NUMB
From my heart to yours–

As I sat on the floor of her 4' x 10'-room that accommodated 3 adults and 6 children, I listened and saw the sights and sounds of suffering. Her 6-year old daughter was injured then infected below the knee, and the infection reached the bone. While in Syria, the daughter, Wala'a وَلاء, witnessed a man blown to pieces by a bomb, her husband now is a shoeshine, she invited her neighbor (the 3rd adult) who was living on the street with her son and pregnant with a baby girl, to come and live with them. This lady gave birth to the new baby in the same room where they live. That's giving when you have nothing to give. This unedited version, spoken in Arabic with English translation, gives a snapshot into the soul crushed by suffering. Her daughter is being cared for at a Christian organization with which I was familiar. The little girl who looks four insisted on coming to school to learn with the other kids. The organization has four schools that serve an informal curriculum, keeping the kids off the streets, giving them shelter and care. If you visit the website, I'm sure you know how you can help. If you are invited by God to visit, to listen, to look within, and learn up close how to love God again, please let me know. Don't let the emotions drive you, but do let His love constrain you to take action. *(Tuesday, October 21, 2014 at 9:32 A.M. CDT)*

DESPAIR DEFINED
From my heart to yours–

Here is the midwife who never did the procedure before, and the mom-to-be who came off the street to find shelter. The baby cries because she doesn't have the proper milk, and has been trying to digest to no avail powdered milk that causes more pain unnecessarily. Both were loved by others during the past year, others who know Him who loved the world. The leading person who took us to visit this lady has experienced a more traumatic pain and loss, and knows firsthand how a heart can be ripped apart. But she also knows a Savior who died for love's sake, and a Father who has enough love to cover a world soaked in suffering and pain. Love always gives until it hurts, and obedience always leads to suffering. That's where all meet, just like the cross where everything was settled. *(Tuesday, October 21, 2014 at 9:45 A.M. CDT)*

EMBRACING THE WORLD
From my heart to yours–

There is no human capacity that can embrace the world. But He who embraced the world can give his followers all the capacity He deems necessary to accomplish His purpose. He asks for three things (F-A-O): Faithfulness, Availability, and Obedience. He certainly doesn't ask for money. That's dumb and insulting to even consider. He prompts, He leads, He blesses, He moves...like none other. *(Tuesday, October 21, 2014 at 9:56 A.M. CDT)*

TRUE SHAME
From my heart to yours–

If you think about it, the entire incarnation experience has been one experience of shame after another until the culmination of shame when he was crucified in the complete shameful nakedness on the cross so that you and I have a covering forever. His complete emptying gave us fullness; His complete humiliation gave us a crown of righteousness; His complete separation from the Father gave us adoption and union; His complete surrender made it possible for us to surrender to Him so that He will always be the "All in All" and that He might have the "preeminence in all things". And, He is worthy! His name is Jesus Christ, and He is my Lord. *(Wednesday, October 22, 2014 at 2:28 A.M. CDT)*

"DON'T ABANDON US"
From my heart to yours—

Richard and Sabina Wurmbrand were voices in the wilderness of the persecuted church to the comfortable church worldwide. He died in 1901 at the age of 95. He tasted suffering at the hands of the Nazis and the Russians in Siberia for 12 years at the latter. He concluded that "pain does not know national origin". In his book, "*Tortured for Christ*", Richard Wurmbrand said, "The message I bring from the Underground Church is: "Don't abandon us!", "Don't forget us!", "Don't write us off!". "Give us the tools we need! We will pay the price for using them!" "This is the message I have been charged to deliver to the Free Church" (pg. 144) "Pray for one another". *(Thursday, October 23, 2014 at 7:42 A.M. CDT)*

WHEN GOD GOES TO JAIL
From my heart to yours—

He was known in the Russian jail in Siberia as "Prisoner Number 1". "In 1945 Romanian Communists seized power and a million 'invited' Russian troops poured into the country. Pastor Wurmbrand ministered to his oppressed countrymen and engaged in bold evangelism to the Russian soldiers. In the same year, Richard and Sabina Wurmbrand attended the Congress of Cults organized by the Romanian Communist government. Many religious leaders came forward to praise Communism and to swear loyalty to the new regime. Sabina said, "Richard, stand up and wash away this shame from the face of Christ." Richard warned, "If I do so, you lose your husband." She replied, "I don't wish to have a coward as a husband." Thus Richard declared to the 4,000 delegates, whose speeches were broadcast to the whole nation, that their duty is to glorify God and Christ alone. Between 1945 and 1947, Richard distributed one million Gospels to Russian troops, the books often disguised as Communist propaganda. Richard also smuggled Gospels into Russia. On 30 December 1947, the Peoples' Republic of Romania was proclaimed." He died on 17 February, 2001. *(Thursday, October 23, 2014 at 8:12 A.M. CDT)*

INTERCESSION
From my heart to yours–

Do you have someone praying and interceding on your behalf? The secret and joy of taking trips like the recent ones is that I'm only the mouth piece, but the actual effectiveness is that of the many who prayed faithfully every day. That's where it is appropriate to say that "the effectual fervent prayer of the righteous [i.e., someone praying the right thing] avails much (i.e., makes a big difference where things matters most)". We are very thankful for everyone who partnered in prayer. We just landed in Chicago :). One more leg of two-hour flight and I'll be home. :). YES!!! *(Friday, October 24, 2014 at 1:50 P.M. CDT)*

UNEXPECTED "I LOVE YOU"
From my heart to yours–

I woke up early for my "time", and found a text message Jonathan had left after I started looking at the inside of my eyelids :). They have already picked me up at the airport, we hugged tight and sensed the contentment in their heart, as he sat in the front I had to give him a "high-5" several times (wonder why!?), giggled, told me how he took his mom to dinner while I was gone, proud of how he treated her, told him how proud I was, told me how much he loved me, already had dinner together, talked in snippets about everything we could think of, laughed at times, serious at other times, concerned if the subject matter called for it, but I really was very tired (jet lag, popping ears, etc.). Then I woke up this morning and found the message he left: "I love you, Father". I should not have been surprised because he did that in the past. But my eyes welled up again because I was glad he hasn't changed in that regard. I never doubted that he always loved me, but was thankful he thinks of his dad even when his dad provided for him all he needed and more. "I love you, Father." "*I love you, Lord; and I lift my voice, To worship You, Oh, my soul, rejoice, Take joy my King, In what You hear, Let it be a sweet, sweet sound in Your ear*" *(Saturday, October 25, 2014 at 5:59 A.M. CDT)*

WHY GRACE MATTERS
From my heart to yours–

She was a nobody and poor who lived here and there, sickly-looking, fragile and broken, alone and sad, shaken at the slightest unexpected sounds from unknown sources. She went from place to place looking for food and love, and always found herself settling for crumbs. She was thirsty and often settled for rain water in the fall or sipped on collected stagnant waters many times. She needed a robe to cover but her slender form was not cooperating much. She looked beyond the hills wishing her lot could change, but the sun never rose and her tears fell often. Unfulfilled promises from many lovers found her returning to the same starting point at the intersection of "Nowhere Corner" and "Bizzie St." Isolated and ashamed, she desperately searched for meaning, for acceptance, and for love. She found none with whom to be, and with whom to identify. She looked in the mirror and thought she found the panacea, until the mirror cracked, once and again. Then she sank into her personalized pit of despair, and wrapped herself with filthy rags for the night was long, and the way home was far, far away. Then, the Prince found her and loved her, and said, "Will you marry me?" And life was never the same again. *(Saturday, October 25, 2014 at 6:43 A.M. CDT)*

LOVING FOR NO REASON
From my heart to yours—

It is easy to love when I have reason to love - nothing wrong with that. But to love for no reason, that says little about the object, but finds more than is needed in the loving heart. We lack little in the first, but lack much in the second. That's why Jesus came close, and His name was called Emmanuel. (Hebrew): Emm- "with", Anu- "us", El- "God". *Isn't He Awesome*?! *(Saturday, October 25, 2014 at 7:45 A.M. CDT)*

"OLD", A MATTER OF PERSPECTIVE
From my heart to yours—

She said she waited every day and prayed every day. Then I came in, sat next to her, and life is back to where we left off. She couldn't believe that I was home. I had to double check too. I made the mistake and said, "Mom, I missed you" :). She went on and on about how she spent her days waiting and wanted to meet me outside. Then I asked, "What about Baba (Dad)?" She replied, "He's getting old, of course." My Mom -- hasn't changed much. Navigating through the twilight years is always manageable with a cup of coffee in hand. *(Saturday, October 25, 2014 at 1:41 P.M. CDT)*

Two days later, she seems more rested than before, not without some silly moments, like the picture in which she insisted to fix her hair a bit. I offered her to take a minute and freshen up some, but she said "Too late now". At 89, I'd say, Click! Next! Ha-ha. She earned the right to say anything, and usually it's correct whether it is or not (ha-ha). *(Monday, October 27, 2014 at 1:13 P.M. CDT)*

MAKING THE DIFFERENCE
From my heart to yours—

I looked at the Yazidis of Kurdistan up close and personal, and I looked at the beautiful people at the Birmingham church; and found that the only difference between the two groups is: Jesus. One group knows him, the other needs Him. What a Name: Jesus Christ! *(Saturday, November 8, 2014 at 2:34 P.M. CST)*

DOING BUSINESS
From my heart to yours—

Why we do God's business God's way by spending time, not with people, but with God? Here's why: From Acts 13:1-3, we learn that the Holy Spirit is sovereign (key word) in:

- Choosing whom He pleases
- Leading all who are obedient
- Directing all operations
- Charting course of action
- Filling with His power
- Enabling them to focus
- Instilling in them a sense of awe.

In summary, we worship! *(Friday, November 14, 2014 at 10:46 A.M. CST)*

HOW CAN I PRAY FOR YOU
From my heart to yours—

Would you consider (1) Asking someone "how can I pray for you?" And if they come and ask, "Would you pray for me", reply, "Can I do that now?" Don't look around wondering who's watching. Don't say, "I will". Just Do it right there and then. You owe it to that person. And the Father is listening 24/7. (2) Praying while you wait, at traffic lights, in line at the bank, at security check, waiting to order at Starbucks, while the offering is taken up at church (before and after you give, while you're on hold on a call, while you're waiting for a meal to be ready, and every other such occasion? (3) Praying for people, especially those you dislike, No, those you can't stand, and ask God to love them through you? (4) Making a meal and take it to someone who needs it ... before you eat yours? (Find someone)

(5) Being still before God, totally quiet, just meditating on His goodness, His mercies, His love that will not let Go? Would you consider doing that every day for 7 days? He is worthy. His name is Jesus. He chose to be separated from the Father for an eternal moment so that you and I will never be alone again, *Ever. (Sunday, November 16, 2014 at 4:27 P.M. CST)*

MANY PRAYERS ANSWERED
From my heart to yours–

Thank You to *all* who prayed for the missions conference in Boston. It was a true visitation of the gentle Spirit. One man said, "Would you pray for me? I am a follower of Christ, but I learned that I need to obey." Another said, "I need to let Him take full control of my life." Another said, "I'm beginning to have a good idea of how important prayer is." Another said, "I just want to tell my Heavenly Father how much I love Him." I listened, and in my heart I longed for heaven again. The words of the song say, *"Sweet Holy Spirit, Sweet heavenly Dove; Stay right here with us, Filling us with your love; And for each blessing, We lift our hearts in praise; Without a doubt we'll know, That we have been revived, When we shall leave this place." (Sunday, November 16, 2014 at 4:49 P.M. CST)*

DIFFICULT TO GIVE GLORY
From my heart to yours–

It's very easy to give glory to people. It happens all the time. But to give glory to God is far more difficult. Here is why:

(1) The Holy Spirit is the only Person who adequately and fully brings glory to God. The Holy Spirit does not need human help. And when He indwells a human heart, He remains the only one bringing glory.

(2) When Isaiah saw God's glory (Isa 6), he also saw his utter sinfulness. We don't see that today. David Brainerd did his whole life.

(3) When John saw God's glory (in Revelation), he fell flat on his face. We don't see that today.

(4) When Moses saw God's glory, well, (partial view in the Mountain), he was told to take his shoes off, and again he was hidden in the rock, and still his face radiated, but he didn't know it. He pursued God, and God knew it.

(5) When Jesus gave glory to the Father, He died on the cross. We always choose not to. Today, we are content with clapping, and when the service ends, we go back to the way we were.

Glory means Presence. Presence means Fire. Fire changes things. It means everything will burn up except that which God has changed in our character. *(Wednesday, November 19, 2014 at 8:36 A.M. CST)*

THE SPIRIT'S WORK
From my heart to yours—

How do I know that something happening is the work of the Holy Spirit? Here is how: If what is happening gives the right emphasis at the right time on the right thing and for the right end, it's from the Holy Spirit...every time. And only He is able to do that. *(Wednesday, November 19, 2014 at 8:39 A.M. CST)*

CONFIDENT, NOT SO FAST
From my heart to yours—

I was awakened this morning disturbed by the thought of God's glory. Bear with me. We want to go, seemingly in a hurry, into the Presence of God to behold His glory. We decide when and how long we wish to stay. We overlook the fact that entrance into His Presence is still guarded with fire and judgment. The only way we *can* enter is when we have the cover of Him who offered Himself as a sacrifice and took the fire of the altar and drank the cup of judgment on our behalf. Then He became our entrance into the Presence of Him who is an "all-consuming fire". *(Wednesday, November 19, 2014 at 8:53 A.M. CST)*

HORSE RACE
From my heart to yours—

When we compare any detail in our life in Christ to whatever the world has to offer as an alternative for living, it would appear like we are in a horse race, trying to bring someone from one horse to another (e.g., from one religion to another, from one faith to another). The fact is, the horse died. And it's a whole new life that began in Christ. *(Wednesday, November 19, 2014 at 9:11 A.M. CST)*

TO SEE, TO LIVE
From my heart to yours—

To see His glory is for us to die and for Him to live...die to self, die to the world, die to sin. Jesus on earth constantly reflected the glory of the Father *as the Son of Man* (i.e., as man, like us) by dying to self, dying to the world, and dying to sin. He did that so we *know* that we *can* glorify Him constantly if we, like He, live in the full power and dominance and working of the Holy Spirit in every detail of our life. *(Wednesday, November 19, 2014 at 9:12 A.M. CST)*

DOING GOOD
From my heart to yours–

"Doing good" is easy to do if one has resources. There are two problems. First, is that not all people have resources, and that creates an imbalance and inequity. Second, "doing good" also seems to give the impression that "being good" can be safely and comfortably implied and can be derived by conclusion. Not so fast! Reason being, human pride and unrelenting arrogance seem lately to easily get in the way and remain tolerated and unnoticed for the most part. That's how deceptive sin is. And that's why it took God to know satan's heart. To dismiss God would be pure evil. For even though He cast Adam and Eve uncompromisingly out of the Garden, He did not discard them the way people do to people today. *(Monday, November 24, 2014 at 7:18 A.M. CST)*

EMPTY AND LONELY
From my heart to yours–

How can a person be empty and lonely yet cluttered in life? Easy! Just look around. They have but are still looking. They grasp and catch handfuls of air. They own but leave everything behind. They talk but it's mostly echo. They ask, but ask again. They knock but no one is there. Jesus said, "*Come unto me … And I will give you rest… My yoke is easy; my yoke is light.*"

Paul in the Philippian jail redefined the meaning of "stocks and bonds". And The Church of Jesus Christ of Everyday Saints is not a Facebook social media platform. It's real. *(Tuesday, November 25, 2014 at 9:51 A.M. CST)*

DYING TO SELF (1)
From my heart to yours—

Did Jesus, the Son of Man, "die to self" while on earth? Absolutely *Yes*. We say that Jesus had to learn to die to *self* before He died for the *world*. He had to die to self *Himself* before He could say to anyone: "Follow Me". Now, *all* He asks for is: *Obedience*. Not ascetism, not refraining from certain things, not watching what we say, NOT activities or words. Not denominations or combinations. It's a singular mindset lifestyle; it's being like Him; it's being "in Him"; and that's why we say: It's *All about Him*. And that's why He said, "*When He, the Spirit of truth, comes, He will lead you into all truth. He will take of me, and give to you.*" Are you a follower of Jesus? *(Wednesday, November 26, 2014 at 9:25 A.M. CST)*

DYING TO SELF (2)
From my heart to yours—

Jesus did nothing (in pursuit of dying to self) based on how He felt at the moment while living on earth. He did not have a list of daily activities. He did not seek approval or consult anyone on earth. In other words, nothing on earth, to Him, was a consideration. It wasn't about what "He Did", but about "Whose He was". He simply did everything based on the desire of the Father in heaven from where He was born of the Spirit. Isn't that what Mary was told about the "Spirit of the Mighty" regarding Jesus' birth? Isn't that how anyone is born again, of the same Spirit too, and becomes a "follower of Jesus"? *(Wednesday, November 26, 2014 at 10:11 A.M. CST)*

DYING TO SELF (3)
From my heart to yours—

The world rejected Him when the world discovered that He came from God and they had no capacity to be pleasing to God (Rom 8:8). Yet, this "pleasing to the Father" was exactly the very reason why Jesus came to earth. And when the world didn't know what else to do with Him, they killed Him. Gal 4:29 "who is born according to the flesh persecuted him who is born according to the Spirit." 2 Tim 3:12 "they who desire to live godly will be persecuted." (Parenthetical question: can I pray that persecution stops against the believers?) True followers can (and ought to) expect the same treatment. How did Jesus succeed in living a life pleasing to the Father? Here's a thought: He yielded His will to the Father's will. That's why we say that He did not come to "save the world" as a task and get it done, but simply to "do the will of the Father". All his choices had the "pleasure of the Father" at their center. *(Thursday, November 27, 2014 at 11:13 A.M. CST)*

MEMBERS OF ONE ANOTHER
From my heart to yours—

This news piece is about 1-2 weeks old from North Sudan about the persecuted church there. Satan is attacking from the outside and inside. While some are calling believers to consider alternatives to grow the church, the fact remains that suffering is intended to cleanse the church, mobilize the believers, to purify the heart toward God. Prayer is much appreciated. The church there is part of the church where we are, Our brothers and sisters. If one hurts, I hurt, you hurt. God is able to do far more in such events. Many examples are scattered throughout church history. God can do it again in Sudan and elsewhere in North Africa and the Middle East.

This is NOT how a true follower of Jesus behaves, and for one simple reason: he cannot get anywhere even if he tries. :) *(Thursday, November 27, 2014 at 11:51 P.M. CST)*

~~~~~

DISAGREEMENTS RESOLVED
From my heart to yours—

When two members in the body of Christ are not in agreement, the entire body goes nowhere. They must agree, not by talking to one another, but by listening to the Spirit of Christ who fills the entire Body. *(Friday, November 28, 2014 at 12:48 P.M. CST)*

~~~~~

BEAR WITH ME PLEASE
From my heart to yours—

This morning, as I was running an errand, the Holy Spirit brought the attached picture once more and put it front and center before me with a question: "What were you focused on? What caught your attention?" And I thought, "Well, the shoes of course pointing in opposite direction." And the next question rushed in, "Did you consider looking at the FEET?" And then it all came together in my mind. The feet were DESIGNED and INTENDED to point in the same direction AND to work in harmony together; likewise, the members of the Body. But it's the shoes, not the feet that were pointing in opposite directions. And it's the shoes that were forcing the feet to behave contrary to their original design and intent. And I wondered -- how many times do we, in the Body of Christ, try to perform surgeries to match the feet with the direction of the shoes instead of the opposite - every member capturing every high thought and enslaving it to the obedience of Christ!!! And without exception, harm is brought to the Body. And all along, the feet should have been yielding to the Head and not to the shoes that were never designed as part of the body. *(Saturday, November 29, 2014 at 12:08 A.M. CST)*

～～～

PATIENCE - THE GIFT WRAP OF FAITH (1 OF 2)
From my heart to yours–

(For a bit more light on details, please read #2) The book of Job is not a dramatic illustration about Patience, but the truth about Faith. By way of Introduction: For me to think that God is "righteous" may be proper and reasonable. But for HIM to testify that I am righteous, then He must have made that possible by a means outside myself. That's the secret of the Book of Job in the OT. The reasoning behind it gives insight into the "Gospel" that Job came to "know", and now is fully declared in Christ and always proclaimed in the NT. The Book of Job is far more than a book about "patience". To write an entire book about patience may lift human aspirations somewhat, and that's...uh..."nice". But when God steps into a book (a nuance of the concept of "inspiration"), the whole picture changes. And to remain consistent with biblical precedent, we must begin our thinking now with God in the story of Job. Here is what the text says: "Job said to God, "You asked, 'Who is this who hides counsel without knowledge?' Therefore I have uttered what I did not understand, Things too wonderful for me, which I did not know. Listen, please, and let me speak; You said, 'I will question you, and you shall answer Me.' "I have heard of You by the hearing of the ear, But now my eye sees You. Therefore I abhor myself, And repent in dust and ashes." (Job 42:3-6 NKJV) Stepping in summary through the text, here is the flow of thought: In summary: God spoke ---> Job heard ---> Job lived in misery ---> His trusted friends failed him miserably ---> But Job held on to what he heard ---> His friends had no clue about what he heard ---> God could not lie ---> God fulfills his promise ---> Job confesses ---> Job lives to see faith become a reality in his lifetime ---> now there is no need for faith anymore because the eye has seen the promise fulfilled. Job, like Isaiah, discovered his sin when he stepped into the Presence of God; and it was too much to absorb. Yet, God justified him -- but he did that because of his Faith. *"The just shall live by faith,"* right? *(Saturday, November 29, 2014 at 7:58 A.M. CST)*

PATIENCE - THE GIFT WRAP OF FAITH (2 OF 2)
From my heart to yours–

(For a summary, please read #1) The book of Job is not a dramatic illustration about Patience, but the truth about Faith that works. By way of Introduction: The Book of Job is far more than a book about "patience". To write an entire book about patience may lift human aspirations somewhat, and that's...uh..."nice". But when God steps into a book (a nuance of the concept of "inspiration"), the whole picture changes. And to remain consistent with biblical precedent, we must begin our thinking now with God in the story of Job. Here is what the text says: "Job said to God, "You asked, 'Who is this who hides counsel without knowledge?' Therefore I have uttered what I did not understand, Things too wonderful for me, which I did not know. Listen, please, and let me speak; You said, 'I will question you, and you shall answer Me.' "I have heard of You by the hearing of the ear, But now my eye sees You. Therefore I abhor myself, And repent in dust and ashes." (Job 42:3-6 NKJV) Stepping through the text in detail, here is the flow of thought: (1) God spoke what could not be understood by mere human comprehension; (2) Job "heard" but did not "understand" (3) It was not because human capacity to "understand" hasn't developed yet; (4) But it was because what God "spoke" was "too wonderful" to Job; (5) And Job was beyond "knowing" that on his own. (6) But no one denies the fact that Job did "hear" it; "I have heard of You by the hearing of the ear." (Job 42:5 NKJV) (7) And no one denies that Job did not "understand" but he could not let go either. (8) He "believed". (9) THAT was what Job was holding on to, not that something was said but because it was GOD WHO SAID IT; (10) He (Job) stepped outside the limitations of human knowledge which is always limited, and entered into the realm of God when he attached himself to what God said. (11) In other words, as a believer, he became a "partaker of the divine nature" (2 Peter 1:4). Faith became the basis (in the legal sense) for limitless knowledge. (12) And THAT was what God could not take away from Job because He (God) spoke it. (13) And THAT is what FAITH is - exactly - It is "hearing and holding on to what God said, simply because GOD SAID IT." (14) Hebrews 6:18 God cannot lie if He makes a promise (quoted from Numbers 23:19). (15) And that's why His promises are "great and precious" (2 Peter 1) (16) This experience led Job to "abhor" himself and "repent". In summary: God spoke ---> Job heard ---> Job lived in misery ---> His trusted friends could not help him ---> But Job held on to what he heard ---> His friends had no clue about what he heard ---> God could not lie ---> God fulfills his promise ---> Job confesses ---> Job lives to see faith become a reality in his lifetime ---> now there is no need for faith anymore because the eye has seen the promise fulfilled. Now, moving from the Old to the New (Testament): Job is a type of Christ. He points to Jesus Christ who is "the Author and Finisher of our faith" - that is, Jesus is the

Fountainhead and the Perfecter of all faith. No one can add to the meaning and foundation of faith more than what Jesus laid. So much so that He (Jesus Christ) can make "real faith" a daily reality if we are "in union with Him"; that is, He in us and we in Him. Notice the words: "In the beginning was the word (the word spoken), and the word was with God (the word's fountain/source), and the word was God (the word's nature).... And the word became flesh (the word expressed)." (John 1) The fact of the Word ---> the Source of the Word ---> the Nature of the Word ---> the Expression of the Word. Paul takes this matter of faith a step further. He said to Titus that there is the promise of "eternal life"; thus, bridging the past with the future (Titus 1:1-2). Likewise, Peter writes to, "those who have obtained like precious faith with us by the righteousness of our God and Savior Jesus Christ: Grace and peace be multiplied to you in the knowledge of God and of Jesus our Lord, as His divine power has given to us all things that pertain to life and godliness, through the knowledge of Him who called us by glory and virtue, by which have been given to us exceedingly great and precious PROMISES, that through these you may be partakers of the divine nature, having escaped the corruption that is in the world through lust. (II Peter 1:1-4 NKJV) The question is never "Do you understand?" - when it comes to God; but rather, "Do you believe?" For faith is simply dwelling in the realm of the knowledge of God. That is, living where God is. But Paul said, "know ye not that you are the temple of God and God dwells in you". So faith now is "dwelling in the realm of God, fully expressed in Jesus Christ, who is dwelling in me, in the power of the Holy Spirit". So the Word says, "Faith comes by hearing, and hearing (comes) by the word of God." (Romans 10:17) Job, like Isaiah, discovered his sin only when he stepped into the Presence of God; and God's holiness was too much to absorb. Yet, God justified Job -- because of his Faith. Likewise Jesus discovered the full reality of OUR sin when He glanced into the cup and stepped into the furnace of God's wrath. Jesus was perfected - patiently - because He held on to the Father by FAITH, and saw the "joy set before Him" (Heb. 12), right? *(Saturday, November 29, 2014 at 8:39 A.M. CST)*

A SONG IN THE NIGHT
From my heart to yours—

Someone can always give me a song in the day to sing, but I know of only One who gives a song in the night. The difference? When I sing the one in the day, I go to the next song --maybe. But when I sing the song in the night, it leads me to worship, for I know he holds my hand, and I know He also holds tomorrow. During the day, there is work. At night, all I want, is a song. For I know that He walks with me and He talks with me, and He tells me I am His own. And that's all I want to hear. *(Monday, December 1, 2014 at 8:30 P.M. CST)*

EXCLUSIVE PREROGATIVE
From my heart to yours—

Jesus Christ reserved few things exclusively for himself to see that they happen exactly and completely. All else that we can think of is included. May we never forget these things:

(1) He reserves the power to SAVE the sinner, and He does, because the dead only need life and He is the Life.

(2) He reserves the power to BUILD the Church, and He does, because He paid for her, and He is the Way.

(3) He reserves the power to KEEP us holy, and He does, because He is Holy, and He is the Truth.

He accomplish the first through the power of His cross; the second through the power of His Name; and the third through the power of His Spirit. Eternal life is what the dead need. Eternal power is what the believer has. Eternal Spirit is what holiness demands. All three, without exception, demand *Obedience*. He himself obeyed, and He gives us daily the will to obey likewise. Do you believe? May we never forget, because He also reserves the final word to *Himself*. *(Thursday, December 4, 2014 at 1:13 A.M. CST)*

ARE YOU REALLY LISTENING? (1 OF 2)
From my heart to yours—

One of the things I discovered in 2014 that I needed to seriously commit to learn is: Listening, and "to listen carefully". Here's why: (1) There is too much religious chatter going on all over the place, I think. (2) What God wants me to hear may take place only once. He's not committed to repeating Himself. Now, THAT brought me real quick to a different reality. (3) People have become skilled in "saying things right". Just depends to whom they are talking. He, on the other hand, is different. He always does and says the right thing. (4) Listening means I need to stop thinking about what I'm going to say next. So hard, I caught myself red-handed. Maybe that's why I often walk away empty-handed. (5) Listening brings me face to face with whether I'm committed to "change" based on who He is and consequently what He says. (6) Listening maybe through people I never expected would say anything. When they spoke, it wasn't what I was expecting either. And few times they spoke without words.

The heartache was too much to bear. When I listened, here is what I heard... (...Next post). *(Saturday, December 6, 2014 at 11:48 P.M. CST)*

$$\sim\!\!\sim\!\!\sim$$

ARE YOU REALLY LISTENING? (2 OF 2)
From my heart to yours–

When I listened and knew I was just listening, I stood in awe, I bowed in silence, and I was fully wrapped in the wonder of His amazing love and grace. And there was a hush, a holy hush, as I looked into the eyes of a helpless sick patient with pneumonia in South Sudan whom I asked if I can pray for her. I could barely see inside that one room house. One small window, couple of pieces of old furniture, two partly broken chairs with plastic backing, and no electricity or even wires. I asked myself, "Can God be here too?" She was too tired to speak, but when I asked, her tired eyes wanted to speak. She closed her shaky red-lined eyelids in agreement then opened them, only to find her eyes welled up. My fellow pastor who accompanied me said she waits for someone to come and pray with her each time. He said "you have no idea how much she longs for that". I prayed - broken English, broken Arabic, broken Sudanese, some something I blabbered with my mouth. What they didn't hear was that I was really praying for God to help me and teach me to pray and not lie with words I memorized and formulas I'm comfortable with. I was done praying. I looked at her as she mouthed without audio the words "Thank you". I saw how helpless I am without Him, even when I prayed. Walking out, I remember that I stepped over the threshold at the door and looking back only to see her eyes close. Maybe she was praying for me. I wished it with all my heart. *(Saturday, December 6, 2014 at 11:52 P.M. CST)*

$$\sim\!\!\sim\!\!\sim$$

HEARING LOSS
From my heart to yours–

Why don't we *listen* when God speaks? Consider these reasons: (1) The haunting fears - some known or unknown, some transferred by others or are self-generated, some are real or not so real, and some natural to sharpen character and propel us forward. (2) The past, where many reside without realizing how much (3) The daunting prospects of the future, where many wish they reside but never manage to reach. Then we read, "*He who has an ear, let him hear* (as in, *listen*). It *is* possible then to listen, for with God all things are possible. May He give us today a listening ear because he said, "*I know the thoughts that I think toward you, says the LORD, thoughts of peace and not of evil, to give you a future and a hope.*" (Jeremiah 29:11). *(Sunday, December 7, 2014 at 7:35 A.M. CST)*

FOLLOWING AFTER HIM
From my heart to yours–

Being a True Follower of Jesus Christ is serious business and not a religious fad, mantra, cultic, or bathed in ritualistic waters of many flavors. Following Him has two parts. The first is that it always presents Him to us *alone* as our example so that we are not tempted to follow or be swayed by people. The second part it serves is as a reminder: (1) to walk humbly before God; (2) to remain submissive to the Spirit; (3) to be transparently accountable to godly people; (4) to remain true to his/her calling; (5) to use the gifts God has given remembering that it's not the gift but the given who makes thing happen, and (6) to be wise in the stewardship of the body - this earthen vessel that carries precious cargo. The rest is mere details that vary by experience or circumstance. But He remains the same, and forever. His name is Jesus Christ. He alone is worthy of worship. What do you say! *(Tuesday, December 9, 2014 at 1:48 P.M. CST)*

PRAYING RIGHT (1)
From my heart to yours–

Thinking right about prayer begins by thinking right about God. We always miss the first when we always ignore the second. And when we learn the second, we better watch out because the first will never be as we expected. *(Thursday, December 11, 2014 at 7:37 A.M. CST)*

PRAYING RIGHT (2)
From my heart to yours–

Thinking right about prayer begins by thinking right about God. So, when the disciples asked, "Lord, teach us to pray", they were confessing: (1) Lord, we don't know about God. Would you please teach us anew? (2) Lord, we are not asking for the words. We are asking about the Word for we believe. (3) Lord, we don't want to pray like the Pharisees, and not like the Gentiles. We want to pray like you. (4) Lord, we have been to the Temple and synagogue. Would you take us into the Presence of Him who we cannot speak His Name for it is too holy for our lips. (5) Lord, we have heard you pray. Teach us THAT. And Jesus said, "Since I've been here on earth, as the Son of Man, He's been my Father in a way that you too can know the same relationship with Him. And I want you to know that He IS your Father. I wanted to be human like you so much, because I want you to share in my divine nature too. That's the only way we (you and I) can be ONE. And you all can also be ONE like I and the Father are." So, when you pray, say, "Our Father who art in heaven ....." He is my Father like you can never imagine. Stay with me, and I will show you everything about Him. And you will love Him just like I love Him. I have already asked Him for that." Do you understand? And Peter said, "*Lord, to whom shall we go; You have the word of eternal life.*" And the Voice came from heaven saying, "This is my Beloved Son in whom I am well pleased. Listen to Him." *(Thursday, December 11, 2014 at 11:31 A.M. CST)*

WHAT DO YOU SEE WHEN YOU LOOK?
From my heart to yours–

When I look at someone who is dirty, ugly, below my social level, uneducated and dumb; When I come across someone I hate, unwelcome, always distant, highly opinionated and a pure rebel; When I gaze at someone who hates me, shows no respect and disregard about anything I try to tell him (because I am far better); When I intentionally push him away or avoid him; Then I remember how much God loved me in Christ and accepted me as I was. Then He showed me His Son on the cross to show me the image of what He wants me to become. Then He embraced me, and His Spirit engulfed me, and brought me to Him who died for me, and taught me to say, "I love you". "*How can I say 'Thanks' for the things you have done for me? Things so undeserved, yet you came to prove your love for me; The voices of a million angels, could not express my gratitude; All that I am, or ever hope to be; I owe it all to Thee. 'To God be the glory.'*" And I'm still learning ... *(Thursday, December 11, 2014 at 12:17 P.M. CST)*

EMMANUEL (GOD WITH US)
From my heart to yours—

Clarifying this business of being "called by God", I know its definition and summary is not man-made, but heaven-sent. Yes, I'm thinking of Christmas! I'm still asking and pondering on my own journey as I think of Emmanuel (God with us), as I think of Jesus the Son of Man, as I think of many unknown nameless messengers of the cross. I remembered a song from many years past; the words say: "When I think of how He came so far from glory Came to dwell among the lowly such as I To suffer shame and such disgrace On Mount Calvary take my place Then I ask myself this question Who am I?" "Who am I that The King would bleed and die for Who am I that He would pray not my will, Thy Lord The answer I may never know Why He ever loved me so But to that old rugged cross He'd go For who am I?" Yes, it IS Christmas. And I'm glad He prepared the delivery room when "there was no room"...long, long time ago. So, I share my thoughts so far. For I'm convinced that "being called" depends: - not on where I'm going next, but on if I'm listening first - not on what I want (even if it's doable), but on what He wants (even if it's impossible) - not on what needs to be done, but on what needs to be done in me - not on what the message is, but on where the message is from - not only on the depths of my sin, but also on the heights for His grace - not on the questionable value of my love for Him, but on the indescribable value of His love for me. *"Behold, what manner of love the Father has bestowed upon us that we should be called the children of God."* (1 John) Merry Christmas!
(Wednesday, December 17, 2014 at 10:09 P.M. CST)

WORTHLESS SACRIFICES
From my heart to yours—

David said, "I will not sacrifice to the Lord my God burnt offerings that cost me nothing." (2 Sam 24) "For You do not desire sacrifice, or else I would give it; You do not delight in burnt offering. The sacrifices of God are a broken spirit, A broken and a contrite heart— These, O God, You will not despise." (Psalms 51) The error of the church today is that we offer, and gladly, sacrifices unto the Lord that cost us nothing. "Therefore, when Christ (the Anointed One) came into the world, He said: 'Sacrifice and offering you did not desire, but a body you prepared for me; with burnt offerings and sin offerings you were not pleased. Then I said, 'Here I am - it is written about me in the scroll- I have come to do your will, My God.' " (Heb. 10) *"How much more shall the blood of Christ, who through the eternal Spirit offered Himself without spot to God, cleanse your conscience from dead works to serve the living God?"* (Heb. 9) "And by that will, we have been made holy through the sacrifice of the body of Jesus Christ once for all." (Heb. 10) *"Therefore, I urge you, brothers and sisters, in view of God's mercy, to offer your bodies as a living sacrifice, holy and pleasing to God - this is your true and proper worship."* Acceptable sacrifices to the Lord are only those that cost; the one, who offers them, pays. *(Thursday, December 18, 2014 at 5:28 A.M. CST)*

HOLY LIVING
From my heart to yours—

HOLY practical living is done individually. It is not customizable to my liking, because God is HOLY in name and nature and anything He touches. And He is changeless. Has He touched you lately? For with His touch there is healing, there is newness in life, and there is power to stop Him in His tracks like in the story of the woman who touched the hem of his garment. My prayer is that the One who touched the broken and fallen, diseased and rejected, distant and lonely may touch you before end of 2014. I would strongly encourage you to touch - even the hem of His garment, for His name is Holy. *(Friday, December 19, 2014 at 10:38 A.M. CST)*

STRANGE THINGS HAPPEN
From my heart to yours–

Forgive me, but I am still thinking of Christmas. For I recognized that unusual things happen when people come face to face with Jesus - just Jesus, nothing else, no one else. Here's what I mean:

A. Wise men in search of a King, they – (1) Came persistently with the right attitude (2) Worshipped completely the right person (3) Departed rejoicing to begin a journey that never ends

B. Mary in virgin existence, she – (1) Sensed the Presence of the Holy Spirit (2) Received overwhelming Peace, Grace, and Blessing (3) Heard clear and consistent prophecy regarding the baby in her womb (Lk 1:32ff) For Everyone on whom the Spirit comes and in whom the power of the Most High works, comes into a personal communion with God that never ends.

C. Shepherds in the field, they – (1) The last shall be first for the Gospel by design is "for all" (2) The least deserved a royal presentation (3) They came puzzled, they went rejoicing

D. Simeon in the Temple, he – (1) "Knew" the Baby was not the vehicle by the sum total of God's redemption (2) Was in the Spirit, waiting, praying, and full of unwavering faith (3) Magnified God by serving the purpose which summarized the reason for his existence

Many others came face to face with Him, until today. Many will see Him face to face, for eternity. Are you one? Or, are we "done" with Christmas? *(Tuesday, December 30, 2014 at 7:38 A.M. CST)*

TRUE UNION
From my heart to yours–

True Union with Christ prepares a true follower of Christ for true communion with Him. Both, the union and communion are the work of His Spirit in me. He brings me to Him and brings Him to me. The Spirit places me in Him and shows me the wonder of His love all of my days until my cup overflows. The difference between "talking the talk" and "walking the talk" can be compared to the three men, experts in all fields of human knowledge and experience, were in the waiting room discussing the merits and challenges of childbearing... Until a woman in her ninth month walked in and hobbled her way to the delivery room". "And there was silence for a span of 30 minutes," seemed like eternity there for a moment. *(Tuesday, December 30, 2014 at 10:26 P.M. CST)*

SPIRITUAL WARFARE (1 OF 2)
From my heart to yours–

Spiritual Warfare, strictly speaking, is the war that rages daily between the Spirit of Christ and the spirit of Satan which is in the world. The follower of Christ is the field where the war is being fought viciously. Both, the Spirit of Christ and the spirit of satan have committed all their resources to win the war of *daily living.* These are NOT electronic war games we play, but this war and every battle in it is a matter of life or death, Every-Single-Day. There is NO political correctness or "tolerance" acceptable, and *no* negotiations proposed. One side must win in real life. My *Identity Alone* defines my position and determines which side I am on. My *Obedience Alone* defines my character and determines which of the two I am resisting. The rest is mere details. My *obedience* reflects in me the true character of Christ, nurtured daily in my relationship with the Spirit of Christ. It is carried out daily through my complete surrender to Him. *"To Be like Him"* is what life in Him is all about. *(Tuesday, December 30, 2014 at 11:16 P.M. CST)*

SPIRITUAL WARFARE (2 OF 2)
From my heart to yours—

My *surrender* (mind, soul, body, emotions, will) is one sure thing demanded by the two sides whether we are aware or not. Surrender to the Spirit of Christ brings us uninterrupted fellowship with Christ. On the other hand, Surrender to the spirit of Satan in this world will certainly break the Spirit's fellowship, will grieve Him, and renders me useless in my daily service. Nothing I can DO, except total and complete surrender of my mind, soul, body, emotions, and will is acceptable. Talking the talk with precision alone is fake and qualifies me for the "*Most Miserable*" Award. True songs are not what's on my lips but what's in my heart. My lips may make me sound like an angel, but the groaning of my heart may make me sound like a lonely owl in the night. That's what Jesus Christ the Son of Man did to the Spirit as He lived on earth. That's what He expects me to do likewise. And He reminds me in my spirit saying, "Yes, you can!" "*Love not the world!*" *(Tuesday, December 30, 2014 at 11:18 P.M. CST)*

INEVITABLE STORMS (1 OF 2)
From my heart to yours–

I always began to worry after a while when everything in my life appears to be going perfectly well. Nothing to complain about! Nothing seems "out of place". Yet it has written all over it the absence of any wind for my sail, and the floating of dead fish in the same waters where they were intended to swim always, not as a sport but as a matter of life or death. Storms in real life are inevitable. Storms in the life of a true follower of Christ are the "stuff" out of which real life is made, and character is shaped. To be certain, I don't need to invite storms; for coming, they will. First, are Storms caused by my *disobedience*. These are discounted because they are not part of a living faith, not by day, not by night. They simply need to be settled at the cross, acknowledging my sin specifically, confessing my sin without excuse, passionately hating the very thought of it, and completely casting myself upon the mercy of a holy and righteous God who hates sin, and reminding myself that the same fountain that flowed from Calvary to wash me clean and save me is the one that continues to cleanse me from every sin (1 John 1:7). Other storms are definitely in the forecast. (Please see 2 of 2) *(Tuesday, December 30, 2014 at 11:41 P.M. CST)*

INEVITABLE STORMS (2 OF 2)
From my heart to yours–

Other storms are not invited but can be expected. But why do these happen in the life of a true follower of Christ? After all, some may think, "If I'm following Him, why are these happening to me?" Some erroneously think that following Jesus will *prevent* storms from coming. This is SO *untrue*. Here are some reasons why these types of storms come –

(1) To Discipline: just because I confessed my sin and am sure of its forgiveness, doesn't mean that there are no consequences that still must be paid. Regardless of how repentant a criminal may be, before the judge there still are consequences.

(2) To Remind: to remind the follower of Christ that it is "the will in heaven" that comes to earth, not the will on earth that gets executed in heaven. Experiencing His will in my life does not rule out pain. Jesus, the Son of Man, is our example.

(3) To Anticipate: this is what every follower of Christ looks forward to, namely, the day when we see Him face to face and all earthly suffering will come to an end. Meanwhile, we along with all of nature "groan" anticipating a day when things change (Romans 8).

(4) To Assure: this is a clear statement of affirmation from Him to us, a promise, that as our spirit was quickened through the indwelling Holy Spirit and as our character and personality are being transformed daily through the same Spirit, the day is coming when our faulty bodies will be transformed, and the "corruptible" shall put on the "incorruptible" (Thessalonians)

(5) To Watch: this is the nature of daily living by faith as followers of Christ. We cannot sleep or be distracted. Satan intends "to steal and to kill and to destroy". Refining our life and traveling light (Heb. 12:1-2) is what the Spirit does. Sometimes through suffering He gets our attention and keeps us focused by faith on Him, not to inflict but to refine and transform as by fire (1 Peter 1 and 2 Peter 1).

(6) To Wait: this is waiting, not because we understand, but precisely because we do *not* understand. And even if He tried to explain, our capacity to comprehend is very limited. That's when He

wants us to simply "trust and obey", not because I see the light at the end of the tunnel, but because He walks with me even through the valley of the shadow of death (Psalm 23).

(7) To Pray: this is when the unexplainable happens, for no earthly reason or rhyme. Holding on to Him by faith, through the tears, will give us His peace that passes understanding. His peace which no one can explain will be delivered to me as a follower at the right time and in the right measure. *(Wednesday, December 31, 2014 at 12:08 A.M. CST)*

GREAT AND PRECIOUS PROMISES
From my heart to yours—

Just to list these promises would remind me of what I have, then I will likely move to the next thing in my daily life. But to take them one by one, one day at a time, (like One-A-Day + Iron), chew on it, and spend the day thinking, praising, thanking, and trusting that promise for that day, now *that* makes me look forward to 2015, and is worth looking forward to meeting the Lord day by day. I encourage you to do likewise. He's worth it, right? Just one promise, each day! We know that He is the only One who has kept all his promises; not because of who we are but because of who He is. His name is Jesus Christ. All my love is due Him. What about your love?? *(Wednesday, December 31, 2014 at 11:53 A.M. CST)*

MY FIRST THOUGHT
From my heart to yours—

I asked as I laid down last night, "Lord, please give me a first thought for 2015 as I wake up tomorrow morning. I don't want 2015 to be tempted with the clutter of religious trappings acceptable to those on earth. I ask that you anchor my heart in you." I woke up this morning humming a few lines from an old song that says "*Worthy Is the Lamb That Was Slain*", taken from Revelation 5:12 *"In a loud voice they were saying: "Worthy is the Lamb, who was slain, to receive power and wealth and wisdom and strength and honor and glory and praise!"* I smiled and thanked Him for answering my prayer. My prayer for you who carry His Name is that throughout your 2015 days you discover the wonder of His grace and the splendor of His majesty, for He is worthy. It's simply an eternal kaleidoscope of Who He Is. A more recent song has these lines: "Name above all names You are worthy of all praise And my heart will sing How great is our God." Happy New Year! *(Thursday, January 1, 2015 at 11:02 A.M. CST)*

THE DAY MOM STOPPED BEING MOM, MAYBE
From my heart to yours–

I knew I was going on yet another journey, unexpected to be sure, but that's how God works. He prefers journeys, unplanned for us, but as for Him, he's always there. One recent morning I saw a picture of my nephew's newborn little girl, Ruth, laying in the infant incubator, oxygen tubes in her little nose, resting, asleep and the machine helping her breathe. Then later that morning I went to my parents' home and saw my dad sitting in his chair, with oxygen tubes in his not-so-little nose, resting, and the machine helping him breathe. And I thought, "My! My! Many years have come and gone, but not much has changed." Today, I was sitting with Mom (89) after helping her with some needed tasks as her strength is failing her in many respects. Over the past several months, when she was still strong, she noticed "some things" have been happening to her, couldn't explain it, catching her by surprise every time, and she looks at me puzzled and says, "what's happening to me?" Those who know Mom, all her life she never asked those kinds of questions-- Always in charge, always running circles around the rest of the crowd. But now she realizes that her engines are starting to slow down. She would say the words -- I can cook, I can clean, I can have people over, this is what needs to be done, we need to go visit so and so, etc., but she started to catch herself not able to do hardly any. She looks at me and smiles, and says, "I was able to..., but... (Pause)...I know." Then she leans forward, runs her fingers through my hair, and whispers..."but I know I'm not alone." I remembered one time, while walking with her up the stairs to her room, she paused in her faltering steps, turned to me and said, "Do you know that all these years, we have been living in the grace of God? I know He will never leave us. Don't ever forget it." That was months ago. And since then, siblings and I could see how her engines were showing more and more signs of wear and tear and significant slowing down, and her sense of her surrounding was fading rapidly. As I sat back in the chair next to her bed, I wondered, "Is this the same Mom I had? It can't be! By what the eyes could see and judge -- *No way*! The body is still there, the eyes, the smile, and the hands. Granted, she slowed down. But was the vessel that I saw for years -- the real person? I see: No more taking charge; No more "sure step" or confidence in her speech; No more snapping to attention of everything around her. The shell is failing. The tent is being shaken by the winds of change. My Mom is not the Mom that my eyes always told me, but now I see that they lied. Then I realized that my eyes didn't lie. I realized that they were simply not the proper measuring stick in the first place. I realized that my Mom is always there. I just needed a vision adjustment of my own, and a reminder that we really don't walk by sight--never have, never should, for we never can. How do I know? After she showered, got dressed, hair combed, her night gown buttoned up, and with my hands at her waistline she hobbled toward her bed, she turned around just enough for me to wrap my arm around her. She leaned her head on my chest and kissed me as I kissed the top of her head. "Mom, do you feel better now?" "I know I'm much better." She sat on her bedside and gave me her hands. She leaned again and nuzzled her face into my head as I was trying to clip her fingernails. "Mom, hold on, I need to finish." "I know, but I needed to kiss you once more." Dinner was being prepared. I gave her the first bite, and remembered some sixty years ago when she did the same to me -- clipping nails, dressing me, feeding me, making me look handsome, hair combed, shoes on my feet, initiating a conversation that hasn't ended yet. Now, things are....., well, just about the same. Her hands are soft as ever. Her fingernails trimmed nicely. "Do you like how your fingernails look, Mom?" "Oh, yes." "Ready to eat?" "Eat? I have everything right here." Then I knew that the shell never was my Mom. The shell was simply the *visual*, for my sake, of who she has really been all these years. Regardless of what happens to the visual, the real person will always be there. Just like the baby in the manger, he became the visual and the full expression of what God has been from eternity past. We just needed to see for a short spell. Then He said, "Close your eyes now and know that I am with you until the very end." I helped her up, hugged her close, and thanked God for the years, for the conversation, for his never ending love. At the start, she helped me make sense. Now, the tables turned, and I can see God navigating her through life with grace and pure love, enough to sustain her until she sees Him who is the same yesterday, today, and...

"*Let the Word of Christ dwell in your richly.*" Here is a good place to begin :). It would be a GREAT encouragement to others to know who finished well. Why? *Because it's all about Him.*

～⌒～

PURE LOVE, PURE WORSHIP
From my heart to yours—

I'm not ashamed of the Gospel of Christ because it is the power of God to save to the uttermost. Nothing short of the full power of God is able to save a runaway. Nothing less than the full justice of His wrath was needed to be poured on sin. Nothing less than His love is able to motivate anyone to live for Him alone. For it was the prime motive behind our redemption, his incarnation, his resurrection, and our life in Him. All made possible at the wondrous cross on which the Prince of glory died. My prayer is that ONLY my unquestionable nonnegotiable irreversible unconditional love for Him be the motivation that always and passionately kindles the fire in my heart-- not shame, not family, not people, not country, not politics, not peers, not guilt, not book, not sword, not any other allegiance. He did the same, and it's only reasonable for Him to ask us to do likewise. In case we can't, he says, "not to worry, I am with you always, my Spirit is in you, and you will know when your love has been purified." Pure love breeds pure worship! *(Saturday, January 3, 2015 at 10:39 A.M. CST)*

～⌒～

"I LIFT UP MY VOICE"
From my heart to yours—

Twenty nine years ago, when he was but few hours old, his Mom and I handed him back to God. Since then, we've never been disappointed nor tried to look back to review our decision, for God always does something beautiful, something good. His cousins call him "Jona". We call him "Son". Always beloved. He taught us to love God with a pure heart. A chorus that Jona composed 10 years ago sums it all up: "*I lift up my voice, to You for ever more; I sing with my mouth, the praises of my King; He reigns in my heart, for others to see; The glories of God, shining through me.*" *(Tuesday, January 6, 2015 at 6:50 A.M. CST)*

SIMPLE THINGS
From my heart to yours—

My two joys - having a quiet birthday dinner with the them. THANK YOU Everyone for your love and friendship, and for being part of our life. On many occasions, when Jonathan prays, he asks God to bless -- and here there is no telling who he mentions, most times by name, dear people from Egypt or Sudan, Lebanon or Jordan, Syria or Iraq, Morocco or Algeria, Tunis or down the street from our house. What a blessing to me/us when he prays. Much appreciation and love to you, our family and friends. *(Tuesday, January 6, 2015 at 7:19 P.M. CST)*

SERIOUSLY, WHO ARE YOU? (1 OF 2)
From my heart to yours–

And the evil spirit answered and said, *"Jesus I know, and Paul I know; but who are you?"* (Acts 19:15) Summary: The "spirit world" is where the real war has always been, and it is the world where Jesus won the battle against satan, and satan knows it. That's why he is raving mad and furiously angry. As long as I think that the visible world is where the war is waged, I lose. Btw, the war has been won, soundly, completely, and eternally. Where? On the cross. Then Jesus said, "*All authority is given to me... Go...I am with you until the very end.*" (Matt 28) From the verse above, here are some observations: (1) Jesus doesn't need introduction where it matters (i.e., in the spirit world). (2) Real followers of Jesus don't need introduction there either. (3) Jesus expects His followers to be (outwardly) who they really are on the inside, and only His followers can. The rest are fake as fake can be. (4) That's why His followers are never known by any denomination but content with the simple truth of being "his followers". How do I know? He said, "My sheep hear my voice and follow me because they know me." (John 10) (5) If evil spirits know who Jesus and Paul really are, they definitely know if I am real or fake. What people think, therefore, is...well, irrelevant. (6) Jesus confirms who we really are by embedding the whole of his Holy Spirit in us completely. Jesus: "I will ask the Father, and he will give you another comforter - one just like me" - so you never have to miss a beat. Not only this; there is more, much more. (Please see #2). *(Friday, January 9, 2015 at 9:13 A.M. CST)*

SERIOUSLY, WHO ARE YOU? (2 OF 2)
From my heart to yours—

And the evil spirit answered and said, "Jesus I know, and Paul I know; but who are you?" (Acts 19:15)

(1) Jesus and Paul had no doubt about what really matters: their identity, who they really are. Paul: "I know whom I have believed..." Jesus: "I am the way, the truth, and even the life...I am the bread of life...I am the living water...I am the good shepherd...I AM that I AM...I am the narrow gate...I am the light of the world...I am the resurrection and the life...I am the true vine

(2) They both operated internally (in their heart) in that same spirit world, and reflected what people cannot see to the visible world. That's why the Scriptures say, "As a man think in his heart, so is he."

(3) Jesus will not judge man based on what man *does* but on who he *is* first ("he who searches the heart" Rom 8:27; "he who searches the minds and hearts" Rev. 2:24; "until the Lord comes, who will both bring to light the hidden things of darkness and expose the motives of your hearts" 1 Cor. 4:5; "the word of God is quick and powerful, and sharper than any two edged sword, piercing even to the dividing asunder of soul and spirit, and of the joints and marrow, and is a discerner and judge of the thoughts and intents of the heart.").

(Friday, January 9, 2015 at 11:16 A.M. CST)

FAITH, THE MISSING GEM
From my heart to yours—

In the words of A. W. Tozer: "To court a Christian for his financial contribution is as evil a thing as to marry a man for his money." *"Then will follow coldness and spiritual sterility which we will try desperately to cure by wild appeals to God for revival."* "The people of the world will not much care what we believe and they will stare vacantly at our religious forms, but there is one thing they will never forgive us—the presence of God's Spirit in our hearts. They may not know the cause of that strange feeling of antagonism which rises within them, but it will be nonetheless real and dangerous. Satan will never cease to make war on the Man-child, and the soul in which dwells the Spirit of Christ will continue to be the target for his attacks;" and, *"For My people have committed two evils: They have forsaken Me, the fountain of living waters, And hewn themselves cisterns—broken cisterns that can hold no water."* - Jeremiah 2:13 God help us if we truly carry the name of Christ. *(Friday, January 9, 2015 at 10:32 P.M. CST)*

RELIGIOUS ROMANCE
From my heart to yours—

Romancing the Holy Spirit of God to secure his favor is a deadly sin if we have no intentions to submit, to surrender, to change. Seduction of the Spirit (e.g., Mr. and Mrs. Ananias in Acts 5, and Simon the magician in Acts 8) is sure to fail, and will carry with it a double portion of God's wrath (Jer. 2:23). The three-fold reason is that (1) it always fails in attracting a person to the crucified Christ; (2) it gives a false impression of salvation; and (3) gives a false conviction that we are doing the right thing. God help us if we indeed carry the name of Christ. *(Friday, January 9, 2015 at 10:49 P.M. CST)*

THINKING OF JESUS (1 OF 2)
From my heart to yours

This morning, I woke up thinking about Jesus. I noticed this about Him: (1) His days were never cluttered, and he was intentional and deliberate, ALWAYS. (2) He always looked for and found a solution. (3) He always spent a significant amount of time in prayer. Period! (4) He passionately had the Father as his top priority, ALWAYS, and never compromised that. The Father's presence, the Father's heart, the Father's will. The rest was details. Maybe that's why he wasn't impressed with being made king on earth. (5) He "finished the work he was sent to do". No questions asked. His "exit interview" was on the cross on earth and in the Holy of Holies in heaven. Still want to be a follower of Jesus?! *(Tuesday, January 13, 2015 at 9:39 A.M. CST)*

THINKING OF JESUS (2 OF 2)
From my heart to yours–

In thinking further about Jesus, I noticed that He was able to accomplish everything without exception – (1) Not as the Son of God (although he was always aware of his divine nature, as all his followers ought to) but as the Son of Man (2) Not by "pushing his way through", but by emptying himself and yielding to the Spirit of the living God (3) Not by rising above the crowd, for all were dead in sin, but by being separate from the crowd to do the will of the Father completely (4) Not by his teaching but by His obedience unto death (5) Not by going after what He wanted but by going after what mattered, "to seek and to save that which is lost" (6) Not by taking the lives of others, but by giving his own life a ransom for many. I looked in the mirror and thought: "Martha, Martha ..." (*Tuesday, January 13, 2015 at 9:46 A.M. CST*)

I DON'T KNOW WHY
From my heart to yours–

(1) Jesus never helped anyone "feel good about themselves. I don't know why people say that. (2) Jesus never helped anyone "find themselves", especially since every true follower must lose himself/herself. (3) Jesus never promised what He could not deliver on. HIS promises alone are "great and precious". I don't know why many take the liberty from their pulpits and make promises saying "Jesus told me to tell you". (4) Jesus never started with the individual to introduce him/her to the love of the Father. He always brought the person to an "alone" place, face-to-face with Him first. Pharisees didn't know what to do with Him; publicans and sinners did. (5) Jesus never taught doctrines, but began and concluded with himself. I don't know why we think we know better.   (*Tuesday, January 13, 2015 at 2:37 P.M. CST*)

IN SUMMARY ABOUT JESUS
From my heart to yours–

After the last two posts "thinking about Jesus", I realized a slight wordiness. So, here are twenty (20) single-word descriptors to wrap our mind and heart around, and consequently around Him: Simple, Intentional, Deliberate, Transparent, Passionate, Focused, Clear-headed, Creative, Saving, Prayerful, Realistic, Prioritizing, Human, Gentle, Separated, Obedient, Surrendered, Giving, Ransoming, All-Loving, Not a typical workshop material, but a good start toward *worship.* Do I love Him enough to give up everything to be like Him?! No excuses! *(Tuesday, January 13, 2015 at 2:48 P.M. CST)*

EVIL AND GOOD
From my heart to yours—

Desires and choices (good and evil) are first cousins from parents who are not blood-related. The only common factor between them is that both have a price and their owner must pay. Both have consequences taking a person on a path of irreconcilable differences. "*Love not the world.*" *(Saturday, January 17, 2015 at 7:30 A.M. CST)*

WORSHIP, RELATIONSHIP, LORDSHIP
From my heart to yours—

My relationship with God is irreversibly anchored in the cross of Calvary. If I minimize the impact of what happened at the cross, I will trivialize the depth of the relationship with Him, and render most of it as optional. As I survey the cross properly, I am driven not to work harder but to explore the necessity of true singular worship of Him. This is where I cry out, "Remember me, Lord". For it is not what I've done that really matters at the end of my days, but what you've done. A line of a song I learned in the '70s says: "*Oh, the wonder of wonders that thrills my soul, is the wonder that God loved me.*" His name, His precious name, is Jesus Christ. *(Wednesday, January 21, 2015 at 5:33 P.M. CST)*

CROWDING SATAN OUT (1 OF 2)
From my heart to yours–

The daily desire of God for me as a true follower of Christ is to BE like Jesus by means of the power of the Holy Spirit. Since the Father, the Son, and the Holy Spirit are committed to this, this - their commitment - is a non-negotiable on Go's part. Pure and Simple! As Jesus succeeded, YES, you and I can too. Life is not about *doing*, but it's about *being*. For *being* is what's invisible; *doing* is what's visible. The rest is details. *Being filled*: To the *true* follower of Jesus Christ, (Not the fake one), being filled with the Holy Spirit is not optional, not an elective course, and is not one of the routes on a GPS screen. Walking in the Spirit, Living in the Spirit, and Being filled with the Spirit of God is imperative in its command, and indicative of an awakened soul passionate for God and everything that God - not I - is about. True passion can only BE for one. To think that I can be made alive and can say, in effect, "Thank you Lord for this and that, but I intend to live my life my way, and please clean up after me because you love me", is a delusion right out of hell, a deadly virus from satan that spreads across Christendom and its members. *Being Ready*: The reason for this is one. The *Spirit* (divine nature: worshipping, loving, sacrificing, serving, trusting, hoping, loving more), and the *Flesh* (human nature: my thoughts, affection, will, desires, wants, etc.) are at war with one another (Romans 8). Whether I realize it or not, the Holy Spirit who delivered me from the grip and dominion of satan is determined to preserve and protect those who are saved and are under His control. *Being True*: A cup that is *full* is a cup that has no room, not for even one drop. If a drop of liquid is poured into the full cup, it has to roll out because there is absolutely no room for one more drop. Likewise with satan. If I crowd him out of my life, he will have no room to stand. This does not mean: "get religious" because that's disgusting and evil. Jesus didn't die on the cross so I can be religious, but so I can be resurrected from death, revived in the Spirit, and reformed from the grounds up in the image of Christ. Jesus said, "The ruler of this world comes and he will find nothing that belongs to him." How did Jesus accomplish that? Simple! Here is how: (we want to be like Him, right?) (Please, see part 2). *(Thursday, January 22, 2015 at 5:25 A.M. CST)*

∽⌒∾

CROWDING SATAN OUT (2 OF 2)
From my heart to yours–

The daily desire of God for me as a true follower of Christ is to BE like Jesus by means of the power of the Holy Spirit. Since the Father, the Son, and the Holy Spirit are committed to this, this - their commitment - is a non-negotiable on Go's part. Pure and Simple! As Jesus succeeded, YES, you and I can too. Jesus said, "The ruler of this world comes and he will find nothing that belongs to him." How did Jesus accomplish that? Simple! Here is how: (we want to be like Him, right?) (1) PASSION: He was loving and passionate about the Father, about the Lost, about the Church, about the Word of God, and about the thing called "Obedience". We can BE likewise. (2) LOVE: He loved to the uttermost, without exception, without question, without hesitation, and every day of Him life. He died full of pure love. Nothing is like that on earth. Don't bother looking. If I look, I pay, and the price I pay is heavy. We can BE likewise. (3) SURRENDER: He completely, consciously, and without looking back, surrendered to the Holy Spirit of God to whom, while in His earthly days and like us, Jesus surrendered

because He loved to the uttermost (see # 1 and 2). We can BE likewise. (4) WARFARE: He was very conscious of the war to be waged with evil, with satan, with the flesh, with the world system. Although His eyes were wide open going in, although He was attacked frequently by satan and ultimately at the cross, He fixed His eyes not on the shameful cross but what's beyond the cross. We can BE likewise. (5) FAITH: He lived His whole life as the "Son of Man" (meaning, like us) by faith, not knowing what to expect at every turn, but trusting the Father, the One who said, "This is my Beloved Son in whom I am very pleased". We can BE likewise. The line from a song says: "...and He walks with me, and He talked with me, and He tells me I am His own." The question is not: Who am I and what am I to do (even though I don't know exactly who I am), but *why would He even care so much for me and love me*?!!!
(Thursday, January 22, 2015 at 5:45 A.M. CST)

<hr>

SPIRIT-FILLED PRACTICUM
From my heart to yours–

I'm learning that a person's life is made rich because of events woven into stories with places and people and experiences. One such story is that of Pastor Bill. He and Maxine, his wife, wandered into our worship time one Sunday morning in the mid-80's and sat in the back, reserved and quiet. That was the first time we lay eyes on this couple. During "guest recognition" time, I asked them if they would kindly tell us about themselves. Pastor Bill: I'm Bill, this is Maxine my wife. We were driving in this direction and saw cars in the parking lot, and decided to stop and worship with you. John: Are you pastor of any church now, brother Bill? Bill: well, I was, up until this morning. Choking on his words, he went on ... Bill: the church where I was pastor asked me to leave after the morning service at 8 A.M. after I shared with them that I needed their prayers because the doctor gave us the bad news that I have bone cancer in a very advanced stage and it's expected to spread. The church deacons said they couldn't afford my insurance and needed to leave. So we didn't know where to go, and it seems the Lord led us here but we don't know why. Silence! John: Can we pray for brother Bill right now and ask God to intervene?! We all stood and prayed, some choking in tears from this sudden unexpected news. It really disrupted everything, EVERYTHING, and we knew it. I don't recall how we finished "the service", but we did, and went home. We shook hands with Bill and Maxine, welcomed them, embraced them, promised to continue to pray for them, and someone invited them for a meal that day. During the following few weeks, Pastor Bill and Maxine continued to come every week. Church people started providing meals for them to help, visiting them, encouraging them often, and praying with them. Very sweet spirit, no doubt. Then, something different, something strange, almost spontaneous, started happening. Not sure where it started, but starting, it did. Bill's condition worsened. His doctor visits were giving bad reports every time. His cancer spread to his spine, his head, lymph nodes, and extremities. If he and wife happened to walk in late during the church's prayer time, we knew Bill has just walked in, because we could smell the devastation taking place in his body ... and soul. Moving 350 lbs. became much more difficult. Also, over a period of 2-3 weeks, individual members during the week or on weekend would ask to see me, or call, or wait until everyone left the service, and individually would say the following, one way or another, "pastor, we've been studying about the Holy Spirit for over a year.

We've been studying about prayer for the past six months. Do you think God sent us Bill, wanting us to apply what we studied and pray?" One by one, more than half of the membership, even guests, as if all became part of "one", woven into one body fabric, fasting, restless, hushed, and wanting God to do something. John: yes, we need to continue to pray trusting God in this. I didn't know yet that I'm about to learn a massively BIG lesson expressed by an elderly lady of prayer one time: that, "when I pray for rain, I better carry an umbrella"! Few weeks went by, until one Sunday night I stood up as usual and, unrehearsed, said, "I'd like to change the program tonight." Then I shared with them what they individually have been burdened to share with me, how they'd like to spend time in prayer specifically for Bill, how they felt God sent him specifically to us, how they're uncomfortable with doing things business as usual. "I'd like us to pray, 2 or 3 but not more in each group. Go anywhere in the building. Pray until the Lord says stop. The last person in the building, please lock the doors and turn the lights out before you go home." Amaui and I left around 10 P.M. Many stayed after that. I knew there was fire, fire in the soul, at the core, that cannot be quenched easily!!! Few weeks went by. No one dared say anything; ask anything, not even a whisper. Loving and praying continued each in his/her home. Then, one Sunday evening I asked if anyone would like to share anything - a verse of scripture, a prayer request, anything. There were a few who raised their hands, and were heard. Then Bill raised his hand, then raised all 350+ lbs. of body weight and stood up. Pastor Bill: well, this past week I went for my regular checkup at the specialist to see how much worse the cancer has gotten. They took blood samples, did many other tests, and we waited in the waiting room. Two hours went by, felt like eternity.

The doctor walked out to meet us and said, "Bill, I think we need to run some more tests to check few more things." So we went back in, drew more blood, checked other stuff, and we went back to the waiting room, and we waited more." After an hour or so, Bill continued, "the doctor came back out." Doctor: well, I really don't understand what's going on. We checked and double-checked, and all I can say now is that there isn't one cell in your body, Bill, that is cancerous. But I don't know what happened". As Bill finished sharing that Sunday night, things were not normal for a while. Tears flowed, many "Amen" were heard all around, even from one elderly "conservative" man who stays tight-lipped normally and expressionless, he even broke out in laughter and rejoicing; a release of a flood of anguish and the waiting has come to an end. The Lord heard from heaven and brought joy to his people. Few weeks later, during ordination, pastor Bill laid his hands on my head, clean, whole, no smell, and prayed, and we wept as we prayed, and felt the sweetness of Him who is sweeter than the honeycomb. Prayer! That's what Church life is all about! God moves, always to accomplish His purposes, especially when we least expect it. Our role model, Jesus, prayed, and he paid the price in full throughout ALL his prayers, always keeping his eyes on Him who sat on the throne. That's why "nothing shall separate us from the love of God through Jesus Christ our Lord." His name is Jesus, and that's yet another reason why I love him so! *(Friday, January 23, 2015 at 12:54 A.M. CST)*

STILL THINKING OF HIS LOVE
From my heart to yours—

I'm still thinking of His amazing love. One of the reasons I love Jesus Christ far beyond my own comprehension is not that He gave me things but that He gave me Himself. No one else has done that. No one else needs to bother trying. One was enough, and will always be enough. Another reason why I love Him so is not that he died on the cross of shame, but that He didn't come down from the cross of shame. Shame is what others see in me; Shame is what He took from me. He covered my shame and gave me His Name. He hovered over me and made something new out of the chaos. He loved me that much. I can't love Him enough. Another reason why I love Him passionately is not that He came once, but that He is coming again. Look up! Look up! Few lines from an old song say: *"Something beautiful, something good; All my confusion, He understood; All I had to offer Him was brokenness and strife; But He made something, beautiful, of my life."* His name is Jesus. The beautiful became ugly so that the ugly can be beautiful; The holy became sin so that the sinner can be holy; The loving One was hated, so that the hateful one can love again. *(Friday, January 23, 2015 at 7:24 P.M. CST)*

GIVING A NEW SONG
From my heart to yours—

Anyone with a good voice can sing. We call that "practice". But Jesus came so that the one with no voice and no beauty can have a song in their heart and beauty all the days of their life. He took the stink of shame and the sting of death so that I can be clothed and accepted in Him. That's another reason why I love Him so. *(Friday, January 23, 2015 at 8:03 P.M. CST)*

～～～

ON BEING IN HIM
From my heart to yours—

To be "IN HIM" means: (1) To have residence and identity (2) To have reference and security (3) To have confidence and serenity. Isn't that what people are looking for? Isn't that what loneliness is yearning for? Isn't that what the world is offering as counterfeit? His name is Jesus. He personally answers all who call upon His name, 24/7, is not affected by global warming or frigid weather, not seasonal, and His love is not conditional. *(Friday, January 23, 2015 at 8:06 P.M. CST)*

～～～

ENEMIES TO THE END
From my heart to yours—

Jesus and satan have a very clear understanding of who the other is, which led them to a divorce. Reason: Irreconcilable Difference. It is best not to try and bring them together to coexist or cohabitate. They both have agreed NOT to just settle their differences amicably and shack-up. It is a waste of time and of eternity. It won't work. For satan, it's plausible. But for Jesus, it certainly is out of character. "Love not the world". *(Friday, January 23, 2015 at 8:41 P.M. CST)*

～～～

BEING LIKE NO ONE ELSE
From my heart to yours–

To BE like Jesus means to be like no one ELSE. To BE like Jesus means--not TO DO, but TO BE. To BE means there is a beginning. And in the beginning...GOD. May we never be tempted from within or seduced from without into thinking that He will accept what we do as a fair substitute. *(Friday, January 23, 2015 at 8:49 P.M. CST)*

THE SPIRIT OF THE LORD
From my heart to yours–

If God saw it necessary for Jesus, the Son of Man, to have the Holy Spirit constantly with Him on earth as His guide, His strength, His refuge, His source of power, His means of constant communion with the Father, His protector from temptation, His comfort when all left Him, His affirmation by His continuous presence that the Father is pleased in Him, His assurance that every word, every thought, every desire, every emotion, every glance, every step and even His death on the cross is destined to be successful... *Who do we think we are* to think that we can do any of that on our own in a world of dog-eat-dog, and many dogs have gone mad and become wolves who seek to destroy our very soul, if they could??? !!! *Who do we think we are* to be deluded into thinking that we can strut into God's eternal holy presence by our own merits or by whatever credentials to claim ???!!! What arrogance!!! Yet, He loved us just as we are, and invites us to be whole again, at the cross! At the cross is where His blood was shed, and it's still flowing to save and redeem. *(Friday, January 23, 2015 at 9:10 P.M. CST)*

JESUS AND HOLLYWOOD
From my heart to yours—

The difference between Jesus Christ and Hollywood is that Jesus takes the fake, the counterfeit, and the wrong and makes him authentic, original and true...in Him. Hollywood ... is just about acting and knows how to put on a big production. The difference between the true and fake followers of Christ is that the true follower can be, and therefore can do...through Christ. The fake follower thinks he can be by doing it "all by himself" while all along using the name of Christ. Jesus gives hope and home. The world gives audacity to be hopeful but never arrives. *(Friday, January 23, 2015 at 9:22 P.M. CST)*

THINKING OF HEAVEN
From my heart to yours—

I woke up this morning with heaven on my mind. And the Holy Spirit brought a song to my mind that I learned about 40 years ago. I did not have it written down anywhere. But I thanked Him for reminding me of it. *"Oft' times the day seems long, And trials hard to bear, We're tempted to complain, To murmur and despair, But Christ will soon appear To take his Bride away, The Tempter will be over In God's celestial day Chorus IT will be worth it all When we see Jesus All trials will seem so small When we see Christ One glimpse of his dear face All sorrows he'll erase So bravely run the race Till we see Christ."* *(Saturday, January 24, 2015 at 6:42 A.M. CST)*

INTIMACY: INITIAL THOUGHTS
From my heart to yours–

Jesus Christ calls his followers into an intimate relationship with God. Nothing less! And we immediately have a serious problem. The reason is we have never been in an intimate successful pure holy relationship with anyone much less God to compound the problem, The baggage we bring to the table does not help in building a successful relationship with God. And this creates the second problem and that is if we cannot build the successful intimate relationship with God, It would be impossible to expect to have a successful intimate relationship with another person. What is the solution? How can we get into an intimate relationship with God and we don't know where to begin? Jesus Christ came to give us a successful intimate relationship with God, but also to give us the beginning of such intimate relationship with him. He did that at the cross. *(Saturday, January 24, 2015 at 9:25 P.M. CST)*

PLEASANT SURPRISE
From my heart to yours–

A Precious Moment with a Very Special lady. She is 93 years old, went on her last mission trip at 87. As I was speaking yesterday about "lesser known" people, I asked, "how many know Billy Graham?" Everyone's hand went up. Then I asked, "How many of you know Mordecai Ham?" No one! Then this beautiful lady raised her hand. I was surprised and asked, "Are we talking about the same Mordecai Ham?" She said, "Yes we are. He was the one who led Billy Graham to faith in Christ, and me too." Everyone applauded. Mordecai Ham (born 1877, died 1961). Billy Graham came to faith in Christ in 1934 in Charlotte, NC. *(Sunday, January 25, 2015 at 11:03 P.M. CST)*

CONFUSION HAPPENS (1 OF 3)
From my hart to yours–

"I CAN" doesn't mean "I MUST". (1Timothy 5) "*I can*" speaks of: Possibility of something getting done, Freedom of doing something, Availability of options, Liberty for personal expression, and such ideas. So, I can. "*I must*" speaks of: Something is Required to be done, Action is Very important to happen, something is not Optional, Hindrances need to be addressed which might prevent something from happening, and such thoughts. Sometimes, (maybe many times), in the life of the church or individual follower of Jesus Christ, we get "*I can*" and "*I must*" confused. And, even worse, we swap their meanings. Here is what I mean: many times, what MUST be done, I treat it as option, and that's wrong; and other times, what *can* be done, but doesn't have to, we think it really absolutely *must* be done, and I go to all extremes to make something happen, even if it hurts someone else, or damages a relationship or friendship. And *that's* wrong as well. At least, we can say, such conduct is not really consistent with the Spirit of Christ in the life of the church, all or one. Only the Holy Spirit can guide through the differences. If I work independent of Him, I'm likely to fail because I will be very likely depending on self *even if I succeed*. If I totally implicitly depend on Him, I will very likely be a good follower of Christ because that's what Jesus did too all His life while on earth. We want to be like Him, right? That's what Paul addressed very clearly in First Timothy, chapter five. Please take time to read it, and then read post # (2) (*Monday, January 26, 2015 at 8:52 A.M. CST*)

CONFUSION HAPPENS (2 OF 3)
From my heart to yours–

"*I can*" doesn't mean "*I must*". (1Timothy 5) The difference of heavenly treasures and earthly pleasures -- In post #1, I spoke of some nuances of meaning, how easily confusing it can get in daily living, and the simple truth that it takes nothing less than the Holy Spirit of God to guide me and lead me *practically* to be *in real life* a true follower of Jesus Christ. In summary, in First Timothy 5, Paul addresses several areas in the life of the church with clear directions how we ought to behave in order to reflect the mind of Christ. He talks about: (1) Speaking (addressing, admonition, sharing, etc.) with an older man, young men, an older lady, and young ladies. (5:1-2) (2) Honoring widows, honoring and serving some, and warning and mentoring other widows; the reasoning and methods behind helping some, and possible pitfalls when not paying attention to conduct. (5:3-16) (3) Speaking about leaders in the church: multiple leaders, levels of leaders, priority of leadership. Getting that confused has gotten many in lingering trouble. (5:17-18) (4) Accepting complaints on others, and how to behave. (5:19-20) (5) Warnings and Precautions to Timothy as leader. (5:21-22) (6) Caring for personal details. (5:23) (7) Being a leader doesn't mean being concerned about all the actions of people. Personal responsibility and related consequences are essential to keep in mind, to the very end (5:24-25). *(Monday, January 26, 2015 at 8:52 A.M. CST)*

CONFUSION HAPPENS (3 OF 3)
From my heart to yours—

"*I can*" doesn't mean "*I must*". Or, what is the difference between heavenly treasures and earthly pleasures - in the life of Jesus follower, the family, the church? (1 Timothy 5) In post #1, and in view of 1Timothy 5, we highlighted by way of introduction some misconceptions about the differences between "*I can*" and "*I must*". In post #2, we highlighted an informal outline of the chapter, and the different areas it presented. Here, in the last post, we highlight the five (5) principles offered to keep in mind. To be true to Scriptures, I cannot customize the text and interpretation/principles derived to a local context (country, language, requirements, social status, etc.). What makes a biblical principle a biblical principle is that we can take it anywhere in the world, and it would apply just fine. If it cannot apply everywhere, it shouldn't be applied anywhere. Otherwise, we have earthly variations that dictate biblical truths, and we customize biblical treasures according to earthly pleasures. That's wrong! Two examples: (1) To be a true follower of Jesus Christ, I must believe in Him as my Savior and Lord. Can I take this principle to any person anywhere and apply it? Definitely Yes. (2) To be a true group of local believers and call ourselves a local church, I must have a building to meet in. Can I take this principle to any place anywhere and apply it as a requirement? Obviously not. *Must* we have a building to be a church? No. CAN we have a building in which to meet? Absolutely, Yes. The *only* way to be guided toward BALANCE in life between CAN and MUST happens when I/we continually yield completely to the Holy Spirit, without a hidden agenda or ulterior motive. Here are some guiding principles that can be applied anywhere. I can ask: Is the action, or Are the instruction, or is the agreement promoting: (1) Sufficient and proper organization to accomplish something? (2) أوّلاً الترتيب Consider the impact church as a group first, before the individual. (3) أوّلاً الجماعة Keep the Main Thing the MAIN THING. In the church, it's always "so that the ministry doesn't get hindered". (4) كي لا تُعاق الخدمة . أوّلاً الهدف The Spiritual always takes priority to the temporal/physical. God first, Man second, Always. الروحيّات أوّلاً، ثم الجسديّات(5) In ALL things, Jesus Christ FIRST. Is He the center? Is He receiving all the glory? Is He coming first in what really matters? Am I willing to change for His sake? Is my thinking and attitude reflecting how much I want HIM (not me) to be first? أوّلاً يسوع. *(Monday, January 26, 2015 at 8:55 A.M. CST)*

SUBTLE IDOLATRY
From my heart to yours–

"He is the Alpha and the Omega" in its simplest form..... Means: It's All about Him. That's why He is "the same, yesterday, today, and forever." Anything else (or less) is equivalent to creating a god in my own image. "Little children, keep yourselves from idols. Amen." (I John 5:21) And, *Yes We Can* keep everything about Him, in the power of the indwelling Spirit. His Blessed Name is: Jesus. And He is Wonderful. *(Monday, January 26, 2015 at 10:47 A.M. CST)*

THANK YOU FOR PRAYING. THANK YOU FOR TAKING PART.
Doctor said the little princess will be running in a month :) On one of the 2014 trips, we met a little girl who "stole the heart". We will call her "Sama". But the name is not what matters, but the story. It's a true story. She insisted on going to school and not staying at home. She had no place to call home. She's been displaced multiple

times. One day, Sama fell and scratched her leg. Parents ignored the scar even though it got infected after few weeks. The infection got so bad; it started to affect the bones. She couldn't walk anymore. Her parents brought her to school with a cast on the whole leg. Then everywhere she needed to go while at school, she had to be carried...EVERYWHERE. She said she wanted to learn and not stay at home. The doctors said we may have to amputate her leg at some point. The infection reached deep into the bone. Surface treatment will not help at this point. To treat the infection, now at the bone level, they have to embed medicine with a tube, remove the infected part, and inject the medicine through the tube to the bone area to keep the infection from spreading. Surgery was out of the question. Too expensive, and parents were not sure where they will be. They sold all they had only to buy the injectable medicine, with no solution in sight. Several people (some of you took part) contributed to help Sama. She had the surgery. After few weeks, Sama came to school, wobbling like a little duck, walking like a little princess.

(Tuesday, January 27, 2015 at 7:39 P.M. CST)

❧

SERIOUS TRUSTING
From my heart to yours–

"Trust in the Lord with all your heart and lean not on your understanding." (Proverbs) What does it mean to say, "I trust in God"? Do I (you) really trust Him? Here are some thoughts: (1) I KNOW whom I trust because "He is" and He gave me His name – "I know whom I have believed" (2) I know He IS ABLE because "Nothing escapes Him" (Isaiah 40) – "*I know whom I have believed and He is able to keep what has been committed to me.*" (3) I know that I cannot trust *always* in anything or anyone else, even myself, my strength, my mind, my emotions, my will, my decision-making skills, my relationships, future, possessions, body, everything – EVERYTHING, not because they don't work, but because they are unreliable like God. I yield to Him – Alone. (4) I know He has my best interest at heart because He loves me AS I AM with His whole heart. (5) I know He cannot LIE or DENY Himself. I'm not sure I can trust my fractured heart all the time. But Him? YES. His promises are too great and too precious, and He is too much for me to comprehend. Maybe that's why He came to me, and loved me as I am and gave me life. Do you trust Him? I am learning, with Him: (1) I cannot play games. He didn't with me at the cross. (2) I cannot say "NO Lord". It's illogical. (3) I cannot give up on Him, therefore on me either. (4) I don't want my way. His way is always better. (5) He began with me, and never left me until now. I serious doubt He will, not because of who I am, but because of who HE is. His name is Jesus, and He died for me. Yes, He is trustworthy! That's why I love Him! And, You?! *(Wednesday, January 28, 2015 at 11:13 A.M. CST)*

"PRAYING IN THE SPIRIT"
From my heart to yours–

What does it mean? Here are some thoughts: Being immersed in the spirit; Listening to the Spirit; Being led by the Spirit; Seeking the mind of the Spirit for wisdom, discernment, and refuge. For discernment, as A. W. Tower said, is not knowing the difference between the good and the bad, but "knowing the difference between the good and the almost good." Only the Holy Spirit can make that happen continuously, successfully, and to the glory of the Son of God. Expecting the Spirit of God to bring about answers and joy in the Lord, strength while waiting, confidence that God will answer, and longing for God... ... and nothing else. Nothing less. I have determined in my heart that I do not want the results that I desire. Continuous surrender to him allows and enables me to remain in him. Having a mind to pray when I choose and having a mindset of prayer as a breath of life is the difference between praying in the flesh and praying in the Spirit. *(Thursday, January 29, 2015 at 6:55 A.M. CST)*

PRAYING AND TRUSTING
From my heart to yours–

Prayer is not a sign of giving up but a call to looking up. Trusting Him is not what I do until I get my way, but a self-transformation until His will be done on earth (in me) as it is in heaven (in the image of His Son). Fervent desperate prayer takes place only when the pain is sharp and when the wound is deep. Then I take hold of Him and never let go. Until then, the average prayer bounces back from the ceiling, and forms a spiritually stagnant swamp in the bottom of my soul. *(Wednesday, February 18, 2015 at 12:08 A.M. CST)*

BALANCE - THE MISSING INGREDIENT
From my heart to yours–

I was arrested early this morning by what A. W. Tozer wrote. He said, "Never let any man become necessary to you. Christ alone is necessary." My thought sequence was: "that's nice" --> "let me read it again" --> "Wow, really?!" --> "let me read further". But I could not. I paused, then stopped in my tracks because the question came to me: "Is Jesus Christ really my sufficiency, the only real necessity in my life?!" The grace of God alone enables me to keep the balance between: (1) receiving help from Him through others, and (2) at the same time remain independent of them. His indwelling Spirit in me does that in my life every day. Paul said, "I have learned that whatsoever state I am in there with to be content." We make a mistake when we think the balance to be kept is between confidence in Christ and confidence in self. That's why Jesus emphatically asserted that to be a true followers of His, we must deny EVEN self. Anything else is simply unacceptable. The same idea is expressed in the words of Jesus in John 17:15, "The world has hated them because they are not of the world, just as I am not of the world. I do not pray that you should take them out of the world, but that you should keep them from the evil one." All that a house built on a ROCK needs is -- the ROCK. The rest of the house is simply details. So is life. *(Thursday, February 19, 2015 at 5:04 A.M. CST)*

KEEPING THE BALANCE
From my heart to yours—

Life is a balancing act. But it's not an act; it's reality in all its details; it's the real thing. Political correctness is navigating of self through a maze (taking risks) that gradually becomes a disciplined life in the art of telling lies - (بياض وجه، تمسيح جوخ، وما شابه ذلك). One of the aspects of the kaleidoscope of real faith in Christ is that it's the first step toward real balance in practical living. So we begin by faith. We also must continue by faith because "without faith it is impossible to please Him" (Heb. 11:6). Faith, that's what "Balance" is all about, where the invisible becomes visible. It's not faith in self (because self is affected negatively at times by outside factors), but faith in Him (because He is able, and He is good, and His mercy endures forever). It is not a game of risk-taking. I win some, I lose some. But it's a daily walk of complete surrender to Him, empowered by His

Spirit - in faith, in hope, in love. The greatest of them is _____ (fill in the blank). *(Thursday, February 19, 2015 at 5:27 A.M. CST)*

INTENTIONAL LIVING
From my heart to yours—

From observing current and recent events around the world in the last two decades, I am determined and am learning to live intentionally in the new reality that the amazing God my Father is able to accomplish anything and everything that He purposed through Christ and in the power of His Spirit without human instrumentality and without being bound whatsoever to man's dimensions of time and space. In all this that He IS doing, He invited me, through Christ, to be filled with His Holy Spirit, to see what He does and to worship. And if it pleases Him, He may use me, but He is never required to do so. I'm not shocked by how small I am, but I am incessantly amazed by how AWESOME He is. That's yet another reason why I love Him so. *(Friday, February 27, 2015 at 5:28 A.M. CST)*

WHAT'S THE BASIS?
From my heart to yours—

I've learned that God does not operate on the basis of "more or less". He does not have a basis; He IS the basis for everything. For we humans always operate from a certain point of reference - Always. God never does that because He always has been, is, and always will be - in Himself - the only point of reference. That is why he is never impressed by the high and mighty, by the full and expanding, by the rich and famous. In fact, he is only attracted to the weak and lowly, the bruised and broken, the alone and the shattered. We are too familiar with these people. There - there - is where His whole character is manifested each time in completeness and perfect power that drives me to be in constant awe and to worship Him. To top that, He invites us through the cross of Christ, nothing more nothing less, to be grafted into Him to be one with Him as He is eternally the Triune One alone. We dare not glory in anything but the CROSS. *(Friday, February 27, 2015 at 6:57 A.M. CST)*

Dad UPDATE, (2 March): Got in at 9:00 A.M. CST.

Toxins are garbage that is processed out of the body by many filtering stations. Carbon Dioxide (CO2) is one of the main bad toxins. Normal range is around 40%. Dad came in with above 75%. This morning he's at 55%. Kidney function is about the same (40% of normal). Heart slightly enlarged. Cardiologist didn't come yet to read the EKG, but not in the "critical range". Air is being forced into the lungs via mask to force the lungs and body to release unneeded fluids and put more Oxygen in his system. In summary: His system has been for a long time "out of balance", and it caught up with him. Prayerfully, the professional assistance will restore what they can. YOUR prayers matter, regardless. Thank You! What keeps "BALANCE" front and center in the life of a true follower of Christ is a good, clear, focused, intentional, and desperate view of the CROSS. That is where glory and shame met, and where the debt was settled forever, where all won except one. That's why: it's all about Him.

Dad UPDATE- 2 March 4:15 P.M. CST:

This afternoon has been rough; systems struggling; confirmed pneumonia that required aggressive antibiotic treatment. Opted also to add 2 units of blood to increase the red cells count to carry more oxygen throughout the body. He is being maintained in all systems, and waiting for body to release more fluids. Your prayers are appreciated I'm trying to post simple factual updates at least once a day, and avoid words that trigger emotional response or inaccurate assumptions. One thing, and only one thing, we can be sure of at all times is that God invited us to call on Him anytime, and to trust Him all the time regardless of what the eyes see or the ears hear. He IS - ALWAYS our Father.

Dad's UPDATE - 10:30 A.M. CST; 3 March: (Text from my lovely brother Kamal)

"Dr. Just left dad, very happy with his status today...much better than yesterday...she is pleased and is much nicer. She said that giving him blood was a good thing; it helped. X-ray still foggy...wants to make sure his kidneys are back to normal...Still not there." .... more later.

Dad UPDATE 11:20 A.M. CST –

Oxygen mask is off, breathing well on his own, systems within normal range, CT scan to be reviewed, handsome, oooops (not a medical term :), fed him breakfast, sat up and is conversant. I gave him 24 hours to be shaved and hair combed :). Barring anything else from happening suddenly, he will remain in ICU another day. I call that "special measure of grace" as we help them write their remaining chapter - not sure of the number of pages. Of course, having a granddaughter with him is encouraging too. She asked him, "is it because I'm here, Jiddo, (Grandpa), that you're getting better?" :). That's Maya! Better yet, that's Kamal's daughter (my niece). THANK YOU for prayers. One of the reasons for the church to pray is for the church to reap together the fruit of the Presence and rejoice in HIM for no reason outside of Him and regardless of details.

ONCE MORE
From my heart to yours—

As we left, Mom turned around and had to have one more hug and kiss. :). Yes, for everything there is a time. Now, it's time to love, because love is always better - ALWAYS! *(Wednesday, March 4, 2015 at 2:49 P.M. CST)*

OLD PARENTS
From my heart to yours—

One thing I'm learning about our parents at this stage of their life is that it doesn't make sense to give up on them when they are at their weakest point. That's what love is about. That's what Christ is all about. We're still learning. *(Wednesday, March 4, 2015 at 3:30 P.M. CST)*

ALL OF GRACE
From my heart to yours—

All my life I learned from Mom at every turn of circumstances. She was capable, smart, some would even say she was shrewd. She loves people, but always loved the Lord more. She had no problem expressing herself fully, even when she didn't need to use words. Last week, we were taking a walk outside and she reminded me that "all our life, my son, we lived because of the anointing we have from His hand". And, like Mary, I was keeping those things in my heart. Especially during the past year or so, Mom's ability to focus (on anything) started to deteriorate, her words at times were not totally connected, her thoughts were not instantly ready as before to verbalize. And she asked me often, "What is happening to me?" I wasn't sure she was looking for answers. I'm not sure I had an answer ready. Yet, she somehow knew that "the Lord will not leave us". I knew that too. *Then*, a couple of days ago, she was sitting with us in the living room, and unexpectedly said, "Can we pray? I'd like to pray." We glanced quickly at each other quizzing not sure what she was going to utter, what disconnected thoughts or words were about to come out of her mouth. And like Thomas the doubtful, we said so piously "sure mom, we can pray. You sure you want to pray, or want me to pray?" For you see, I thought, I was the one educated to pray and read many books and prayed in meetings etc. etc. she said, "No, I'd like to pray." She bowed her head, not waiting on us, and raised her hand not like a beggar asking for alms but like a princess talking to her Father the King, and began to pray. Her prayer wasn't short. I couldn't help but crack one eye open slightly to make sure it was the same woman praying. Her entire prayer, every word, every thought, every sequence of words was perfectly aligned with proper flow and meaning. She prayed asking the Lord "to help us because we are weak and we need him every day of our life; thanked him for He is good to us always," and she went on and on. Then ended, asking for His blessing upon us. Then during and after her prayer on my way home from my sister Samia's home, I noticed that the Lord had few words and questions for me to chew on. As if the Lord was saying: - Do you really think that she needed to line-up her words just right for me to understand her heart? - Do you really think that even if her words and thoughts didn't make any sense to you, that I wouldn't understand her? But I gave her logic of expression for your sake so you might believe that I'm still sovereign where human logic and diction fail. - Did you really have to crack your eye open while she was in my Presence? - Do you know why she was prompted to pray? It was Me. - and, Yes, without anointing, you can do nothing. I wanted, like Peter, to go outside and cry bitterly. He and I knew that I failed the test. He extended His mercy and grace for His Son's sake yet again, because I knew His desire was, and is, to keep me in His Presence, under His wings, and "know that He is God". So, as I leave for this my journey, all I'm praying for is anointing, a touch of the hem of His garment, a kiss of His feet, and maybe His fragrance will come back on me to His glory. The rest of the trip, or life for that matter, is mere details. *(Friday, March 6, 2015 at 11:31 P.M. CST)*

BREATHE ON ME
From my heart to yours–

I'm learning, when I sin and want to run away and hide, that the best place to run away to, and hide in, is the Lord himself. One line in a song says, "No one understands like Jesus." For, you see, at the cross and under his wings there is rest for the weary, healing for the broken, acceptance for the rejected, forgiveness for confession, and there - there is everlasting love. I'm learning, unless I learn THAT about Him, that all my words are just that ---words, words in vacuum, words in desperate need of life, words that echo emptiness from the ceiling back to me. So I pray often the words of the song entitled, "Breathe on me": "When the battle makes me weary It seems that I've lost ground; It's so hard to hear Your voice Lord With distractions all around; I try to lift my hands, to give You praise But then a spirit of heaviness Tries to shield Your face, so I'm saying breathe [Chorus:] Breathe into me oh Lord, the breath of life So that my spirit would be whole And my soul made right Breathe into me oh Lord, day by day So that my heart is pure before You, always, always." *(Saturday, March 7, 2015 at 12:29 A.M. CST)*

<figure>◦◦◦◦◦◦</figure>

EVANGELICALS CONFUSED
From my heart to yours–

I'm inclined to think these days, instead of bashing the president that the evangelicals - first - would do well to pay a visit to the cross of Christ, the cross we hang around our neck and prevents us from seeing the beam in our proverbial eye. Here is why: I might be first to cast a stone, but I'm noticing that we seriously suffer from chronic religious myopia and so we lash out at him making him the "whipping boy" simply because, in my humble assessment, he took away from us our ecclesiastical religious pacifier that we use and, like babies, give it to each other and giggle when we have more babies in our corner with our color of pacifier. We forgot that "the way of the cross leads home"- ALWAYS the cross, ONLY the cross. I'm not bothered so much by the 72 virgins as much as I am by another set of 72's (or so) we have concocted in the hollow halls of our imaginations, and like in the OT we have "erred" in our ways and gone after other gods. Why should we panic when prayer is removed from the schools when there is no real NT prayer happening in church- *in the church*? Why do we shed tears for ones who died for their faith, yet we gleefully read or recite portions of Hebrews 11, when we are not willing to "throw off everything that hinders and the sin that so easily entangles us"? Why do we insist - *insist* - on retaining our whatever version of the "form of godliness" and consistently "deny the power"? I would dare presume that the vast numbers of evangelical churches, as churches, do not pray for the president and all those in presumed power, and we don't truly acknowledge that God is truly sovereign and that like in Daniel's days God is - *is* -the true authority in the kingdom of man? He lifts up and He brings down, and all like the king of Assyria of old are "His messenger Angels"? Why do we fault the Muslims for reciting their book when we do everything to ours except "hide it in our hearts"? Why do we blame them for wanting to tear down the cross from our symbolic buildings, when we barely do seasonal homage to ours driven by whatever piety we possess? Are they onto something and are not realizing it themselves in their hearts, that God wants to and has branded the cross from eternity past on the tablets of their hearts and they cannot escape the all-time reality of the cross and the shed blood for sins, and they lash out again and again, wanting to destroy, not realizing the *many* attempts before that, like the birthday candle that keep lighting up after we blow on it, the Light of the world keeps lighting up again and again, here there and everywhere? Have we forgotten that He is not like us in any conceivable way? Have we forgotten that His word does not return void - *ever*? Have we forgotten that His Spirit always makes beauty out of chaos when He hovers? Maybe, just maybe, we need to stop considering the pharisaic ways of the snobbish Pharisee praying - and in the Temple of all places - and beat our chest and confess how desperate we are for a fresh look at the cross of Christ. That's where His love was demonstrated and abounded. That's where God met man in Jesus; that's where His Spirit fully exhibited grace and justice and mercy and holiness and faith and love. I have a sneaking suspicion that not all heaven's occupants, when all is said and done, will be evangelicals; and not all evangelicals will have a permanent residence status as they figured. That's why the pictures I snapped and attached always remind me, that orphans, widows, and children will likely make it first. Nothing but the cross of Jesus! In that, we glory! In Him we are safely abiding! *(Saturday, March 7, 2015 at 9:20 A.M. CST)*

～⌒～⌒～

THE CHURCH: STEADY AS SHE GOES
From my heart to yours–

A sampling of the longing for home -- Jesus said, ""I have told you these things, so that in me you may have peace. In this world you will have trouble. But take heart! I have overcome the world." (John 16). Here is a song from years gone by entitled: "The King is Coming" (It's on YouTube). The lyrics: "*The Market place is empty No more traffic in the streets All the builders tools are silent No more time to harvest wheat Busy housewives cease their labors in the courtroom no debate Work on earth has been suspended As the King comes through the gate.* Chorus: "*The King is coming The King is coming I just heard the trumpet sounding And now his face I see The King is coming The King is coming Praise God He's coming for me*". "*Happy face line the hallway Those whose lives have been redeemed Broken homes that He has mended Those from prison He's set free Little children and the aged Hand in hand stand all aglow Those who were crippled, broken, ruined Clad in garments white as snow*" (Chorus). "*I can hear the chariots rumble I can see the marching throng And the flurry of God's trumpets spell the end of sin and wrong Regal robes are now unfolding Heaven's grandstands all in place Heaven's choir is now assembled Start to sing Amazing Grace*" (Chorus). *(Saturday, March 7, 2015 at 12:57 P.M. CST)*

THE RELEVANCE OF GOD
From my heart to yours—

I was unable to find a connection with the facts that God created the world, or that He is able to create many more world(s), or that He is so powerful and all- knowing, or that he can be everywhere, or that he is majestic and great, or that He is in heaven, or that he has a trillion angels, or that he has a golden throne, or anything else. I didn't care, and it didn't mean anything ... In fact nothing had true meaning and relevance... UNTIL ... I heard of this great God... that He came down, that He loved me and that He came to forgive my sin and to erase the stain of my guilt, to wash me clean and remove my shame, and give me life again, to clothe me in white To bring me back to Himself and give my life meaning and adopt me as His child forever. Forgiveness -- ah yes, Now I'm listening! Now, THAT'S good news!!! The words of a song put it this way: Out from heaven's palaces, Splendor filled and bright! Came the King and He came to bring, To the world new life and light. Chorus: What grace is this that brought my Savior down, That made Him leave His glorious throne and crown. The one who made the earth, the sky, and sea. Who put the stars in every galaxy! What condescension, oh how can it be! What shame He suffered oh what agony! And then the death He died, For sinners crucified, What grace is this! What grace is this! *(Sunday, March 8, 2015 at 6:08 A.M. CDT)*

DAD UPDATE: In keeping up with Dad's condition by phone before departure, it became clear that his status is unstable (details unknown yet). So, I decided to cancel the trip. Prayer appreciated.

DAD UPDATE 1:30 P.M. CST: After a lengthy conference with the lung doctor, here is a summary: (1) Dad's lungs and heart are struggling but he's not giving up (2) Overall condition is fragile at best (3) We are taking things one day at a time, with advisement (4) The next 24-48 hours will give us more insight about proper "next step" overall course of action (5) I was content to cancel this trip We pray and wait on the Lord through this valley. After all, it was grace that brought us safe thus far, and we have no complaints at all but gratitude.

EXTRA GRACE
From my heart to yours—

Making a good decision when there is none - is something that God the Holy Spirit enables us to do by granting an extra grace-filled measure of perfect peace, strength, assurance, and His Presence, especially when it's very dark and no light at the end of the tunnel, when all knowledge and expertise are exhausted. He is there. How? Simply because "*My God will supply all your needs according to his riches in glory in Christ Jesus our Lord.*" It's His promise! How do I know that to be true? Because I'm there, and I'm still learning. *(Sunday, March 8, 2015 at 3:02 P.M. CDT)*

HIS FORGIVENESS IS MORE
From my heart to yours—

I cannot see the awesomeness of His forgiveness without seeing the awfulness of my sin. That's why the cross of Christ is absolutely indispensable. That's where all debts are settled. That is where all accusations are refuted, and satan's mouth is shuttered forever. To forgive one wrong for one human is very kind. To forgive all wrongs for all mankind is so wonderful to sleep on. Isn't Jesus Awesome?!!! *(Monday, March 9, 2015 at 12:52 A.M. CDT)*

❧

ENTIRE LIFE
From my heart to yours–

It was brought to my attention very vividly these days, in summary, that throughout my entire life I have been in one form or another and on many levels spending my existence till now between the living and the dead. That's another reason why I'll be eternally grateful for the resurrection of Christ. There IS another chapter coming!

❧

DAD UPDATE: Today, since late last night, Baba had a stable time. His condition was encouraging enough that the doctor recommended going to a "step down" room, which is less intensive than ICU. It appears that he will need an oxygen breathing mask almost always, and take a break from it few times. He will need attention and constant care, but not sure for how long. His lungs and other systems are stable and he will be monitored 24/7 for a while. Pneumonia treatment results have improved a tiny amount. Toxicity in his blood is better. In the "step down" room, he will have time to gain some strength. Very thankful for all those who are praying. *(Monday, March 9, 2015 at 11:13 A.M. CDT)*

❧

DAD UPDATE, 10 MARCH, 1:50 P.M.: Doctor pleased with progress, waiting to move to a "step down" room; vitals are good, sat in chair for couple of hours, conversant and interactive, asked for his Bible and glasses, lung fluids are decreasing steadily, kidneys functional. His one problem is that he doesn't listen to me :). But I think I'll keep him. Anyway, he looks OK for. 90 year-old.

~~~

DAD UPDATE, 8 P.M., MARCH 3: The doctors are prepared to release him from the hospital. He will be transferred to an intensive nursing rehab facility for up to 3 wks. Stable enough in general; treatment to be maintained; many details to work out tomorrow. THANK YOU, one and all, for praying. Our debt of love and gratitude is huge. We accept his workings in life's events as they happen, but most of all we are eternally grateful that our names are written in the Book of Life. I pray more diligently that I don't live one day beyond my usefulness to Him who loved me and gave himself for me...and you! More update tomorrow.

~~~

BE CAREFUL HOW TO PRAY
From my heart to yours–

A true Scenario that actually took place: (in summary) A diabetic missionary to South America was kidnapped by a rebel group known for their atrocities. His daily medication was going to run out within few days. You and I will probably do what all his family, friends, and mission agency did: prayed that God would set him free, that he would remain safe, that God would protect him, that he would not suffer, that somehow God would heal him so he wouldn't need treatment until he gets released, and.....you know, that kind of praying. It's amazing how we have become so predictable when storms come. But the truth about our missionary friend is that God did not answer any of those prayers. And I'm glad more and more these days that when He wants to do something ... or anything, He does not ask for our advice. Tomorrow is the rest of our missionary friend's story. *(Wednesday, March 11, 2015 at 5:51 A.M. CDT)*

UPDATE: A true Scenario that actually took place: (The Rest of the Story) If you read the last post about our diabetic missionary friend to South America who was kidnapped by a rebel group. Here's what happened: After several days, the medicine of our diabetic missionary friend ran out. He didn't panic. As they interrogated him repeatedly, he shared why he was in the area (serving as missionary). He shared with them about the love of God who sent His Son to die on the cross, and that he was burdened to share that story of God's love. They were constantly monitored him in his cell. He was starting to lose his strength due to not taking his medication: eye sight failing, pain in legs and arms, tingling, numbness, burning sensation in the feet, etc. In his cell, he continued to pray audibly sometimes, unshaken (like Daniel in the lions' den). He was brought to the leader of the gang often, shared his testimony consistently, and even prayed for rebel leader. Back home, people prayed. God wasn't listening to them but to his faithful servant. He was like Daniel who, in the midst of attacks, "continued to open his window toward Jerusalem and prayed three times every day." The break came, and the Lord softened the heart of the rebel leader. He sent a couple of gang members and got the diabetes medicine for the missionary. Then after few months, the missionary was released in the city. What happened during that time? The gang leader and 37 of his followers accepted the Gospel message and were saved totally captured by the Love of Christ which set them free, and gave up the "rebel" business. How does God work? LIKE GOD, of course!!!! :) Aren't you glad prayers were

NOT answered back home? I know in my own life I prayed often and thanked God for NOT answering my prayers. Like children who become advisors to their discerning parents, at times we act like advisors to God. Yet, He continues to love us and continues to do what He purposes in His mind. So, how should we then PRAY? Have you thought about praying intentionally for the president to be saved (if he is not truly saved?), or for the demon-possessed ISIS goons that somehow they see/hear about the love that covers multitudes of evil and to be saved? Or have we determined in our hearts that they don't deserve heaven? Do they (like we) deserve just punishment? Absolutely YES. Do they (like we) need to know the love of *Christ*? Absolutely YES. That's called: GRACE. For the first proper thought about grace is when I think erroneously that I deserve heaven, because I *don't*.

∞———∞

DAD UPDATE, 9:00 A.M., 11 MARCH: Dad was scheduled for transfer to a nursing rehab facility. Plans changed. Nurse came in early morning today to give medicine and wash him. He was not responsive as usual, very sluggish. Something changed overnight. CT scan came back negative. One pupil was wide open, non-responsive to light indicating neurological changes in the brain. He is on his way now to have MRI done. It will be 2-3 hours for results to be read and know what happened. Will keep you updated. Still in the valley of the shadow. Still thankful and prayerful.

∞———∞

UNION MEANS "BECOMING ONE"
From my heart to yours—

For over a month, Mom has been living at my sister's house being one level and easier for Mom. Dad, living one mile away, was coming almost daily to visit with her. Many days he called one of us and said "I'm ready, when are you coming?" "Coming for what! Dad?" "To take me to see your Mom" was his answer. I never thought that my dad was *that* romantic and wanting to be with Mom. But on certain days I even noticed that he fixed himself up a bit and dressed reasonably well. At 89, I called that "handsome"! I was glad I wasn't around when he was 23 :). But, it crossed my mind that there had to be more to this than just a romance. For during the past several days, both of them, totally separately and independently, would ask one of the kids about the other. Mom about Dad, Dad about Mom. Both expressed desire to "go back home", and even after Mom went to my sister's house, Dad really thought that she will come back home at some point. All she talked about was wanting to go home. Almost each time he went to visit her he would insinuate or comment to her about coming home at some point. Almost every one of the kids tried to convince him and her that "you're only one mile – *one mile*" apart. That's good." But to them it was not even close. Home! What IS so magical and mysterious about "home"?!!! The only explanation I could come up with, beyond the romance, is that "*Home*" means "*Union*" and nothing less. It's far beyond emotions and the mushy stuff. It's deeper than words can express. It's "*Home*"; it's *Union*"; it's becoming "*One*". There are no possessions or things, even if the whole world were wrapped up in a Walmart bag, that can add one iota to what is "*One*", not even children. Totally self-contained, sustained, and self-sufficient. Even God knew he was onto something when He declared, "And the two shall be ONE". And He could only know that if He knew what "ONE" and "UNION" meant. Now we are part of another "UNION" that will last forever; it's the

Union of *Christ* and the *Church*. There is nothing like it or even close. In Ephesians 5, Paul talked about the union between the husband and wife, then he brought it to the greater Union, that of Christ and the Church. Anything -- *Anything* -- the world has to offer as alternative is at best *an imitation*, but in most cases it's a corruption of the original. Now, I'm inclined to think that we would do well to discover what it means to *go home*. For Jesus said, "I am the way, the truth, and the life; no one comes to the Father but by me." The song says, "The way of the cross leads home". It does! *(Wednesday, March 11, 2015 at 10:06 A.M. CDT)*

EXISTENTIAL LONGING FOR HOME
From my heart to yours—

Regardless of culture, there is always an existential longing to "go home". Something will always remain missing; something is mysteriously incomprehensible and enigmatic about *Home*. It has a perpetual attractiveness that doesn't fade or is easily replaceable. In fact, there is nothing beyond *Home*. What is more enigmatic is that when someone is not home yet, deep in the fiber of his existence, he knows. Even in experiments done on the salmon, and regardless where they are transported, they will not stop their return migration until they get "home". That's why Jesus said with a loud voice, "*If anyone thirsts, let him come to me and drink. He who believes in me, as the Scripture has said, out of his heart will flow rivers of living water.*" (John 7) *Home* - that's where thirst is quenched, hunger is removed. There is contentment, warmth, truth, transparency, sweetness, and indestructible love. *(Wednesday, March 11, 2015 at 10:49 A.M. CDT)*

STEPPING THROUGH
From my heart to yours—

According to the doctors' recommendation as of now, Dad will be going through the "Comfort Stage" of care in his life. He has been taking one step forward and two steps back for a while. Now he is extremely exhausted and cannot go one step forward with any expected success or improvement. He will remain at the hospital ICU for "a day or two" until we work out the best next step for us to take. Hospice is being discussed. There is further consultation among the doctors to make sure he is receiving the best option and treatment. He will very likely NOT make it for very long. We remain trusting God to do what is pleasing in His sight...as He has in their 89 years. Be praying that the journey will end well and grace-full. With much gratitude for your love and every word of encouragement. PS: We are asking that only prayer is appreciated (NO VISITS to the hospital) at this time, allowing him plenty of rest. *(Wednesday, March 11, 2015 at 4:10 P.M. CDT)*

DAD UPDATE, 12 MARCH, 10:30 A.M. CST:

- Please keep in mind that anything can change at any time. - Had a good night last night, no incidents - Vital signs average (for him) - Still some persistent issues - Good doesn't necessarily mean "always good", and Bad doesn't necessarily mean "getting worse" - We are taking his situation day by day, hour by hour, incident by incident - The plan now is to make sure he remains stable for 2-3 days - He and I talked for a while. He had many questions that we discussed and he understood everything. - His lungs have limited function, but he's managing. - Barring anything drastic and sudden, the plan is to move to a step-down room in few days then to rehab facility. -

We remain thankful for the medical care and the continuous prayers.

~~~~~

THE FUNNY SIDE
From my heart to yours—

During one of my visits with Mom to the ER, I rushed her in, sat her down, and went to the counter to fill out all the paperwork. When I was done, the receptionist said, with a sense of confidence, "Sir, you're done now. You can go now and sit with your wife, and we'll call you shortly." ha-ha. The nurse nearby whispered with similar air of confidence, "That's not his wife. That's his sister." Spoken like an expert! Ha-ha I went back and sat with Mom, and told her what happened. She chuckled and said, "They have no clue what they're talking about". I'm afraid at times that I judge based on what the eye can see and the brains analyze, but the truth of the matter is that, like those two, "I have no clue what I'm talking about." Ouch!

~~~~~

ON BEING A FOLLOWER OF CHRIST
From my heart to yours—

To be REAL and AUTHENTIC as a follower of Christ requires the transformation of the Mind and Heart and Will, not to be better, but to be Christ-like. For only at the cross are the lines drawn between "rebellion of the heart" and "complete surrender". The rest are futile attempts at capturing the wind. I am eternally thankful that Jesus remained until the very end on the cross, and did not listen to his mockers when they said, "He saved many. Let him save himself and come down." He was not so concerned ever about saving one because his eternal plan has been to give himself as a ransom for many. Today, I long to kiss His feet and worship Him anew.

How much does He love us? When we marry, we say, "...until death do us part". But he said, "...even death will NOT us part." Now, our turn! *(Saturday, March 14, 2015 at 8:36 A.M. CDT)*

WHY DO I LOVE HIM MORE?
From my heart to yours—

Why would I rather have Jesus than anything? If the way to heaven was paved with gold, and I can collect all the gold my heart desires along the way, I will never arrive on my own because getting there is no TomTom. Jesus said, "I am the Way." The cross and the Christ is where it begins and where there is entrance. And some still don't get it and have carved to themselves dangerous paths and think of it as a heavenly safari. Yet, the lowest of the low longs to kiss his sacred feet and look to Him and be saved. That's why I love Him so. His name is Jesus! *(Saturday, March 14, 2015 at 9:11 A.M. CDT)*

WHY DO I LOVE HIM?
From my heart to yours—

Why do I love Him? Here are some reasons: Because He looked at the rejects of the world and accepted them; at the despised of the world and He became despised like them; at the woman who lost everything in life and He simply gave her power and life eternal; at the thief and He restored him; at the dead and He raised Him; at the poor and He blessed them; at everyone who came to Him to deliver them, and He did not turn away; at the hungry and thirsty, and He said "Come unto me." He attached Himself to us for love's sake. THAT's why! ...and there is more. *(Saturday, March 14, 2015 at 9:11 A.M. CDT)*

∽⌒⌒⌒∽

NICE DOCTRINE
From my heart to yours–

In Christianity, religious theory and doctrinal discussions will always remain "Nice" to have, but will never become practical and life-transforming until one comes to the cross of Christ. That is where one discovers that *Christ* is where the beginning and end reside, and He requires Complete Surrender for a new life to begin in Him. The amazing and sure thing about this picture is the absence of alternatives. *(Saturday, March 14, 2015 at 11:23 A.M. CDT)*

∽⌒⌒⌒∽

JESUS AND MARKETING DON'T MIX
From my heart to yours–

Jesus is not something or someone to be advertised or promoted. Here are some reasons: (1) He cannot be like Priceline where "You Name Your Price". He already did that. (2) He does not say like Nike, "Just Do It", because He completed what needs to be Done. (3) He doesn't do the McDonald's "Lovin' it!" thing, because I cannot be "Lovin' It" if I'm not "Livin' It". (4) He despises Wall Street so much that He redefined the terms "stocks" and "bonds". He doesn't have a treasury department because he IS gold through and through. (5) He is not to be traded, sold or bought, not into mergers, shuns being on "Charts" of popularity. One tried to sell Him once and lost even his life and hung himself. (6) He doesn't have a "Weather Channel" because it's always "Sunny" *with* him even when it's dark and not "Funny". (7) One of his favorite words is *ever*. We can even say he is for-EVER; not just forever but for forever and EVER; his mercies and love are forever; He is EVER-ready to forgive and receive; he is EVER Present in time of need; he is EVER-living, EVER-interceding, EVER-giving, and EVER-lasting. His arms are open to whom-EVER, when-EVER and howEVER he/she comes. And you ask me why I love Him so?!!! My heart's desire for you and me today is to give Him "*Blessing and glory and wisdom, Thanksgiving and honor and power and might ... forEVER and EVER. Amen.*" (Revelation 7) His name is Jesus! *(Saturday, March 14, 2015 at 12:08 P.M. CDT)*

LOVE'S TRUE NATURE
From my heart to yours– (extended)

From passages such as Philippians 2:5-11, it is reasonable to conclude that Jesus Christ gave up everything to accomplish the will of the Father and save me as part of the eternal plan. Am I willing to give up everything for the sake of Christ and the Gospel in order to accomplish His complete and perfect will in my life? Put differently, am I willing to surrender completely and allow the Holy Spirit to apply the Gospel of Jesus Christ to me, and lead my life as to how I should think, feel, decide, and act? This is not being religious; it's being Christ-like. I can give, sing, travel, speak, be friendly, be kind, and be as pious and religious as I please. The truth is that He accepts nothing less than total surrender before I am able to perform the "first act of kindness" to His pleasure. The good deeds never drive the character. In fact, I can be paralyzed and be completely surrendered to the Lordship of Christ to His satisfaction. In other words, I must die in order for Him to live in me empowered by His Holy Spirit. For *it* is not what I do that matters, but rather what He does in and through me. How much I do does not matter. What pleases Him does. Short of that, the truth of the matter is that I'm playing games with Him, knowing fully when he was crucified that he was dead serious. And when He died, his intention was not to make me or Him "feel good". So He said to Peter, "*Do you love me?*" I'm inclined to think also that He is asking the same question to those who claim to be His followers. May this day in your life and mine, March 15, truly be the Lord's Day! *(Sunday, March 15, 2015 at 3:14 A.M. CDT)*

A SUMMARY OF LOVE'S TRUE NATURE
From my heart to yours–

From passages such as Philippians 2:5-11, it is reasonable to conclude that Jesus Christ gave up everything to accomplish the will of the Father and save me as part of the eternal plan. Am I willing to give up everything for the sake of Christ and the Gospel in order to accomplish His complete and perfect will in my life? Put differently, am I willing to surrender completely and allow the Holy Spirit to apply the Gospel of Jesus Christ to me, and lead my life as to how I should think, feel, decide, and act? This is not being religious; it's being Christ-like. *(Sunday, March 15, 2015 at 3:36 A.M. CDT)*

GRACE MOMENT
From my heart to yours–

A moment of Grace through many years. We were sitting for breakfast at Hani and Samia's home. Mom slept well and is very glad. So, her heart opened up in a sacred moment. As the song says:

"T'was grace that brought me safe thus far; And grace will lead me home." *(Sunday, March 15, 2015 at 12:22 P.M. CDT)*

$\sim\!\!\sim\!\!\sim$

DAD UPDATE, MARCH 16, 11:15 A.M. CST: The plan NOW: (per Dr.'s instructions) Dad will be discharged to Rehab facility later this afternoon, for up to 21 days. Will be evaluated at that time for "what's next". Good Morning! Thank you for prayers!

$\sim\!\!\sim\!\!\sim$

DAD UPDATE, MARCH 17, 11 P.M. CST: Finally, the time came and he was transferred to a rehab facility with skilled nursing. He will be receiving a variety of therapies as his health allows. Thank you for your prayers! We ask to hold off on any visits for few days until he regains some energy. He loves to see especially friends and church members. Meanwhile he needs most of all to adjust to the new environment. Your cooperation is much appreciated. I will definitely keep you updated as to his progress. Sincerely in Christ, John

$\sim\!\!\sim\!\!\sim$

TRUE PARENTHOOD
From my heart to yours–

Seeing that my parents are approaching the age of maturity so much that they are about to fall from the tree of this life, I'm eternally thankful for a few things they taught me and the precious 6 siblings: (1) That their names are written in the Book of eternal life and their passion has been laser-focused on Him who loved them, and the rest is mere details; (2) That it is very possible to be used by God with extremely limited resources because He is still looking for that little boy with bread and fish; (3) That I'd rather work with someone who is thoroughly transparent and genuine yet weak and broken in many places than with the high and mighty in ministry; (4) That the Holy Spirit is definitely not interested in finding someone who is 30-something to use him/her for 40 years, but He chooses broken and yielded vessels in His own time and in His own way, a task that He never entrusts to anyone. In fact it's not necessary. Maybe that's why Jesus said, "I will be with you [.....] I will build My church..."; (5) That loving the unlovely and people deemed worthless in the eyes of others is God's way of showing His glory more fully where there is nothing to look at; (6) That degrees don't qualify and/or equip, but a downpour of the Spirit does every time . Otherwise, what happens is mere rumbling bones. I'm reminded that I still need 32 degrees to add up to Zero; (7) That working in single-hearted and single-minded teams, driven by the Spirit is far better than anything done single-handedly. Even man's redemption took Father, Son and Spirit. (8) That I shouldn't burn a bridge of a relationship, even if another person does. For by doing so, I give the Holy Spirit time to intervene. That's faith and hope driven by love. (9) That loving unconditionally whatsoever is a reality that anyone can discover daily when we are true followers of Him. (10) That being spent for the sake of Christ alone, always pays dividends in time, because it is still true that the seed must die in order to bear fruit. My first sin every day is when I remotely think I can do anything without Him. And just because He said, "I am with you always", doesn't automatically mean "I am with Him always". Pride is always a killer. So, I'm still going one day at a time, even after 60-something years, because I've found that if I "plan" anything, I'm tempted to follow the plan and move my eyes from Him who said, "Follow Me". *(Wednesday, March 18, 2015 at 12:40 P.M. CDT)*

GIVING WHEN THERE IS NOTHING
From my heart to yours–

I was thinking all day today about the idea of "giving". I discovered in review of the past 60 years that Giving begins when I run out of "things" to give. That's when the character of the heart reveals its true quality. Then I discover that in fact God is the true "Giver"; hence, every good gift is from "above", from the "father of lights". King David knew it deeply when he said in praise to God, "and from *your* hand we gave." I discovered and was annoyed greatly by my own selfishness that deprives me of loving God from a pure heart. *(Wednesday, March 18, 2015 at 8:41 P.M. CDT)*

SNAPSHOT OF GRACE
From my heart to yours–

If people condescendingly look down on King David and always remember his horrible sin, why do they for centuries keep going back to his psalms to sing, to read, to memorize, and to enjoy them? Always!!! Isn't it strange?!!! To enjoy his psalms sincerely, we must understand his sin completely. And that can never happen outside the cross of Christ. When we view his psalms against the backdrop of sin, then we understand the meaning of *grace*. Amazing grace! -- As much as sin drives me away, the attractiveness of His grace creates in me the desire to stay near. Grace makes me run, not away from, but TO His cross. No wonder satan hates the cross of Christ with passion and vengeance! No wonder Paul said, "If anyone glories, let him glory in the cross of Christ!" The cross of Christ is the symbol of Victory. *(Thursday, March 19, 2015 at 6:14 A.M. CDT)*

WHICH CLOUD FORMATION?
From my heart to yours–

I cherish the moments when I look at the skies and snap pictures of cloud formations, wondering which will be the perfect formation that will gladly part and make way when He, my Lord, appears in the clouds. My heart yearns for that day! *(Sunday, March 22, 2015 at 6:09 P.M. CDT)*

THE JOURNEY
From my heart to yours–

Continuing the walk we started many years ago, intending to stay on the concrete path until our feet step onto streets of purest gold. :). Meanwhile, "surely goodness and mercy will follow me"... because every time we turn around, we see His fingerprints, His footsteps, of pure mercy and grace here and there and in many places, totally undeserved. This teaches me to stay the course and worship Him alone and anew every day. The company is awesome too! *(Monday, March 23, 2015 at 12:01 A.M. CDT)*

TRUMPET SOUNDING
From my heart to yours–

Just imagine: (picture) - The trumpet sounding, - The clouds parting away, - The sky all blue, - Even the mountaintop draped in white ... The King Is Coming! Some may think: "This is Crazy!" My only reply is: "As I look around the world over all I see is *far* crazier stuff going on than this, and it's pure evil. Is it really crazy to think that my Lord is coming again?!" His name is Jesus Christ. Is He your Lord yet?! *(Monday, March 23, 2015 at 12:08 A.M. CDT)*

WOULD YOU DO THAT?
From my heart to yours–

If I knew beforehand that: - by being put in jail unfairly - because of my witness for Christ - and I stayed in jail 28 years, Then I discovered as a result of my stay that: - an inmate became a true followers of Christ - his life was radically transformed, and - that change was confirmed over the last three years of my stay in jail. Here is the question: Would I be willing to pay that price and go to jail for that long? Would you? This was a real story that I was told. It took place in a ME country, and left my heart in shambles - again! *(Monday, March 23, 2015 at 12:48 A.M. CDT)*

LAYING WEAPON DOWN, NOT GOOD ENOUGH
From my heart to yours–

This morning, I was reminded that to surrender completely to the governance of the Spirit in my life, it takes more than laying down all my weapons of war. It takes putting on Christ. Otherwise, I will only be a naked fool. One of the reasons I love Him so is that He gave me His Spirit to guide and walk with me fully, and is not measured by number of scoops. *(Monday, March 23, 2015 at 10:37am CDT)*

MARRIED AND HAPPY, YES!
From my heart to yours–

We heard it said that any male and female can make a baby. But it takes character to make a home. In thinking further and reflecting on our journey, here are few more thoughts: (1) As a husband, I don't gain anything if she loses; Spirit-filled reality says: we either both gain or both lose. (2) I must always prepare to be my best - so *she* can succeed, is happy, content, and always loved. (3) She never has to wonder what my intentions are. They are her domain too. Keeping the conversation going. "Whatsoever things is ... These Do" (Phil 4). (4) I must learn all I can, even about why she's so special, to know her more, to love her more. That's a lifetime journey none of its days can be postponed. Walking together - Hand in Hand. (5) We ought to plan on being vulnerable to each other, and to no one else. "Husbands love your wives" NOT "if she blah blah blah". (6) It is always the right thing to do when I apologize, admit wrong, or forgive without a tit-for-tat attitude. (7) Laughter (i.e., being funny, silly) is good therapy, especially when alone. (Proverbs) (8) She will never cry without my tears falling too. (Empathy) (9) Verbalizing emotions takes more time, but is healthy when both are ready. "She knows I love her" is UN-acceptable. That doesn't say anything about her but a *lot* about me. (10) Listening is an art that at the start of marriage is a foreign language. Many die and it's still a foreign language. Rosetta Stone can't help. (11) HONORING parents is always a MUST because it has a promise (Ex 20); Eph. 5). Obeying parents is always a liability after marriage. There IS a difference, unless ... I married the parents too and didn't know it. (12) It's always top priority to be sensitive to each other, not *oversensitive*. Making time, giving preference, and asking questions is an art acquired over time, and regrettably not by many. (13) To claim "superiority in all things" just because we're now married and "I'm the head of the house" is a false pretense...unless I want a maid, it's bad policy, and shows myopic view, especially when I'm still wet behind the ears (lacking experience). (14) If I have to go out of my way to assert anything, I lost before I opened my mouth. Honoring each other with class is better! (15) It's always better to ask for clarification by saying something like: "you said blah blah blah. Did you mean this-and-that, or did you mean something else?", thus giving the other time to elaborate. (16) Re-verbalizing says: "what I understood you to say is 'ABC'. Is that what you meant?" Or, "Help me understand something ......" (17) Interpreting the intentions of the spouse's words is always counter-productive. DON'T even go there. It's shooting yourself in the foot every time. Love tells the truth. (18) To MAKE my spouse submit to me lowers the value of both to what's negotiable. It is selling Christ short, and selling the other something cheap. Submission is a matter of the heart, and is never forced. (19) The best that I can do, is submit completely to Christ. Regarding the other, all I can do is demonstrate my true love of Christ to her. (20) Surrender is laying down all weapons of war down, and NOT picking them back up. This is why Jesus Christ did not come down from the cross. There is always a resurrection morning. (21) Manhood and womanhood need to be treasured by one and for one, and not pleasured by or peddled to any other. Dressing up with class is not seeking attention to self but saving the attention to spouse. Seeking attention from many is intentional by advertisers. Then people come to buy. (22) If Christ has full access to all the rooms of the house, no one else needs an invitation. (23) Four demons need to stay subdued in chains: Pride, Fear, Anger, and Lies. Either all stay controlled by the power of the Spirit of Christ, or any of them can easily give satan a foothold and a new home. (24) Spiritual warfare is a reality, 24/7/365, including holidays and spring breaks. In a marriage, both spouses are required to fight shoulder to shoulder in order to win. When one is weak, the Spirit gives grace to the weary and gives more grace to the other one still standing. (25) It's OK for the husband to say, "I really don't know", especially when the wife already knows that. (26) Neither ought to remotely consider laying like a rug for the other to trample on. Christ died for the Church so that both spouses can uniquely experience standing tall. (27) True love keeps a balance, with a slight intentional tilt toward the other, for love's sake. Nothing earthly takes precedence. (28) Serving is not done through the filter of the other spouse because Christ has already set the standard for service. Anything else is always of lesser quality. (29) Telling the truth may hurt and almost anyone can do that. But telling the truth IN LOVE is to share in the pain and never let go until restoration happens...for love's sake. (30) The woman almost always knows when an embrace is only for love's sake. The husband doesn't need to add artificial flavors. Flowers Welcomed. (31) Giving all is a joy that costs, but the agony of defeat is not there. (32) What is intimately shared is intently and intentionally preserved as intimate. Nothing has an orange sale tag. (33) The "remote" needs to stay like that - remote. (34) Marriage is never about a dream, a right, or a trivia game. Marriage is a battle field. Both spouses are always on one side -- the same side. (35) In-laws are wonderful to keep and cherish, until they become outlaws. (36) Jesus Christ never gave advice. Spouses ought not to start toward each other. It's SO unlike Jesus to "look down". (37) It's better to say "Let Us" instead of "You do this or that", or "I'm not going to do this come hell or high water". Or, "YOU'RE GOING TO DO IT!" (38) I should never make a long-term decision based on a single, short-term event that ended in disappointment. It always backfires. (39) It's always better to lose a battle than to lose the war. I learn from a battle. If I lose the war, learning then is not required. (40) When trouble is brewing, making a baby will only add the expenses, and invite audience to the disappointing performance. (41) Capital Investment is when both spouses don't assume everything is going well and nothing else needs to be done to cultivate the relationship. Instead, both make steady investments over time in ways that will certainly enrich the other, first, and self, next; and the relationship third. This ongoing process is like the daily doses of vitamins many people take so that, when the body is weak, the reservoir of energy naturally provides the added strength. (42) Ongoing fortification and growth is always needed in four areas: physical, mental, social, and spiritual. Fortification takes place alone and together, deliberate and continual, transparently and with focus. (43) When there is a problem, both need to begin the journey at the throne of grace in honest prayerful conversation with Him who hears and answers. (44) Defining the problem is needed next, with time to digest and put forth an action plan. (45) Blame, Shame, and name-calling are a waste of all resources, and will cause moral infection of the soul. (46) No need to pull rank. Christ never did that. In fact, He said "I'm the teacher and I washed your feet." (47) It would be a good exercise to begin at the end, and live life today with the end in mind. It will soon become a new beginning. (48) What needs to be settled, ought to be settled while it is day. The night comes, and time is no more. (49) Gentleness (in hugs, in words, in actions) is always welcomed. And it's more difficult to implement than we think. (50) Leaning to love God is not an option but a necessity; not easy but difficult; not one event but a lifetime journey. (51) Neither ought to make a decision *first*, then backpedal. Let the conversation continue. *(Tuesday, March 24, 2015 at 12:51 A.M. CDT)*

❧

STAYING AND GOING
From my heart to yours—

I'm learning to say, "Going is far better", but staying is for our sake, refocusing the attention of our eyes and hearts on so much and on so precious. Also, as I had a chance the past 5 days to look at other people's journeys through their valleys, ours seemed a light pain in comparison. How and what should I pray? Starting with sitting in numbing silence is good for starters. Listening to Him as He calms the spirit and gives gentle reassurance is like drifting snow. Indeed, "our Father who is in heaven". Then He begins to align our skipping and frail heartbeats, giving us time to stretch our hands toward him like a child does to his loving father. Trusting, Waiting, Thanking always - and for you. *(Tuesday, March 24, 2015 at 10:59 P.M. CDT)*

❧

DAD UPDATE, 27 MARCH, 11:55 A.M., CST:
Short version: Dad spent 3 hours in ER. All tests were acceptable. X-ray was slightly better than before. He was returned to Rehab, getting rest and some physical therapy, and was monitored better. Sincere thanks for your prayers.

Long version: On 24 March, Dad was taken to the ER because his breathing got worse, and he was non-responsive to 3 people who tried to wake him up. Had a heartbeat and very shallow breath. By the time he got to ER, he began to respond. Medical professionals ran several tests and did X-ray. The tests came back w/ average results. His X-ray looked better than when he was in ICU 2 weeks ago. After 3-4 hours in ER, he went back to rehab. My sister and I met with management and made sure specific routines and procedures were in his chart, especially regarding their response in specific scenarios. He was exhausted but slept reasonably well on 3/24. We checked on him regularly. The next two days, he was resting especially after physical therapy (with oxygen). On two visits, he was lying back in bed and talking to the nurse about how the Lord kept them throughout the years. Lacking severely in my pedicure skills, I confess that I nicked his toes a time or two, but was unintentional :). He did thank me at the end. :) The journey of God's grace continues. Thank you for prayers.

RAISING HELL
From my heart to yours—

I cannot raise hell on my way to heaven and expect to get there safe and sound. Likewise, I cannot be a Christian and NOT be a disciple and follower of Jesus Christ, and in intimate relationship with Him. The Holy Spirit who snatched me out of hell will make sure my path to heaven has cooled off, and that all my affections belong to Him. *(Sunday, March 29, 2015 at 6:12 A.M. CDT)*

BEYOND GLORIOUS
From my heart to yours—

My dearest and youngest -- still cherishes a simple kiss from Mom. Can't blame him at all. The true value is not in the kiss, or that this time he was behaving, but in the many years of unquestionable love that will never let go. All he could do is: surrender, close his eyes, and smile :) So is God's incomparable and matchless love, and far more. He said "I have loved you with an everlasting love; therefore I extended to you Mercy." The song says: "Not because of who I am, But because of what you've done, Not because of what I've done, But because of Who you are!" His name is Jesus! He is Risen! SOOO many tombs, Only ONE empty! Happy Easter Everyone -- for love's sake. *(Monday, March 30, 2015 at 6:53 A.M. CDT)*

PAMPERED PARENTS
From my heart to yours—

I'm more in favor of pampering the parents. It's part of honoring them to the very end. It's part of God's love reciprocated! *(Monday, March 30, 2015 at 12:53 P.M. CDT)*

CHARACTER POINT
From my heart to yours—

Who I am defines whether I help you or not. Character is the missing jewel without which the heart is corrupt. True character is not defined by culture or community but by Christ. So, the question that matters is: "Will I surrender completely to Him?" The remainder of life is simply details that reflect my answer. Christ is the only One in human history who requires me to stand up and give the answer that will inescapably reflect my true heart. But what people opted to do, until today, is to crucify him. Then He said, "I will RISE again. Death can't keep me in the ground"! What a Savior! *(Tuesday, March 31, 2015 at 9:30 A.M. CDT)*

IDENTITY MATTERS
From my heart to yours—

Who I am defines whether I help you or not. Who you are, if I'm a true follower of Christ, should not matter at all. This thinking makes me very uncomfortable, outside my comfort zone, outside my religious box, very vulnerable, but with one thing and only one thing

I am left with to enjoy every day, namely, trusting God to do what He promised He will do. No alternative. No fear. No religion. And No name is good enough except the name of Jesus. He is so different that heaven and earth have absolutely nothing to offer as alternative. All the world can do is: Pretend. And the sad part is that some Christians do the same also: Pretend. Is He worth trusting? Really! *(Tuesday, March 31, 2015 at 4:35 P.M. CDT)*

WHICH IS FIRST
From my heart to yours—

"To do", or "Not to do" -- is NOT the question. "To do" -- is self-driven, self-determined, and creates self-driven standards. "Not to do" -- is discriminatory, unhealthy, and creates divisions. To "BE" in order to "DO" is what Christ asks. He also reminds us that we can only do that through Him. We can only "BE" right in Him, the One who matters, in order to "DO" the right thing to anyone including the least important. The question is: Will I obey?! *(Wednesday, April 1, 2015 at 5:48 P.M. CDT)*

COMPLETELY OURS
From my heart to yours—

If the person, presence, power and work of the Holy Spirit is not discerned in private prayer, how am I to discern anything in public ministry?!!! I cannot strive in the presence of people anytime if I don't stand in His presence all the time. *(Friday, April 3, 2015 at 8:01 A.M. CDT)*

THE NORTHBOUND STORY
From my heart to yours—

Summarily, the only *real* and enduring good news in the history of mankind has been the Resurrection of Jesus Christ. It left so many, past and present, totally *stunned*! Everything before the Resurrection flowed toward it like a great river. Everything since the resurrection happened flows from it, "like a river glorious"! At the center of the resurrection is Jesus, the sweetest name I know. That's truly *awesome*! So, to all who truly love Him and look forward to His appearing -- It is high time to live for Him unreservedly, and to love Him without condition. May His Spirit enable, empower, embolden, and embrace His people who cry out to Him day and night. He IS worthy! *(Saturday, April 4, 2015 at 12:26 P.M. CDT)*

NEVER FORSAKEN AGAIN
From my heart to yours—

He was forsaken, so that *we* will never be forsaken. In the Old Testament, God's voice came to Abraham saying, "I know now that you love me because you did not withhold your son from me." In the New Testament, the death, burial, and resurrection of Jesus Christ have given conclusive reason to say to God, "I know now that you love me because you did not withhold your Son from me." His name is Jesus! The old song says: "There have been names that I have loved to hear, but never has there been a name so dear to this heart of mine, as the Name divine, The precious, precious Name of Jesus. Chorus: Jesus is the sweetest name I know, And He's just the same as His lovely Name, And that's the reason why I love Him so; Oh, Jesus is the sweetest name I know. And some day I shall see Him face to face To thank and praise Him for His wondrous grace, Which He gave to me, when He made me free, The blessed Son of God called Jesus." *(Saturday, April 4, 2015 at 12:53 P.M. CDT)*

⌒⌒⌒⌒

PAID IN FULL
From my heart to yours—

The first Resurrection morning affirms payment in-full, and confirms the coming of the second and final resurrection morning. It's only a matter of time, but this time it will be forever! What a day of rejoicing that will be!!! *(Sunday, April 5, 2015 at 5:10 A.M. CDT)*

⌒⌒⌒⌒

THE AMAZING RESURRECTION
From my heart to yours—

- At *death*, the sacrifice was accepted. At *resurrection*, we were accepted.
- At *death*, He invites us to believe and live. At *resurrection*, He invites us to believe and live forever.
- At *death*, He went into heaven to prepare eternal salvation for us. At *resurrection*, He went back into heaven to "prepare a place" for us.
- At *death*, He took our filthy rags of sin. At *resurrection*, He gave us His holy garment of righteousness.
- At *death*, He was alone for days. At *resurrection*, He is with us forever.
- At *death*, He brought heaven to earth. At *resurrection*, He brought earth to heaven. .....and SO much more...

He obeyed and died for us, so that we can obey and live for Him. His name is Jesus. He is worthy! *(Sunday, April 5, 2015 at 11:43 A.M. CDT)*

From my heart to yours *resurrection–*

Dad's last UPDATE: at 1:57 A.M. CST, Dad went home to be with the Lord. As I talked to him yesterday evening at rehab, his last words I remember were: "We have to tell them (about salvation) while we can. We have to tell them." (He was referring to the rehab staff that came to assist him with his exercise.) He was passionate about Him who was passionate about the lost. We worship Him who gave Dad 90 years, and at last held his hand to walk him through the valley of the shadow. Yes, it is after all a great resurrection morning! Your prayers for strength, discernment, and comfort are appreciated. Thank you for standing with us. You were the visible feet and audible words of the Holy Spirit, the Great Comforter!

DATES AND TIMES: - Visitation to Offer Condolences: (at parents' home) (1) Tuesday evening, April 7, 5:00-9:00 AND, (2) Thursday afternoon, after graveside service, April 9, 3:00 P.M. - 9:00 P.M.. - Viewing before funeral service: (1) Wednesday, April 8, 4:30-5:00 for family only (2) Wednesday, April 8, 5:00-7:00 for all (3) Thursday, April 9, 10:00-10:55 A.M. FUNERAL SERVICE: Thursday at 11:00 A.M. (3) In lieu of flowers, the family requests that contributions be made in Dad's honor and memory to help further the ministries of the church he established in Bikfaya, Lebanon in 1953. - Donations can be in cash or check. - Make checks payable to: Arabic Church. - In the notes section, write: "Bikfaya". - All check contributions only are tax-deductible. - Be sure you include your mailing address. Please come prepared to worship. Dad is more alive now than ever before. He's dressed up in incorruptible garments, looking at the face of Jesus and at the faces of those who preceded him. Let us celebrate his life, and the glorious giver of life, the Lord Jesus Christ. Any questions please send a private text or message. *(Monday, April 6, 2015 at 2:53 A.M. CDT)*

~~~~~

TENDER MOMENTS
From my heart to yours—

One of Dad's grand-daughters said, "Always thought he was handsome. Now, even better!" Picture came from another niece and grand-daughter. All beautiful. Dad had great difficulty deciding which was his favorite. Typical Dad! *(Monday, April 6, 2015 at 1:40 P.M. CDT)*

~~~~~

LET IT GO TO CALVARY
From my heart to yours—

Invited To Celebrate and Worship -- From my heart to yours -- In few hours, our family (immediate and extended), our beautiful yet mourning church, and many friends (more than one deserves) will celebrate and worship. We CELEBRATE a life, a seed, very aware of its limitations, bent in its shape, insignificant by most measures, but which allowed a mightier hand to select it, hold it, designate the place, prepare the ground, and guide it deep into the dusty human experience by the fingers of God. The seed went deeper for it pleased Him who planted it that it should bear much fruit, and one final yet gentle push further... until the very last breath was snuffed out and it died. We *worship* because God is worthy, and He enabled us through Christ to always experience His immense love toward us molded by His Spirit, and experience so much, and bring Him compounded glory and praise for generations to come. It's not because of who we are, but because of what He's done (we worship); it's not because of what my Dad has done, but because of who God is, we bow and worship, in Spirit and Truth. You are *invited* now, if need be for the first time, to know the wonder of it all who made all this possible. His name is Jesus. We bow in utter gratitude for one of many things. It is that He was able to keep our Dad faithful in all that he did, and that Dad knew His name. And His name is Wonderful. The peace indeed passes understanding. The joy is truly mixed with sadness. The hope reaches to the very presence of God and touches the hem of His garment by simple faith. His love overflowed toward us, and His grace is truly sufficient. On behalf of the family, I share this song (by André Crouch): "*How can I say thanks, for the things you have done for me; Things so undeserved, yet you gave to prove your love for me; The voices of a million angels, could not express my gratitude, All that I am, or ever hope to be, I owe it all to Thee. Chorus: To God be the glory, for the things He has done; With His blood He has saved me, With His power He has raised me, To God be the glory for the things He has done! Just let me live my life Let it be pleasing, Lord to Thee And should I gain any praise, Let it go to Calvary.*" (Thursday, April 9, 2015 at 3:56 A.M. CDT)

∾⌒〜⌒∿

TRUE VALUE
From my heart to yours–

I asked friends to feel Free to download and print Bible verses that Dad wrote using his Arabic calligraphy skills, to frame and hang on the walls. These verses are masterpieces, not because my Dad wrote them but because Dad just copied what God wrote. These pictures are samples of many verses that Dad wrote during the last three months of his life (more to come). As you can see with some, he wrote on pieces of notebook paper, turned sideways or upside down, and some are pieces attached with tape. I said, "Why don't you use quality paper? Want me to get you some?" He always answered, *"The paper doesn't matter. It's the words that have life. I can write on anything."* Isn't God like that? He can use anything, even a wall, to write with his finger a love story. His precious name is Jesus, and this is yet another reason why I love Him so. *(Thursday, April 9, 2015 at 5:35 A.M. CDT)*

HIDDEN WORD
From my heart to yours–

Feel Free to download and print, to frame and hang on your walls. These verses are masterpieces, not because my Dad wrote them but because Dad just copied what God wrote. When I went to visit him while still living at home, he would whisper in my ear sometimes, "Go upstairs into my study and see what I wrote for you." Isn't that what God whispers in our ears at times, to look and see what He wrote? "Your word have I hid in my heart that I might not sin against thee." *(Thursday, April 9, 2015 at 5:44 A.M. CDT)*

REAL COPYRIGHT
From my heart to yours–

It just dawned on me, as I was posting the pictures of verses Dad wrote in calligraphy, that the idea of copyright laws was in fact started with God. Try changing some part of it, even a word, and see what happens :). Please feel free to download, print, and hang on your walls. Here's why: If God did NOT write his word in legible (readable) form, why are people of the world raving mad about it?

They can try to disregard it, ignore it, and leave it alone to die, tear up all the Bibles, burn them, and try to destroy all they can. They can just dismiss it as fraud if they don't like it. But the truth is, even if they want to dismiss it from their very DNA, they can't, because God left His fingerprints all over it, and it can't be simply dismissed. As if God whispers in the night hours, "Not so fast, friend!" *(Thursday, April 9, 2015 at 5:53 A.M. CDT)*

NEVER RETURNS VOID
From my heart to yours–

Once, before leaving on a trip to the M.E. area, I said "Dad, would you write for me about 10-15 verses that talk about Christ, the blood, heaven, the cross, redemption, God's love, and let me take them with me? I would like to give them as a gift." He asked, "To whom?" I said, "I don't know, but God will show me in time." After arrival, we went to the market (the souk" and got an eye-full of stores that sold gold and silver, and got a nose-full of spices from the Far East. As I meandered on my way to nowhere in particular through the sea of people, I saw from the corner of my eye a little shop that sold few antiques, and went in. Then I noticed in the corner a table with styluses and artistic pens, and some China ink (the best kind to write calligraphy with. I smiled and just knew that this store was it. I asked for the owner, and very quickly our conversation steered its way toward that specific and small corner desk. Then I said, "My Dad is a calligrapher, in his 80s now, but he gave me some things he wrote and I'd like to give them to you as a gift. Or, if you choose, you can feel free to give them away or even sell them. Would you accept?" "Of course", he said with a genuine sense of appreciation. I left his store like the farmer who found a diamond. The next day I rushed back, trying to control my emotions, I handed my friend the verses Dad wrote." "Wow, Wow! This is truly amazing; so perfect. I will certainly take these to my house and frame them, and hang them on my walls. I won't be selling them at all. These are too nice to sell." I smiled and thought to myself, "Now he's hooked! Not that my Dad wrote them, but that God found a way to deliver His word to this man." At the end of the day, It's all about Him. Dad's day just ended. God's day is eternal and bright! *(Thursday, April 9, 2015 at 6:21 A.M. CDT)*

GATE IS STILL NARROW
From my heart to yours–

I begin to worry when Christians think that they found some method or trick by which to get people into the Kingdom. The truth is that it cost God everything to pay for it in full -- His emptying himself, becoming a man, drinking the vengeful cup of wrath to the very end, losing only once the eternal communion with the Father so we will never lose it again ever, meeting all the requirements of the holy law of God regarding sin and paid the price in full; and it still costs blood!!! We *dare not* water it down and dumb it down just so people will accept it by some human means. Even Jesus himself could not have accomplished any part of it without the persistent dominance and hovering of the very Spirit of the living God on His earthly life as the Son of Man. Everyone who comes in requires the conviction and intervention of God's Spirit to snatch them out of hell and darkness into the very light and life of His glorious Son. Yes, his name IS Jesus. *(Thursday, April 9, 2015 at 6:42 A.M. CDT)*

CAN DO ALL THINGS
From my heart to yours–

Later today, I will be on my way to Ethiopia for couple of weeks. Your prayers are much appreciated. I woke up this morning thinking about prayer. The longer I live, the more I think of it as the normal spiritual breathing capacity in the true follower of Christ the enables him/her to do everything else. *EVERYTHING*! Hence, Philippians 4:13. We make a fatal mistake when we want more things then find the artificial means to make them happen. I fear that many who claim to be Christians or in Christian service (which I have no desire or time or capability to dispute its truth), have similar spiritual lungs to my Dad's, with partial capacity if any, to accomplish anything and are always in desperate need of artificial means to sustain their version of Christianity, thinking that that's how life ought to or can be, when in fact it carries only a deceptive appearance of life. And it always gets worse with time. The need for the full breath of the Spirit of God is at a critical level. Then ... life begins! I have faith that God can do much more than I ask. *(Friday, April 10, 2015 at 7:55 A.M. CDT)*

ALL THINGS WORK FOR GOOD
From my heart to yours—

Life's crises and stormy experiences are divine moments which God uses to knock on the heart's door and administer true life. Non-responsive hearts remain in rebellion and in an artificial state of motion, but those who respond will experience true life in Christ. God's desire is life. He's the owner and is entitled to his opinion, but it's the only one that matters. *"I have come that they might have life, and have it more abundantly."* Do you believe?! *(Friday, April 10, 2015 at 8:05 A.M. CDT)*

ALL OR NONE
From my heart to yours—

God will accept nothing less than complete surrender and trust. NOTHING! Just because we don't and can't find Complete Surrender and Trust on earth doesn't mean at all that we treat Him according to our own "terms of engagement". "Complete Surrender" means we lay down all our weapons. "Trust" means that what WE do doesn't amount to anything, but what HE SAYS amounts to everything. For Christ's sake, let whoever hasn't; be reconciled back to God -- at the cross. For that is where life begins and where character is sustained. The rest is mere details. *(Friday, April 10, 2015 at 10:15 A.M. CDT)*

FOUR DAYS AFTER HE WENT HOME
From my heart to yours–

One of the significant things I noticed about Dad over the past 60 years is that he wasn't impressed with himself, especially when something great was done, but he was always impressed and captivated by his Master. Who is yours? Who is mine? I have always learned to ask: "what is impressing me?!!!" Always! *(Friday, April 10, 2015 at 11:04 A.M. CDT)*

CONFIDENCE IN THE POWER OF THE CROSS
From my heart to yours–

When I've settled in my heart that I'm impressed only with the cross of Christ, I discover that I'm not depressed at all in the world regardless of what comes my way, for the cross of Christ has its unique way of leveling the playing fields, and lifting me up again to hope. That's why I'm learning to glory only in the cross. It's imperative for true life in Christ. That's where love happened! *(Friday, April 10, 2015 at 11:54 A.M. CDT)*

CREATIVE POWER
From my heart to yours–

What can one do in 24 hours? Nabeel Emaish, son of Hani and Samia, drew in charcoal a portrait of his Jiddo (Granddad). He showed it to me while in progress. I asked "Nabeel are you able to be done in time for the funeral service? It's tomorrow." His reply was "I got it, it's in my head but just need few more hours and will be done and have it ready to bring with me." When the time came, the portrait was put on display for all to be amazed and stand in gratitude. Still surprised that God created things in 24 hours? Did He not say that he has the whole picture in his mind but took the time needed to perfect it? Isn't Nabeel's love for his Jiddo a sample of God's love for us? Did He not demonstrate His love toward us? Did he not call us to just stand and be amazed and in gratitude? Oh, the love that will not let me go!!! *(Friday, April 10, 2015 at 12:40 P.M. CDT)*

GOOD COMPANY
From my heart to yours–

The balloon message popped up asking: "who are with you?" I smiled and thought: "yes, the Father with His immense love, the Son and my union with Him, and the Spirit with His infilling to accomplish His purpose. And oh yes, the intercessory prayers of many in the family of God". Perfect company, in heaven and on earth! "What shall separate us from the love of God that we always have through Jesus Christ our Lord?!!"... *(Saturday, April 11, 2015 at 3:54 A.M. CDT)*

INCONSISTENCY EXAMINED
From my heart to yours–

"Dissonance" refers to the tension that happens when a person experiences inconsistency and lack of agreement in his thinking (cognitive dissonance) or in his relationships (social dissonance). Cognitive Dissonance happens when there is inconsistency between a person's belief and his/her behavior. So it's personal and internal. It causes disagreement inside the person. Musically, it's called "discordant sounds". Social Dissonance is similar in principle, but happens when there is conflict, tension, and inconsistency where social attitudes and expectations are vague, nebulous. This scenario gives rise to abandon and abuse in failed harmony between what we are told and what we see with our own eyes. Dissonance finds its counterpart in consonance -- from the two Latin words "con" meaning "together", and "son" meaning "sound" - hence, sounding together, or sounding in harmony. Agreement of sounds. Jesus prayed (John 17), and asked the Father that "they [his followers] maybe one", not copycats but in harmony and union. In Job we find the rhetorical question: "how can two walk together unless they agree". *(Saturday, April 11, 2015 at 4:40 A.M. CDT)*

VERY SPECIAL
From my heart to yours–

It's really this simple. My Dad left us for a season, but Jesus said, "I will never leave you orphans...I am with you always." The day comes when we see them both, will see them all, and will be together! He promised. *(Saturday, April 11, 2015 at 4:42 A.M. CDT)*

SO SPECIAL
From my heart to yours–

Everyone likes to have a picture taken for a moment *with* someone we admire. But God did far better-- He loved us so much that he put us IN the picture with the One He loved forever and ever. His name is Jesus! He is SO different, yet SO close to the heart. Are you in the picture?!! *(Saturday, April 11, 2015 at 7:11 A.M. CDT)*

SLEEP IS GOOD
From my heart to yours—

Thank you for prayer! Made it safely to Addis Ababa. Before takeoff from DC, I was already in dreamland. Woke up 3600 miles later for few minutes then went back to sleep. I woke up again to a tap on my arm after couple of hours. The passenger next to me was concerned and said, "Are you ok sir?!" I just gave him the thumbs up then drifted back. Sweet! Arrival was on time; my friend met me on time; and went for breakfast then hotel. Already sensing the sweet Presence of Him who holds everything in the power of his mighty word! *(Sunday, April 12, 2015 at 2:57 A.M. CDT)*

ALL COUNT
From my heart to yours—

Last year, my young and sweet friend promised to pray for me, and she did every trip. Then in the middle of my last trip, her Mom told me that her daughter (nine years old) gave her heart to Jesus. The good news was worth waiting the whole year to hear. This year she made me the same promise. No wonder why Jesus said, "Don't hold the children back from coming to me." I love you Rana, ya Habeebti. I'm praying for you too to be the best that He wants you to be -- for Him. *(Sunday, April 12, 2015 at 7:18 A.M. CDT)*

CALLED FOR HIM
From my heart to yours–

We are only shadows when we stand against the backdrop of His Presence and glory. Individually unique, as peers in ministry bigger than both, yet called to accomplish His purpose. That's what every follower of Christ is called to experience. It is unthinkable for me to complain about anything when parts of God's family don't complain when they have nothing. It's 10:00 P.M. Ethiopia time and noontime in heaven. It's going to be a great bright day in Addis Ababa...for His glory. Continued prayer appreciated. Tomorrow I will be traveling about three hours to destination. The lightness of earthly trials amount to nothing when compared to the glory to come. *(Sunday, April 12, 2015 at 2:09 P.M. CDT)*

"GOOD ENOUGH", REALLY?
From my heart to yours–

Somehow, humans always like to have a way out, and if there isn't one, they create one for themselves. One of those ways is verbally expressed in a way by the phrase: "that's good enough". It disturbs me when I know I'm sure about something, and discover that I'm the only one who thinks that. Here is a sample, when one says/thinks:

(1) I am willing to tolerate everybody, maybe, and that's good enough

(2) I choose whom I love. That's good enough.

(3) "Random acts of kindness" are good enough.

(4) A good moral life is good enough.

(5) "So-and-So" is a "good Christian" is testimony enough, although it comes only from other Christians.

(6) "When you fall, try, try again", and that's good enough.

(7) The minister telling me that I'm saved or am going to heaven is good enough.

(8) Christianity is better than any other religion, and that's good enough. For such thinking, I must ask then:

> (1) "Why did Christ die on the cross?" Could it be that it's because what I think is good enough is really -- not good enough?

> (2) "Why did Christ say 'without me you can do nothing'?" Am I desperately insisting on "my way" to show the world that I am something?

> (3) "Why are Muslims becoming followers of Christ at a high cost to themselves?" Is what they say not true and good enough that the love of Christ shown on the cross is beyond comprehension and they fall at His feet in surrender when everyone discovers that at the cross there is forgiveness of sin, redemption, cleansing of conscience? There is love on display. When one comes to the cross of Christ, he/she discovers that thinking "this is good enough" is neither good nor enough, and discovers also that sufficiency can ONLY be found in the cross.

His name is Jesus Christ! *(Sunday, April 12, 2015 at 7:19 P.M. CDT)*

⁓

UNIVERSAL POWER
From my heart to yours–

If Jesus Christ is not the Son of God, and his claims are wrong and foolish, will someone please tell me... Why do people all over the world, once they hear of him, they come running? Why do people keep coming back to him either (1) to crucify him again or (2) to accept what he offers? And, what does He have to offer, one asks. Here is one to chew on: *Being accepted unconditionally*, as I am, burdens and all, failures and all, sins and all, nagging conscience that won't let me sleep, and the facade I keep holding up so people will think we are whom we really are not. His love only covers a multitude of sins. And that's one reason I worship and adore Him, I surrender and obey him for love's sake. *(Sunday, April 12, 2015 at 7:33 P.M. CDT)*

<div align="center">~~~~</div>

WRONG THINKING
From my heart to yours—

Sometimes it may be foolish, but is almost always purely selfish. Here are some examples:

(1) God loving me completely is required for me to love Him, and I decide when.

(2) God meeting what I think are my needs is required, or else.

(3) I want assurance that God still loves me, although I live in sin.

(4) Loving God is subject to every person's interpretation and where they come from.

(5) What's God's is mine, and what's mine no one dare touch but me.

(6) My good work, as I see it, ought to amount to something in Judgment Day.

(7) I may forgive once, and tolerate seven times, but don't push your luck.

(8) The Bible is for the preacher to keep up with, and sacrifice is for missionaries.

(9) I can't read, so God will have to find another way for me to get it.

(10) The way I live in private is personal, and most likely is NOT how I live in public.

(11) Don't question my salvation, I don't.

(12) "So-and-So" is a "good Christian" is testimony enough, although it comes only from other Christians.

(13) I don't need to bother with the lost around the world.

(14) "I'll try to live by the Sermon on the Mount".

(15) Confession, forgiveness, and repentance are old words.

(16) It's good to think in terms of what I can get back from God if I live for Him as best as I can.

(17) Denying myself, and carrying my cross is subject to interpretation.

(18) I would rather someone else make the big decisions.

(19) God should understand that we're just human when we fail. So we try again.

(20) The Bible is full of good advice.

(21) Loving the people of the world means that we love God.

(22) Getting to God is a personal decision; we create the path for ourselves.

(23) Doing things for God comes from the heart.

ALL of these issues, and so much more, can be resolved conclusively and only at the cross. It's Jesus who not only gives a solution, but He IS the solution.

MERCY IS NOT ENOUGH
From my heart to yours–

When a criminal stands before the judge, very contrite and broken, repentant and willing to do anything, and says with tears streaming down his face, "Your honor, I am SO sorry for what I did. I didn't mean to do it. I beg you to forgive me. I will do anything to make up for what happened. I am a changed person. I need your mercy and promise to be a good person." Why does the judge still have a problem with those words, *even if* they were true? Here is why: Someone *must* pay for what happened, Right? That's why I sing: Jesus paid it all, All to Him I owe. Even more than that, Jesus says, I have forgiven you, I have accepted you forever, I have loved you even before you knew me, I have come in person and did not send an angel, and that's why you will be with me. Do you believe that I did all this and more...just for you? *(Sunday, April 12, 2015 at 7:50 P.M. CDT)*

∽∼∾

FORGIVENESS POWER
From my heart to yours—

A true story: A criminal committed a heinous crime, killing 48 women, without remorse or regret, and admitted he would have killed more. He even led the sheriff to all the places where the killings took place after he did the unthinkable. Needless to say, the jury found him guilty and the judge sentenced him to death. After judgment was passed on him, the families were given the chance to say whatever they wanted to him, to the criminal. With a frozen, cold, emotionless gaze on his face, without any expression, he sat there and looked at every person who spoke. We can imagine what they said. Then one old man whose daughter was one of the worse victim, and has nothing left in the world to live for, stood and said, "I'm not going to condemn you to hell or wish you remain alive and be tortured, because my Lord who died on the cross for me taught me to love and to forgive." (Quoting almost verbatim). The man broke down suddenly and cried bitter tears. Why? The line of a song says, "The cross made the difference for me."

WHOLEHEARTEDLY FOR GOD
From my heart to yours–

I am more convinced today than ever before that God does not believe nor accepts half-hearted ... ANYTHING ... done for Him or in His Name. We ought not either. *(Sunday, April 12, 2015 at 8:23 P.M. CDT)*

TEARS IN THE MORNING
From my heart to yours–

The ONLY way anyone can get me to shed tears uncontrollably at 5:00 A.M. in a hotel room in downtown ETHIOPIA of all places is when a dear nephew of mine gives his heart to Jesus Christ, and decides to obey and follow. What a Gift!!! Jiddo (Grandpa) died, and a grandson came to life eternal. "Truly I say to you, except a corn of wheat fall into the ground and die, it abides alone: but if it dies, it brings forth much fruit." (John 12) What an Awesome Savior and Lord, the GIFT of heaven. He makes my journeying the more worthwhile. Dear Josh, you played "Amazing Grace" so beautifully, and all the while, the amazing grace of God was touching the strings of your heart. I pray for you always that you love God all your life with a pure heart, and let Him mold your character into His image. Let the music begin, for He will never leave you! EVER! *(Sunday, April 12, 2015 at 9:28 P.M. CDT)*

FENCE-STRADDLING
From my heart to yours–

To be in the company of believers is wonderful. But to remain in the company of believers ONLY, is the most unhealthy environment to remain in. The insulation of the follower of Christ is from within, not from without. His Spirit gives power to accomplish it. Jesus prayed (John 17) "Father, I don't ask that you take them from the world, but that you keep them from the evil one." *(Tuesday, April 14, 2015 at 11:55 A.M. CDT)*

THROUGH THE SPIRIT'S EYES
From my heart to yours–

To the true follower of Jesus Christ, everything becomes REAL, for now he can see things through the transparency granted him by the Holy Spirit. "For He [the Spirit] will lead you into all the truth." (John 16) "Becoming real" is never one-sided. Here is what I mean:

(1) The Spirit will show the truth about God's nature -- and the truth about my nature -- so, absorb the first daily, and hate the second daily.

(2) The Spirit leads me to live in His Presence -- and to despise relying on self, because the first is far better.

(3) The Spirit pours over me the love of Christ wherever it applies in daily life, and empties me of my own earthly affections, because darkness and light do not coexist.

(4) The Spirit shows me how holy God is desiring for me to be holy, and gives me a humble spirit to be holy in daily living like Him.

(5) The Spirit gives transforming power to change, and sustaining power to remain changed, for the sake of Christ. *(Tuesday, April 14, 2015 at 11:56 A.M. CDT)*

STILL INCARNATE
From my heart to yours—

As Christ was fully human on earth, he is fully human in glory. That's why He still understands me like none other. That is why He teaches me always to call on Him for He will answer me as He promised. *(Tuesday, April 14, 2015 at 11:57 A.M. CDT)*

TRANSFORMING TRUTH
From my heart to yours—

Learning his truth in my mind is informing, which is good; having the truth in my daily life is transforming, which is too wonderful. That's why His Word says, "...and in His law he [the blessed man] meditate day and night." (Psalm 1) May every true follower be blessed the same. *(Tuesday, April 14, 2015 at 11:57 A.M. CDT)*

WHY WALK WITH GOD
From my heart to yours—

"And Enoch walked with God." - is very true. Here are some reasons:

(1) Walking with God cleanses me of anything that doesn't keep me in His presence.

(2) Walking with God creates in me, as I live my earthly life, the desire and longing to experience more the sacredness of every moment with Him, and not settle for less.

(3) Walking with God teaches me daily something new of His grace, and gives assurance experientially that His mercies will not depart from me.

(4) Walking with God is not a matter of requirement or an option I choose, but a true experience of His abounding grace and abundant love toward me every day.

(5) Walking with God is when I discern the desire of His heart and know it in my daily life. "Thy will be done on earth as ....." *(Tuesday, April 14, 2015 at 11:58 A.M. CDT)*

HEARTBURNS OF THE RIGHT KIND
From my heart to yours—

Seeing fire and having fire are two different things. I see fire and become aware; I have fire and become aflame. The Bible speaks of "holy fire" and "strange fire". Holy fire burns in me what does not please God, and my character changes daily into His likeness. Strange fire is selfish, arrogant, vain, proud, and it self-destructs. Walking with God is congruent to having holy fire within, and a shield of fire around. Then the true follower of Christ is "in" the world and not "of" the world -- always. *(Tuesday, April 14, 2015 at 11:58 A.M. CDT)*

HOLY FIRE
From my heart to yours—

Holy fire has its character. Here is how:

(1) It cleanses the heart daily;

(2) It heals the broken completely;

(3) It purifies the affections internally;

(4) It sets one free to know God and be content in Him;

(5) It grants the desire to serve reflecting his loving heart;

(6) It gives discernment to guard the heart from the world;

(7) It equips so that others advance toward Christ, and Him alone.

(8) It creates repeated hunger for God that keeps the soul within the veil. *(Tuesday, April 14, 2015 at 11:59 A.M. CDT)*

ASKING FOR TROUBLE
From my heart to yours—

When I live a life that does not grieve the Spirit, resist the Spirit, or quench the Spirit, I am well on my way to know the true meaning of the "fear of God". Doing church can be done perfectly well without having any sense of the fear of God. Hence, all are rejected. However, a true follower of Jesus Christ in whom the Spirit dwells, flows like a river and fears God first to remain alive, and is empowered by the Holy Spirit to do His pleasure. *(Tuesday, April 14, 2015 at 11:59 A.M. CDT)*

CHANGE BY SURPRISE
From my heart to yours—

Doing missions does not equip me to change the target audience, but it makes me the target for the Holy Spirit to bring about change -- in me. Then they catch the fire. *(Tuesday, April 14, 2015 at 12:00 P.M. CDT)*

NY LIST - NOT GOOD ENOUGH
From my heart to yours—

Although there are thousands upon thousands of books published so far, why do people everywhere *still* see the Bible like the bright star of Bethlehem, and contains in it the attractiveness of the morning sun to wake up to? The breath of the Spirit that inspired the Word continues to breathe life without limits. The line from the song says, "Spirit of the living God, breathe down on me; Mold me, make me, heal me, use me; Spirit of the living God, breathe down on me" (*Tuesday, April 14, 2015 at 12:00 P.M. CDT*)

INTELLECT NOT GOOD ENOUGH
From my heart to yours–

Sheer intellectual grasp of the gospel gives no assurance of life in Christ. It takes the unceasing power of the Spirit of Christ to bring it to life, always. *(Tuesday, April 14, 2015 at 12:01 P.M. CDT)*

ON THE BEHALF OF
From my heart to yours–

If Jesus the Son of Man is committed to intercede for me at the right hand of the Father for His name's sake, I ought to be committed to intercede on behalf of others around me with equal passion and persistence. Both are done in the full power of the Holy Spirit of God. As the Spirit hovered over the Son in His earthly days, the same Spirit hovers over me when I am on my knees. Trials and temptations, tempests and turmoil are what draws me to call upon Him, and He will answer me as I wait on the Lord God. Amazing grace abounds when I stand between the living God and the dying world (wherever I find myself), because "He can do exceeding abundantly more than we ask or think." *(Tuesday, April 14, 2015 at 12:01 P.M. CDT)*

DOING FOR ETERNITY
From my heart to yours–

The only things I do that are of eternal value are the result of the changes that the Holy Spirit has brought about in me. The rest of what is done, which admittedly and sadly is much has been done in the power of the flesh. What saddens me is not that I haven't done enough or that I haven't changed, but that I have grieved the Spirit in me, and many times quenched Him. My prayer is that He hasn't passed me by and I am still content in my religious circus that has no eternal value, which in the Day of Judgment will turn out to be merely wood, hay, and stubble, and I would be saved by the sheer mercy that He extended toward me. *(Friday, April 17, 2015 at 12:11 A.M. CDT)*

MISSING FEAR
From my heart to yours–

When I live a life that does not grieve the Spirit, resist the Spirit, or quench the Spirit, I am well on my way to know the true meaning of the "fear of God". Doing church can be done perfectly well without having any sense of the fear of God. Hence, all is rejected. However, a true follower of Jesus Christ in whom the Spirit dwells, flows like a river and fears God first to remain alive, and is empowered by the Holy Spirit to do His pleasure. *(Friday, April 17, 2015 at 12:16 A.M. CDT)*

CHEAP WORLD
From my heart to yours—

I either cheapen Christ and the cross to have the world, or I cheapen the world to have Christ and His Spirit. "Love not the world." *(Friday, April 17, 2015 at 12:16 A.M. CDT)*

SWEETNESS OF THE SPIRIT
From my heart to yours—

Yesterday, I had a VERY bad day. In less than 24 hours I was sneezing repeatedly, coughing, nose stopped up, and clear (green) signs of infection :). By noon, I had to stop and go. Stopped by a makeshift pharmacy and picked up "Amox", which sounded good, took it, drank lots of water, and went and slept till the next morning. The group, I learned the next day, spent the night till 2 A.M. and woke up at 6 A.M. till 7:30 and prayed, worshipped and prayed, and then prayed some more. They said the Holy Spirit "was in the place" (one said), and they praised God. The next day, I went in VERY refreshed, and told them Now I feel like a horse ready to go all day. They had a time of rejoicing, clapping, and a holy hush came on the place. I remembered the song: There's a sweet sweet Spirit, in this place; And I know that it's the Spirit of the Lord. There are sweet expressions on each face, And I know that it's the presence of the Lord! *(Friday, April 17, 2015 at 10:09 A.M. CDT)*

LIMITED BUT ABUNDANT
From my heart to yours—

Imagine that all the songs written in English or Arabic are only 30, that's thirty. Not much room to move! Last night after they prayed from noon till evening, a small group got together and wrote a new song! That's #31. They were ecstatic that the others enjoyed the song so much and began to squeal (ز غاريد) with joy. Like a new baby happy making a joyful noise -- to the Lord. *(Friday, April 17, 2015 at 11:47 A.M. CDT)*

∽‿‿‿∾

THE FACES, THE COST, AND THE GLORY
From my heart to yours—

Below are 4 real testimonies of 4 real people. I saw in their faces the face of the One who loved them and us. Lessons for us before the Lord comes!

UNASHAMED: She lived in a grass hut for several years until her early teen years when her father sent her to her uncle in the city. While in the city, she heard the message of Christ's love. At first she refused. After several weeks, she heard the message of salvation again, and she said something happened in her heart, and she decided to follow Jesus. Her uncle was very upset and sent her back home. She went home as a young teen believer. Her father found out that she became a follower of Christ. He gave her the option of returning to Islam or leave the house for good. Her response was that she can't leave Christ, and she urged her father to consider becoming a follower of Jesus Christ instead. She had to leave. So, she went to a small country church where she stayed for several weeks. The church sent her to school to finish 10th grade, then to a two-year program to study Christian-Muslim relations. The she asked to return home. Her father accepted. Her words: "I made peace with my father and the family." After about a year in her father's house, her brother also became a follower of Jesus Christ. --

----

INSIGNIFICANT: I asked him his age. He didn't know. His parents gave him away shortly after he was born. For several years, he moved periodically from one relative's house to another just to have something to eat. He finally met someone who told him about Jesus Christ, and decided to become a follower of Christ. Now he went back to school, in sixth grade. In spite of his quiet demeanor, he bears witness about Christ who accepted him when no one else would. When asked, "Are you sixteen?" He replies, "Maybe". Now all he wants to be is an evangelist for Christ. ---------------------

CORNELIUS AGAIN: I grew up in a Muslim family that passed an idol relic from one generation to the next for three generations until I received it in my home. I had strange feelings about this idol. I threw it in a stream behind our house. I fell ill right after that. I took it from the stream and threw it in the fire and it broke into pieces. That night I had a vision and I heard a voice that said to go to a house and there I will meet a Christian man who will tell me what I need. Although I knew the location of the house, I've never been to it before, and don't know who lived there. The next day I went and met the man of the house whom I didn't know and told him about the vision. He knew what my visit was about, and told me about Jesus. I decided to become a follower of Christ. Immediately, my family rejected me because of Christ and told me to leave the village with my wife and one child. We had our second child who did not survive. At his death, the tribe would not allow me to bury my son in the cemetery. I had no choice but to dig a hole in my back yard and bury him there. After that, we had another son who had the same problem at birth. He lived few months and died too. I also had to bury him next to his brother in my back yard. I wanted to tell people about Jesus. So I became involved in the church, but the church was burned. The elders decided to build another building, and now I work as the guard at the church property and do evangelism work on weekends. ---------------------

PERSISTENT LOVE: I got married as a Muslim and was married for three years until I heard about Jesus Christ. I decided to follow him, and immediately my wife of three years decided to file for divorce in court rejecting the change that took place, and rejecting me saying "this is not the husband I married." (Uncommon to go to court, but allowed by law). No one heard of the woman filing for divorce before. I tried to persuade her to no avail. She went to court and won. She went back to her family, but I tried to call her and beg her to come back but she refused. Then one day the Holy Spirit started to work on her heart and convict her so much that one day she decided to become a follower of Jesus Christ. After few days, she decided to take the first step and call me. She wanted to come back. She told me that she has become a follower of Jesus too. I took her to church and very soon arranged to be married again in church and now we have been together for 10 years. We don't have any children yet and this is getting to be a serious problem especially for her. We continue to serve together and "I want to evangelize" became the desire of our hearts for a while. *(At the conference, everyone got around and laid hands on him and prayed.) (Sunday, April 19, 2015 at 12:58 A.M. CDT)*

PRAYER POWER
From my heart to yours—

Twenty pairs of hands were laid on one whose wife divorced him in court after three years because of him becoming a follower of Christ. The Holy Spirit spoke to her alone and convicted her, and she believed. Then she came to him wanting reconciliation. They have been married (again) and now with no child for 9 years. We prayed asking God to bless their home with a child. There were many tears! *(Sunday, April 19, 2015 at 1:01 A.M. CDT)*

REJOICING ALWAYS
From my heart to yours–

Twenty pairs of holy beautiful hands were laid on me to be one in the Spirit, and for Him to descent on us all. There were many tears also. The man with raised hand prayed. There were many MANY "Amen's. God was glorified! *(Sunday, April 19, 2015 at 1:01 A.M. CDT)*

PRAYER ANSWERED
From my heart to yours–

It almost got to be funny. The past two days, I continued to sneeze due to allergy and much dust, nasal infection, and the elevation of 7500 feet above sea level. However, what my host and I noticed after two days is that I have been sneezing my head off during the 50-minute drive in the morning. I get up to speak between 9:00-5:00, and all my problems stop instantly. At 5:30, we start on the 50-minute drive back, and my sinus problems come back with a vengeance. The first night I had a nose bleed twice. The next day I stand up to speak the four sessions, and my head is clear and sinuses without a problem whatsoever. Pressing on! Praise God! *(Sunday, April 19, 2015 at 1:04 A.M. CDT)*

CHURCH IDENTIFIED
From my heart to yours—

A church is defined:

(1) Not by its charter, but by its character,

(2) Not by its possession, but by its confession,

(3) Not by its membership, but by its fellowship,

(4) Not by its tithing and worship hour, but by its sacrificial giving and prayer power,

(5) Not by the books it supplies, but by the Book it applies,

(6) Not by the big names it brings, but by the Name that it sings,

(7) Not by the people who come in, but by the people who go out. *(Monday, April 20, 2015 at 6:51 A.M. CDT)*

HOW HOLINESS HOLDS HEAVEN -
From my heart to yours—

Heaven maybe a wonderful place, but holiness is required. Spiritual warfare, simply put, can be described as: Satan constantly trying to win the Church, and the Church constantly trying to win the world. Satan seeks to destroy, and Christ seeks to build. Satan is building nothing except his fallen self-image, and Christ is building nothing but His beautiful bride in His image and to His glory. We must remember that when the early believers met, they were known only by the house where they met. ....and the war goes on. Our duty as followers of Jesus Christ is to keep the battle outside the vibrant life of the church. *(Monday, April 20, 2015 at 6:53 A.M. CDT)*

DIFFERENT DNA
From my heart to yours—

The DNA of real evangelism contains, of necessity, the ability to become a growing and maturing disciple of Jesus Christ, with the ability to give birth to other disciples -- not for a certain number of years -- but for life. The church that has an evangelist in its midst ought to pray hard to have a teacher who can spread regularly a full and rich table from God's Word, fully empowered by the One Spirit and not by denominational or partisan affiliation. The world is already divided. We don't need to be active participants in that or bring that mindset into the church. We are not holier by being different from others but by being like Christ. *(Monday, April 20, 2015 at 6:54 A.M. CDT)*

LOVE, LIFE AND DOCTRINE
From my heart to yours—

Doctrinal accuracy never trumps the love of Christ. There is no human being who ever existed and had the final answer on doctrines. And the One who did and could, the Son of Man, who walked among us 2000 years ago, did not teach doctrines but told stories. The reason is simple: it's not who I am, it's not who you are, it's not about me or you, it's not where I stand or sit. *It's All about Him!* Stories are always closer to real life. To be sure, without the Holy Spirit, even the stories cannot be understood, because spiritual things are understood spiritually. Spiritual understanding does not mean intellectual understanding but the kind of understanding that bears fruit and brings truth to life. Therefore, when stories explained by the Spirit of Christ, they contribute far more to the maturity of believers and always without artificial cultural digestive supplements. True spiritual growth is measured, not by reciting doctrines and checking for accuracy, but by the disciple's ability to love God with all his heart, with all his mind, with all his strength, and with all his will; to love the neighbor as oneself; and to reach the world for Christ. Anything else -- is man-made and lacks the purity of the mind of Christ. Being a disciple of Jesus Christ and a disciple-maker is not a specialty trade. It's a Spirit-administered lifestyle and a Christ-like passion that never quits. His name is Jesus! *(Monday, April 20, 2015 at 6:55 A.M. CDT)*

PROVIDENCE AND SOVEREIGNTY
From my heart to yours–

I was brought to my knees when I met someone today with a10th grade education and two-year diploma, who already planted at least 12 house churches (I learned this morning), and was ecstatic to get a 20-year old pair of new shoes, never worn before, so he can use them to visit more. He walks daily for miles, like his Master, who loved so much. One group he visits once each month requires traveling one hour by bus on a dirt road then walking for two hours one-way. He said, "I have to go. I have to go and tell them about Jesus and fellowship with them and encourage them." With a radiant smile on his face, he said after many days to the person who gave him the shoes, "I am very happy today. These shoes don't wear out quickly like my other shoes. These are like the shoes of the Israelites that never wore out in forty years." You see, he was embarrassed often because he had to come asking for another pair. The first one is not good anymore. His income? $50/month. His meals? One-a-day. Anymore complaints? *(Monday, April 20, 2015 at 6:55 A.M. CDT)*

Church Not Out of Wedlock
From my heart to yours–

A church that is birthed by the Spirit is sustained by the Spirit, and the Spirit will always bring it to maturity without any artificial human means. Spirit-led obedience and mutual submission among her people under the Spirit's authority create the only healthy atmosphere that advances the Kingdom of God on earth. Jesus said, "My kingdom is [in this world, but] not of this world." *(Monday, April 20, 2015 at 7:22 A.M. CDT)*

Lost in Translation
From my heart to yours–

My translator (will call him T) was a very energetic dynamic man who became very dear to my heart quickly. One incident occurred when, after I said a sentence, he provided translation but I noticed that he went much longer than what was reasonable for accurate translation. I looked at him with a smile and asked "Did I really say all that?" :). He said, "No but what you said I got excited and I wanted to preach more!!!!!!!" ha-ha Another time, I said one phrase, and his translation went on and on. I said to the people "I ASSURE you that I did not say all that!!!" They laughed. He said, "You say short word! I say *long* word! That's all". And a third incident happened when I said a sentence and stopped waiting for translation. But no translation! Then he looks at me and says, "say again!" So I say it again and ask him, "was it difficult?" He answered, "No, No but I was processing in my head, and WOW! And forgot what I should say, I got too excited!" ha-ha Sweet Spirit. I wish I can clone him! *(Monday, April 20, 2015 at 7:24 A.M. CDT)*

DONKEYS FOR JESUS
From my heart to yours–

A couple of days ago, I was talking about Jesus being the Living Water that all people need. I used an illustration from the local culture, a picture they see many times a day. John: you know the donkeys you have on the streets all day long carrying yellow jugs of water! The people here *need* water *all day*. And these donkeys go to the source with empty jugs, fill them all, then bring them back. They never complain even though the load is heavy for several kilometers. Translator: Yes, we call them here "community donkeys". Then he continued..... Translator: "They are like us, you and me; we bring the living water of Jesus." Everybody laughed!!! I looked at him, motioned to him and me.... "Us?!" Translator: "Yes, we bring Jesus every day and they need Him! So, we are community donkeys" John: كَثّر خيرَك ha-ha But it's very true! *(Monday, April 20, 2015 at 7:33 A.M. CDT)*

RED AND YELLOW, BLACK AND WHITE
From my heart to yours–

I had to have my moment with the heaven-bound young'uns :). The little one I was holding kept looking at me then away, then back to wave her little hand. Jesus loves the little children, All the children of the world, Red and yellow, black and white, They are precious in His sight, Jesus loves the little children of the world! *(Monday, April 20, 2015 at 7:39 A.M. CDT)*

THE POWER OF GOD
From my heart to yours—

Yesterday, Sunday, I went to speak at a church and was told there will be around 130-150. I had to be dropped off at a certain point, walk a bit, then get picked up by someone else who took me to the intended location. Mud hut room with space about 14' x 20'. Inside the hut there was around 70-75 packed like sardines. Outside the hut stood a similar number and some sat on the ground. Two and one-half hours between 9:30-12:00 noon. The space where I stood was about 2' x 3'. You guessed it: no lights or fans. They sang for 45 minutes and prayed for 30 minutes. I stood to speak, and was already "well done". After few minutes of talking, I shared a bit of personal info, then said, "last week on Monday my father died, we buried him on Thursday, and I left to come here on Saturday." I continued for a little over an hour, and sat down. We had a very awesome time in worship. One young man in his twenties walked in from the outside group unannounced with arms spread out and said, "I want to give my life to Jesus Christ because if he came two days after his father died, then the Gospel of Jesus Christ must be more important, and that's what I want." All rejoiced and sang again. What I didn't know and was told later was that in that region, when someone dies, he is buried right away, as in the same day, without a casket even; just wrapped in a cloth/sheet, and turn his face toward Mecca. Then for 14 or 30 days, depending on how important the deceased was, the entire family sits up for that duration and WILL NOT go anywhere, as part of the mourning season. The Gospel of the Living Emmanuel is far more important! It IS "the power of God unto salvation." (Rom 1). *(Monday, April 20, 2015 at 8:04 A.M. CDT)*

SPIRITUAL ALIGNMENT
From my heart to yours–

Every so often, the front wheels of a car need "alignment" to make sure road conditions don't affect how they perform and how long they last. Likewise a spiritual alignment is needed every so often (as in -- Always) by the Spirit in my mind and heart to make sure that my will dissolves into His. Here's what I mean:

(1) The question is not whether I believe God when He speaks, but whether God believes me when I do.

(2) The question is not whether I trust Him but whether He trusts me.

(3) The question is not whether He is listening to me, but whether I am listening to Him.

(4) The question is not if I have Him on my side, but whether He has me on His side.

(5) The question is not whether He changes for my sake, but whether I change for His sake.

(6) The question is never whether He pays attention to what's happening to me on earth, but whether I pay attention to what happened to Him on the cross.

I am to be transformed into His image, and not He into mine. And bragging about Him and his attributes won't change His mind about me without Christ. In fact, He finds that very offensive because He hates counterfeits.

"PUT ON CHRIST"
From my heart to yours—

(1) Nothing of me, but All of Him - always.

(2) The corruptible puts on the incorruptible, not only when we die but while we live.

(3) Not my beauty (or lack thereof), but all of His beauty in me.

(4) Not only Him in me, but also me in Him.

(5) Not my past or present, but my all to Him.

"All to Jesus I surrender, All to Him I freely give; I will ever love and trust Him, In His presence, daily live." Is He not worthy?!!! *(Tuesday, April 21, 2015 at 8:31 P.M. CDT)*

TRANSLATOR NEEDED
From my heart to yours—

When I needed a translator who translated what someone translated also from someone else, I knew then it's because of Calvary and for love's sake. That's how my yesterday went. Had a most sacred time yesterday with beautiful saints who travelled 600 kilometers one-way to spend 12 hours together in a holy hush. It wasn't because they loved me but certainly because they love Him. Not because of who I am but because of what He's done! Then the evening was capped with a 3-hr worship time of the Majesty on high. *(Tuesday, April 21, 2015 at 9:13 P.M. CDT)*

FELLOWSHIP OF THE SPIRIT
From my heart to yours—

One can never even imagine the heights of being in Christ by the power of the Spirit from the depths of sin and shame and death.

However, anyone who scales the heights of Christ carried by the wind of the Spirit can even walk through the valley of the shadow of death. Yet, after meeting new friends who come near death every day, I learned that it's not they who scale the heights but He who dwells on high comes down near them every day and shelters them with His wings. That's the fellowship of the Holy Spirit. He makes Christ available every day to them who cry out. His name is Jesus! *(Wednesday, April 22, 2015 at 12:45 A.M. CDT)*

ETHIOPIAN MOURNING
From my heart to yours–

ETHIOPIA is officially in 3-day mourning for the many that were killed in Libya. May the nightmare end soon! Pray! Pray that even the presence of evil will end. Indeed, the entire world is in the grip of the evil one. But the only good news is that his head was crushed at Calvary. *(Wednesday, April 22, 2015 at 12:57 A.M. CDT)*

FOUR PILLARS
From my heart to yours–

Acts 2:42 points to the Four Pillars: Apostles' teaching, Fellowship, Lord's Supper, and Prayers. No local church can improve on them or add to them or replace them, and remain in an obedient mindset. The common factor that brings them and their meaning together is *Christ.* (1) They are *not intended* to be cultural applications of the Spirit's mind, or interpreted through a cultural filter. (2) They *are intended* for every believing church to implement them if they want to be obedient to the Spirit. (3) They create an attitude of obedience to the Holy Spirit, which is essential in anything related to the Bride of Christ. (4) The *center* of the four pillars is no one and nothing other than the Person of the Risen Lord. His Wonderful name is Jesus. Yes, and Jesus Christ IS wonder-full. *(Wednesday, April 22, 2015 at 7:45 A.M. CDT)*

～～～

THE GOSPEL COST
From my heart to yours—

I sat with someone on this trip who has been serving for about 15 years, and told me about the persecution he endured for the sake of Christ and the Gospel. He had a big cut stitched badly across his left cheek about half an inch below his eye. His head was beaten often and at one time had an opening in it. He said he wants to go back to where he was persecuted because the Lord has helped him to learn their language fluently (one of more than 80 in Ethiopia), and he must go back to tell them about Jesus. I had to ask a mutual friend about what happened to the face, and I was asked if I can send him a cream to soften the scar, but if I didn't find, it's ok. Anymore complaints?! I learned a new phrase on this trip, which is not new. It is: "for the sake of the Gospel". I learned that any other purpose falls short. And only the Holy Spirit can lead in matters that relate to the Gospel or the glory of Jesus Christ. *(Wednesday, April 22, 2015 at 7:56 A.M. CDT)*

～～～

THE ONLY QUESTION
From my heart to yours—

Peter and John went up to the Temple. They met the crippled man. Story recorded in Acts 3. Peter said these words: "Silver and gold have I none, but what I have...", and this is where the Spirit stopped me to ask: What - Do - YOU - have in you and with you?!! I could not finish....then I prayed and asked that only that Name would be on my lips until the last breath I take. *(Wednesday, April 22, 2015 at 8:02 A.M. CDT)*

～～～

POWER IN THAT NAME
From my heart to yours—

A True Story: After several days in jail, the prosecuting attorney asked the follower of Jesus Christ who was distributing Gospel material, "Tell the court, What is your source who gives you the authority to speak and distribute such material?" He was hoping that the man would give him an office name and address. The man looked at him and the judge, and with the gentlest spirit said, "Jesus Christ said in Matthew 28 'All authority is given to me. Therefore, go make disciples, baptize and teach them what I have commanded you'." The prosecuting attorney looked at the judge and said, "Your honor, I resign because I cannot prosecute this man." The judge was so frustrated that he dismissed the case. Anymore complaints?!! Remember, his name is Jesus Christ. As the song says, "No Name on earth has meant so much to me." *(Wednesday, April 22, 2015 at 8:12 A.M. CDT)*

～～～

COFFEE COMPETITION
From my heart to yours—

A dear Sister who has been to Ethiopia in recent years suggested that I check out a special café place in Addis Ababa called Tomoca. My friend in Addis said "Yes! It's the best. How did you know?" I said, "I have connections in high places ha-ha. I really enjoyed the visit there. In Ethiopia it's common to roast and grind the coffee beans fresh and make coffee in a special pot (see pictures). It tastes fresh for sure. But it's STRONG! ☺. *(Thursday, April 23, 2015 at 11:43 A.M. CDT)*

FREE TO CALL HIM "FATHER"
From my heart to yours—

It may not be new news, but the glaring truth of it shocked me enough to jump out of bed when I realized this: When Jesus walked our earth all 33 years; *no one* was ever saved yet - EVER. *No one* could call God "Our Father". *No one* could come in His presence with praise and thanksgiving. *No one*! Not only that, but *everyone*, from Adam to Jesus' resurrection was hanging by the single crimson-colored thread of God's grace and mercy. Only that thread kept God from pouring His wrath on man's rebellion, hatred, pride, and for having completely gone depraved in nature and behavior beyond recognition of his original image. Then Jesus came, and life happened. And there was a new day in heaven and earth. Then a new image was possible - the image of His Son. His name shall be called Emmanuel! No wonder the Father loved the Son so much and was always pleased in Him. But the greater glory and wonder is that, through the Son, the Father poured His love, instead of wrath, on us and made it possible for us to please Him once again when we are in Christ. Now, not a crimson-colored thread anymore, but "There is a fountain filled with blood, Drawn from Emmanuel's vein; And sinners plunged beneath that flood, Lose all their guilty stain." What love!!! *(Monday, April 27, 2015 at 5:09 A.M. CDT)*

MY MOTIVATION
From my heart to yours—

I've concluded that: Only His love for me is what keeps me going, and only His Spirit in me is what keeps me breathing every day. The rest of my life is just details, and my desire is that every detail be in His image and for His glory. Is He not worthy?!! My sister told me last night that a friend of my dad of many years came to her with eyes filled with tears after dad's passing and said, "I've know your dad for many years. When I lost my son, your dad came and was the only one who stayed by my side for three straight days. And I always wondered why." Only the love of the Father, through the Son, can enable us to love others from a pure heart...especially the unlovable, the lonely, the despised, the rejected, and all that society may erroneously think...are doing just fine! *(Monday, April 27, 2015 at 5:30 A.M. CDT)*

A QUIET SPIRIT
From my heart to yours—

Once a dear friend asked, "What does it mean to have a 'quiet spirit' "? I said: "Sometimes a concept can be understood (at least shed more light) by describing what it is NOT. What is not reflective of a "quiet spirit" is: (1) a fretful spirit (2) a fearful spirit (3) a distrustful spirit (4) a spirit that makes choices strictly based on emotions or fleeting passions (5) Trusting in one's abilities driven by love for power and control is not reflective of a "quiet spirit". (6) A "quiet spirit" does not "vent" emotions such as anger Toward a greater understanding of what "quiet spirit" is, here are some thoughts: (1) It's a spirit that has no problem trusting and submitting, because it's at peace with, and it's all about the object of trust. (2) It's a source of strength of character that matures in life. (3) It is a state of the heart that restrains stormy emotions and passions (4) A "quiet spirit" is a characteristic of a heart at rest, at peace, a teachable heart, that finds strength in submission. I have a feeling that in today's world where sometimes excessive assertiveness is the name of the game, there is little tolerance for a 'quiet spirit'" *(Monday, April 27, 2015 at 5:35 A.M. CDT)*

BEING FREE
From my heart to yours—

I find it a very tender and sacred moment whenever I'm sitting with Mom humming a song. This morning it was a song about being free in Christ. Then I begin to sing the words of this familiar song, and I pause at the end of a phrase, and she finishes the rest of it alone. And a smile breaks on her face as though remembering the goodness of Him who loved her all these years. The moment is tender because it's Mom. It's sacred because God dwells in the midst of where 2 or 3 are gathered. It's even reasonably acceptable to stand facing her, humming, embracing her, and dancing with no audience but One, because at 90 she has authentic reverence of Him who walked with her and she's still holding on. And I thought: Is there anything else I would like to remember at 90 years of age? It's not mushy stuff. It's just grace, plain and simple. *(Monday, April 27, 2015 at 4:06 P.M. CDT)*

EXCITED ABOUT JESUS
From my heart to yours—

"Good morning, ladies and gentlemen. We started our descent to Toronto. We will land at 7:40 A.M. That's five minutes ahead of schedule." And I looked around the 787 Dreamliner to see if anyone got in the aisle and was jumping up and down because we will arrive five minutes ahead of schedule. After a 13-hour flight, I will spare the reader the Halloween faces I saw. Now, if someone were to tell me that He coordinated the journey from eternity past, and all factors in heaven and hellish nightmares on earth, and through it all He guided certain people using advanced coordinates of a *star* to the right place and, upon arrival, they came prepared to give precious gifts..., And, on the other end of the social spectrum, I find shepherds to whom the angel said, "I have good news for you. God arrived on time, and has tabernacled on earth in a baby called Jesus; He is Emmanuel, and he is like no other baby." Even the shepherds got so excited that they left their livelihood and came to see the good news. Now, I wondered, would I not become excited? And what would I be willing to leave to follow Him? *(Wednesday, April 29, 2015 at 4:27 P.M. CDT)*

THE ONLY QUESTION REMAINING
From my heart to yours—

Peter and John went up to the Temple. They met the crippled man. Story recorded in Acts 3. The man looked at them. Then Peter said these words: "Silver and gold have I none, but what I have...", and this is where the Spirit stopped me in my tracks to ask: The only question for the true follower of Christ is: What is it that you really have? It's not "that which I have" that I can give, but "that which has me"! *(Wednesday, April 29, 2015 at 5:28 P.M. CDT)*

JESUS IS MINE
From my heart to yours—

If I say "Jesus is mine", does that mean that I own Him? Or that I have a relationship with Him? Or, that all He has is mine? Or that I can have all that He has? All the above may be OK to say. But, the more serious question to ask, and just to be fair, is to consider when He says about me that I am His -- does that mean that He owns me? Or that He's happy to have a relationship with me? Or that all I have is His? Or that He can have all that I have? Maybe, what I really mean is that he's just my "significant other", and we are just "partners"-- a state of things that can change on a moment's notice, and I go and find another "significant other". The truth is, if this is my way of thinking, that all along, this Jesus "thing" has been a figment of my own imagination. The truth is that He doesn't go for "living together" or just "being friends". The truth is that He demands complete surrender before I can even say "hello" or "I love you". The truth is that when He said to me "I love you", He died, and gave me His life. "To reciprocate" is the only acceptable response. *(Thursday, April 30, 2015 at 4:51 P.M. CDT)*

PEER MEASUREMENTS
From my heart to yours—

When the people of God are on their knees, they are about the same height. They are about to touch the hem of His garment. Then, power happens, His power; and heaven stops, because one of the children is calling out upon his Father. A contrite heart is not in the bended knee but in the mended heart, and the branded soul with fire from the altar. *(Friday, May 1, 2015 at 7:49 A.M. CDT)*

～～～

DOING FAVORS
From my heart to yours–

It's very common when we need someone's momentary help to say, "Could you do me a favor?" and we tell then what the need might be. I wonder if that's how we approach God when we need His help! To say "please" doesn't help because He looks at the heart only. We may not say the words, but could it be that that's how we think and that's the basis for speaking to Him? "As a man thinks in his heart so is he." "Let the words of my mouth and the meditation of my heart be acceptable in Your sight, O LORD, my strength and my Redeemer." (Psalms 19). *(Friday, May 1, 2015 at 9:28 A.M. CDT)*

～～～

A QUESTION OF THE HEART
From my heart to yours–

"To honor or not to honor" someone is not really the question, because I'm determined to begin with "to honor", and stop there. I fear otherwise that my heart may get corrupted thinking that "not to honor" is another option, and I sin in my heart and no one knows except me and One who matters most. *"Let the words of my mouth and the meditation of my heart be acceptable in Your sight, O LORD, my strength and my Redeemer."* (Psalms 19). *(Saturday, May 2, 2015 at 4:42 A.M. CDT)*

～～～

ON BEING LIKE HIM
From my heart to yours–

The follower's "being in Christ" is equivalent to what Jesus experienced when He was on earth, and prayed saying, "... *you,*

Father, are in me, and I in you, that they also may be one in us." (John 17) The Son was one in the Father. The Father was one in the Son. And now He desires that we be one in Him. The preposition "in", and not "with" means we are not independent of Him any longer, but have been integrated in Him. Now His oneness includes us, all who believe. The impact: the Son speaks not of himself, but what He hears from the Father. And now, we who are true followers speak not of ourselves, independent of Him in thought and practice, but what we hear from Him, we speak. The full presentation of Christ to the world through the true follower happens in the full power of the Holy Spirit. *(Saturday, May 2, 2015 at 9:23 P.M. CDT)*

REDEFINING WORK
From my heart to yours–

The best and only thing I can DO for Christ is: to surrender completely to Him. That is when His Spirit takes full control of my heart, mind, soul, and strength. Then I live a surrendered life every day to His glory. Moving successfully from theory to practice is what the Holy Spirit alone is able to do. He, the Spirit, teaches me daily how to love Christ with all my heart. The rest is simply details. *(Saturday, May 2, 2015 at 9:24 P.M. CDT)*

BEING ONE
From my heart to yours–

Union with Christ is not what I decide but what the Holy Spirit executes in the heart. The universality of His invitation is what makes it His initiative. The rest of life simply consists of communion with the Spirit of Christ and daily reunion with Him, the purpose of which is to behold the glory of Christ. What other people experience through the senses is the true "expression", that is, the outward visible events, of what happens within. May we never be ashamed of Him! *(Tuesday, May 5, 2015 at 8:42 A.M. CDT)*

"HOLY" IS MEANT FOR GOD
From my heart to yours–

If the angels of heaven hide their faces and cry out "*Holy, holy, holy, Lord God Almighty for His glory fills the whole earth*", I must remember at all times that only the blood of Jesus Christ, and only His blood, is what held back, and forever, the downpour of God's justice and anger on me. Not clapping, not singing, not being religious, not being from a certain country, not education, nothing from earth; All from heaven. Then in Christ, it happened, and we have been accepted *forever*. The holy God has been satisfied with the sacrifice on the cross. And He made it possible for anyone to be reconciled back to God *forever*. *(Tuesday, May 5, 2015 at 9:48 P.M. CDT)*

GOD'S WILL
From my heart to yours–

Romans 12:1-2 "*Be not conformed...but be ye transformed...in order that you may experience God's perfect and acceptable will*". The key is: be transformed...in order to experience and know his perfect will. The problem is not in knowing his will but in our willingness to change (be transformed). No change? God says, "No can do". Maybe that's why many flounder in their walk with God and pursuit of the awesome and wonderful Lord. His name is Jesus. Your comments are welcome. *(Friday, May 8, 2015 at 7:35 P.M. CDT)*

TO BE IS THE QUESTION
From my heart to yours—

Anything the church thinks about *doing*, the world can do *better*, because the trademark of the church is not in what it does in the world, but in *whom* it is *in* the world. The church is not about *doing* but about *being*. The church is not in competition with the world. For the war has been won at the cross. May we always live in the world for Him who died for the world and rose again so we can bring the world, one at a time, to be reconciled to Christ. "Love not the world." *(Monday, May 11, 2015 at 9:44 A.M. CDT)*

CHANGES REQUIRED
From my heart to yours—

Regardless of the good things I do, unless He changes me through His Holy Spirit, I will never know His will. (Romans 12:2). Worse still, I will be deceiving myself if I pretend that I do know and am living in his will. He's not interested in what I do for Him, but in what He does in me. God's intention is not to give me but live in me; not to improve me, but to redeem me. He was so serious that He died for me. Therefore, it's reasonable to think that He expects the same from me in return. His name is uniquely JESUS. *(Wednesday, May 13, 2015 at 10:37 P.M. CDT)*

NEVER EASY, EVER
From my heart to yours—

It's nothing more than an emotional high to think that to be a follower of Jesus Christ is EASY. Clear, but never easy. For all it takes is: FAITH. Here's what I mean: Jesus said: "If you keep My commandments, you will abide in My love, just as I have kept My Father's commandments and abide in His love." He also said, "If you love me, keep my commandments." (John 15) John said, "He who has the Son has life; he who does not have the Son of God does not have life." (I John 5) Jesus is not special because he came from heaven to earth, but because:

(a) He was born on earth like us completely by the power of the Holy Spirit of God,

(b) Was always filled with the same Spirit,

(c) Loved the Father with ALL his heart, mind, strength, and soul,

(d) Was able also by the same Spirit to "keep the Father's commandments" all the days of his earthly life, and thus

(e) Glorified the Father through the Spirit to the very end. WHY? ... in order that fallen man can have the sure possibility to be:

(a) Born "again" by the power of the very same Spirit,

(b) Be also filled with the fire of His Spirit,

(c) Love Him passionately with ALL his heart, mind, strength, and soul,

(d) Keep all His commandments all the days of the earthly existence, and thus

(e) Glorify Him through the same Spirit. Just like Jesus. *(Friday, May 15, 2015 at 6:04 P.M. CDT)*

NOT ONLY A CUP OF CHAMOMILE
From my heart to yours—

It was supposed to be stopping by *just* for a cup of Chamomile. Turned out to be a near-meal experience, cheeses, bread, crackers, cucumber, almonds, home-grown oranges, mixed nuts, and more cheese, tea, coffee, etc. But what stole the show was the excitement and transparency of how God brought John and Janet to a very intimate walk with him, by faith, and by molding their character to be like Christ, Yes through cancer of many kinds, through accidents, through wrong decisions, God saw them through. The joy of the Lord showed on their faces and the fellowship was truly sweet. I came to the affirmation that, Yes, "Jesus Christ is the same, Yesterday, Today, and Forever. The journey continues. Thank you John and Janet for a delightful time in your home. *(Tuesday, May 19, 2015 at 12:17 A.M. CDT)*

MY DANCE PARTNER
From my heart to yours–

I believe in dancing (smile). My teacher was my Mom who taught me to dance when I was a very little boy. Now I'm remembering my dance steps with her at 90 everyday right after breakfast. I think she is doing well. And the day will come when I might dance with her on streets of gold. *(Saturday, May 23, 2015 at 11:52 A.M. CDT)*

WHO WANTS CONTROL?
From my heart to yours–

"Control" and "Trust" are contradictory. They have nothing to do with the object, but completely with the subject, because both are a heart condition, an attitude. One comes with the human nature; the other comes from the Christ nature that the Spirit instills in the follower's heart. Trust, or faith, leads naturally to obedience. Control leads to selfishness. Obedience enriches the Spirit-filled life. Selfishness, intended for self-preservation, in fact, leads to self-destruction. Consider Christ and Satan, and one can see a clear demonstration of control and trust. Satan wanted control; he lost.

Christ desired surrender and trust from the heart to the Father. Even through death, he rose victorious. Now, He calls on us to follow Him. *(Monday, May 25, 2015 at 6:49 P.M. CDT)*

THOSE EYES
From my heart to yours–

Sitting with a small group of friends and interacting with Adrian Rogers in 1982, we listened to his heart, and still remember vividly a warning he gave. He said, "If satan can get you to laugh at what is holy, sacred, or anything that has to do with God, you will never see it as holy again. And you will be a fool if you think otherwise." I never forgot his eyes, burning as having been in the Presence, and burdened as having seen the condition of the church in his days. God help us! *(Tuesday, May 26, 2015 at 4:40 A.M. CDT)*

SPIRIT'S THREE-FOLD OBJECTIVE
From my heart to yours–

In a summary snapshot, the three-fold objective of the Holy Spirit is to take, to give, and to glorify. First, He takes all that Jesus was in His earthly days (in whom dwelt the fullness of the Godhead bodily, and with whom the disciples needed nothing else). Second, He distributes the multi-faceted character of Christ continually to every member of His Body, the Church (not a particular denomination) to perfect those who are obedient and walk in Him with fear and trembling. Third, He brings all glory to Him who descended from glory to save us. *(Wednesday, May 27, 2015 at 5:06 A.M. CDT)*

HEARTBEATS THAT MATTER
From my heart to yours—

The true followers of Jesus Christ listen to His heartbeat and are never deceived. For only through the Holy Spirit are they able to know the truth in Him. No human qualifications are required! *(Wednesday, May 27, 2015 at 5:32 A.M. CDT)*

WORKING WITH GOD
From my heart to yours—

Following Him is a mixing of what I have and what He adds only to the extent that I surrender all (and have nothing) to His overwhelming control in my life. Just because I have it doesn't mean He uses it. What He does is always better! *(Wednesday, May 27, 2015 at 5:32 A.M. CDT)*

ALL VAIN UNLESS THE SPIRIT
From my heart to yours—

Only through the Spirit is Christ truly glorified. He doesn't settle for partial glory. Here's a shocker: Every prayer that Jesus prayed while on earth, the Father answered and was glorified in the Son. Just because I have a need, doesn't mean I must pray, because in my need and weakness and nothingness His strength and His sufficiency and Presence are made manifest! *(Wednesday, May 27, 2015 at 5:33 A.M. CDT)*

LASER FOCUS
From my heart to yours–

If "denomination" is my first thought and my first passion, then Christ is missing. If Christ is my first thought, there is no need for a second passion. Claiming "non-denomination" makes it one by default. Claiming "independence" implies independence "from", either from Christ (which is idolatry), or from other denominations, which makes me a denomination unto myself. And to claim "conservative" is plain silly. Was Jesus conservative? Or are we comfy redefining what following Him is?!! Paul: "For me to live is Christ." With Christ, even death is gain. *(Thursday, May 28, 2015 at 8:09 A.M. CDT)*

EVIL IN THE CHURCH
From my heart to yours–

Fighting for control and position in the church is pure evil, and that is no church. *(Thursday, May 28, 2015 at 8:10 A.M. CDT)*

MISPLACED FRIENDLINESS
From my heart to yours–

The only problem I know of with the church is *not* that the church is in the world, but that the world IS in the church. "Love not the world". The only problem I know of in my life is not that I'm unable to deal with sin, but that I'm unwilling. Christ provides cover for the first, but categorically rejects the latter. "I surrender all". *(Thursday, May 28, 2015 at 8:11 A.M. CDT)*

TENDONS NEEDED
From my heart to yours—

Muscles and bones can never work together without the tendons that bind them together. So we are called to work together in the Body of Christ through the Spirit who binds us together forever. *(Thursday, May 28, 2015 at 8:12 A.M. CDT)*

"POWER UNTO SALVATION"
From my heart to yours—

How is the Gospel the "*power of God unto salvation*"? Here's how (in a nutshell) : Since the resurrection and ascension, the Gospel of Christ made its way around the world unhindered, on time, and on target. And every time He saved with *such* power, it brought the dead to life in Christ. Slight snapshot elaboration is in order:

(1) The Jews reached out to the Gentiles in the early days;

(2) The Gentiles took the Gospel to the world for many centuries;

(3) The reformation brought a much needed awareness;

(4) Revivals (16th-19th centuries) rekindled the fires of clean living of Jesus' followers;

(5) And *now* it's high time for Muslims to come and "taste that the Lord, He is good".

The Gospel hasn't changed. The power hasn't diminished. The relevance of the cross has always been preeminent. "The eyes of the Lord are diligently searching throughout the earth". *(Thursday, May 28, 2015 at 11:05 A.M. CDT)*

THINKING OF RELEVANCE
From my heart to yours—

The relevance and usefulness of the local churches is only to the extent that they deliver the Gospel in their lifestyle and character to the world, and to serve the Muslim world specifically a healthy portion of the real Gospel of Jesus Christ. Further, the relevance of American churches is only as they comes alongside the indigenous churches and invest life in life, not west in east, not high in low, not the able in the nothings of the world. Only then we are able to behold the beauty and power of the Gospel of Christ. Sadly, both churches (local and American) have - for the most part - gone the way of the prodigal son, demanded their portion, bemused by fatness as synonymous to being filled with the Spirit, and now mired in swamps of their own making. The presumption on our part, the audacity of *that that* God is waiting for us to move with the Gospel to the world is sheer religious idiocy or arrogance (am not sure which). We still debate and part company and break fellowship over a Calvinist or Armenian. And we flock between the dignified and the petrified and the calcified of religious establishments unsure of who we are in Christ. *(Thursday, May 28, 2015 at 12:02 P.M. CDT)*

MATTER OF PERSPECTIVE AND CONVICTION
From my heart to yours—

(Life According to the Spirit) + (Life According to the Flesh) is NOT = to (Having the Best of Both Worlds), and is NOT = to (Reaching the World for Christ); But it IS = to (Sub-Zero Life, lost without compass or rudder). That's Not Why Jesus Died. The Math is bad because the cost is far more, and The Wrath is even worse. *(Friday, May 29, 2015 at 5:50 A.M. CDT)*

COMPLETE SURRENDER
From my heart to yours—

I know that if I do not surrender to the Spirit of Christ for a Spirit-filled lifestyle, I have instantly surrendered to a lifestyle of what I know not. The rest is just visible mirage of what seems to be a Spirit-filled life, but is not. To be sure, Spirit-filled actions or activities are not synonymous with a Spirit-filled lifestyle. He sees the heart, and that's what really matters. *(Friday, May 29, 2015 at 7:44 A.M. CDT)*

"COMMITMENT" MEANS
From my heart to yours—

Commitment means "Doing whatever it takes - *always*". The "it" is His will. No excuses accepted; death is. And Change is expected (Rom 12:2). Then Resurrection Life happens.

A Surrendered Life to Christ is a Spirit-filled life in Christ. The two come inseparably together. *(Friday, May 29, 2015 at 7:52 A.M. CDT)*

MY HOUSE
From my heart to yours—

Prayer is Power; Prayer because of Promise; Prayer is where He is delighted to tabernacle. *(Saturday, May 30, 2015 at 11:17 P.M. CDT)*

GOD WALKING AMONG US
From my heart to yours—

I come to the conference for the highlight when God walks among us and is listening. How do I know? It's prayer time. That's when heaven moves! Singing is nice; preaching is ok. But prayer is when we get God's attention. Laying-on of hands is a privilege and best to happen in the family when we pray; Unity, Fellowship, and Love. Laying-on of hands is done for submission, intercession and commission, healing and freedom, and to give glory always! *(Saturday, May 30, 2015 at 11:39 P.M. CDT)*

SAMPLES OF HEAVEN
From my heart to yours—

These delightful ladies haven't seen each other in 30 years. One came from Canada, the other from Tennessee. They worked at the same school, and each has a story to tell of how God walked with them through the years. A sample of how heaven will be like. *(Sunday, May 31, 2015 at 7:49 P.M. CDT)*

RANNO
From my heart to yours—

As he ran to me and hugged me, I asked my little friend, "Do you remember when we met two years ago?" "Yes", he said. His parents waited for him 14 years. Then God gave them "Ranno", which is short for "Asked from God and God gave". His dad, a Sudanese pastor, said he is like Samuel, we prayed for him fervently, and God answered. God is in the business of answering prayer. He waits for us to seek him with our whole heart. *(Sunday, May 31, 2015 at 7:57 P.M. CDT)*

⁓⁓⁓

ACTIVE OBEDIENCE
From my heart to yours—

The popular idea that I can be saved by faith, continue living as I did, without active obedience and Spirit-empowered change in my practical life, is dead wrong, too easy, and is a religious mirage, a lie and a trap by satan to make salvation look SO possible and easy, but it lacks LIFE from and dominance of the Spirit of God. Let's not be fooled; we know his ways. Satan operates from hiding, and is wreaking havoc in persons, in relationships, in homes, in churches. But God is calling his church back to Himself today. *(Monday, June 1, 2015 at 11:06 A.M. CDT)*

⁓⁓⁓

PURE FILLING
From my heart to yours—

To be filled with the Holy Spirit is a must in a world that's filled with everything else. To have or to be filled with anything else other than the Spirit of Christ is unacceptable to follow Him, insufficient to comprehend Him, and renders me permanently ineffective in anything that will bring Him glory. The sad part is that I may still claim to be a "Christian", but everyone wonders what that means. *(Monday, June 1, 2015 at 7:09 P.M. CDT)*

⁓⁓⁓

THINKING LIKE "HIRED SERVANTS"
From my heart to yours–

Someone may have sinned so terribly and irreparable damage happened, that deep in his heart he is convinced and says "I don't deserve heaven, I deserve condemnation". And he begins to engage in pious deeds and gets involved in many worthy causes desiring to please God, but never doing enough. For such person Jesus came, and to such person Jesus says: "*You Are Forgiven. Only Believe!*" Here's why: In the story of the "prodigal son" (Luke 15), upon his return, the son was devastated, and said to his father, " 'Father, I have sinned against heaven and in your sight, and am no longer worthy to be called your son. Make me like one of your hired servants.' "He said the right thing ("I have sinned against heaven and in your sight"). However, he went about restoring their relationship the wrong way. He wanted to be a "hired servant". "Hired servants" in those days are *never*, and will never be, "sons". They are paid by the day and the deed. The master pays them a day's wages. In those days it was pennies. The son was saying, "Father, put me to work and pay me cheap, and I accept that, because I want to repay you and repair the damage I caused and the losses I incurred. Riddled with guilt, he forgot that he is a *son*. Now all he has to do is LIVE like one. That's called: Grace, Mercy, Blessing, and Love! It's called "Being at Home". Now can we behave like "sons" and stop acting like hired hands?!!! The son never determines whether he is a son or not; the Father does! The son never repays the father; the father always has plenty. The son always lives from the riches of the father that never run out. The son will always be a son. He just needs to live like one, and not like a "hired servant"! "Blessed be the God and Father of our Lord Jesus

Christ, who has blessed us with every spiritual blessing in the heavenly places in Christ" (Ephesians 1). *(Tuesday, June 2, 2015 at 8:04 P.M. CDT)*

OLD HABITS
From my heart to yours–

They say, "You can easily take the boy out of the country, but can never take the country out of the boy." Others say, "Old habits die hard." Jesus says, "If anyone wants to follow me, let him deny himself, carry his cross..." we know the rest... Now, the key word is "Obedience". The rest is Him, All Him. And "He is able to do more than we ask or think." Only Obedience to the Spirit of Christ bring Change. *(Tuesday, June 2, 2015 at 8:25 P.M. CDT)*

REBEL AT HEART
From my heart to yours–

Rebellion in the heart is always selfish, and will always say "NO" to anything that has to do with God. Anything and Everything! The sad part is that the heart can be so deceptive that, for self-preservation's sake, the heart hides its rebellion from the conscious mind, and the person never knows. In fact, the person goes on defending himself, thinking he is right. That is why it takes the Spirit of the Living God to uncover to the heart its deceptive nature so that it receives the covering of the blood of Christ. That's called "Grace". *(Tuesday, June 2, 2015 at 10:16 P.M. CDT)*

WE ARE WINNERS
From my heart to yours—

By submitting to the Spirit of Christ, we never lose. Satan never wants us to know that, because he loses, and he knows it. When the heart cries out, "Lord, I submit to your Lordship in my life, to save me, to guide me, to fill me, to let me praise your holy name from the bottom of my heart"-- will never render me a weakling, a failure, a coward, or a loser. In fact, in Him I have all I need, and that's "Contentment". *(Tuesday, June 2, 2015 at 10:24 P.M. CDT)*

DISTRACTIONS UNACCEPTABLE
From my heart to yours—

Anything in me that distracts and redirects the attention from the character of Christ in me, attention to my looks, to who I am, to what I have, to what I can do...saddens the Spirit, and saddens my Lord. "Grieve not the Spirit." It can be what I wear (or not wear), what I say (or not say), my attitude, my tradition, my accomplishments, or even my aspirations. Better for me to judge myself, to subject everything to Christ, than for anyone else to judge me. Through Christ, I can do all things. My desire is not to do as I please, but to do His will "on earth as it is in heaven". *(Tuesday, June 2, 2015 at 10:35 P.M. CDT)*

IMAGINARY CHRISTIANS
From my heart to yours—

It is misleading to think that I have become a Spirit-filled person by reading many "spiritual" books. It takes the full power of the Spirit of the Living God to bring about change that glorifies the Son.

Anything else is fake and renders my service to Him unacceptable.
(Tuesday, June 2, 2015 at 10:37 P.M. CDT)

⤛⤜

ON BEING FUNNY
From my heart to yours—

If Jesus Christ did not even try to be a "funny" guy, why do preachers tell jokes from the pulpits? Are they trying to "connect"? Then I thought, maybe they are trying to be "accepted" by their audience. I shuddered at the very thought of it, because Jesus demanded that I "deny myself", and realized that I might have a touch of idolatry in my heart. Furthermore, Jesus has established the fact that he is attracting millions and millions to Himself all over the world. And He did that *after He died*. Fancy that!! No wonder we fail every time we try to simply "connect" when presenting Christ. Our efforts render the message worthless, ineffective, and earthly. It takes the Spirit, nothing less. Nothing else! The song of olden days says: "All is vain unless the Spirit of the Holy One comes down". *(Wednesday, June 3, 2015 at 5:12 A.M. CDT)*

⤛⤜

ATTITUDES REDEFINED
From my heart to yours—

I read a recent article in Forbes magazine on leadership. It highlighted "Positive Attitude", and said, "You want to keep your team motivated towards the continued success of the company, and keep the energy levels up. Whether that means providing snacks, coffee, relationship advice, or even just an occasional beer in the office, remember that everyone on your team is a person. Keep the office mood a fine balance between productivity and playfulness." Except for the beer, I figured Jesus kept the "fine balance between productivity and playfulness" indeed. Paul and Silas in the Philippian jail found that to be effective. Had good results too. I call that "success of the company". And, talk about keeping up "the energy levels", the jailer definitely got over-excited, but he also ended up with a "positive attitude" indeed! *(Wednesday, June 3, 2015 at 5:27 A.M. CDT)*

MY FIRST THOUGHT
From my heart to yours–

In a world that competes for my attention from the first waking moment, I desired this morning with all my heart that HE (Jesus Christ) is the FIRST thought in my being, so that I can be still and worship Him in my spirit. *(Thursday, June 4, 2015 at 5:51 A.M. CDT)*

DYING ALONE FOR ME
From my heart to yours–

The cross of Christ made it possible for me to cross over from darkness to light, from death to life, from being alone to being in His Presence - forever. So I sing: "He took my sins and my sorrows; He made them his very own; He bore the burden to Calvary And suffered and died alone. When with the ransomed in glory His face I at last shall see, 'twill be my joy through the ages; To sing of his love for me." "He that glories, let him glory in the cross of Christ." *(Thursday, June 4, 2015 at 5:59 A.M. CDT)*

From my heart to yours—

The King born in a manger so that am born from the womb of His Spirit,

- became a pauper so that I can be satisfied in Him,

- hungered so that I may partake of the Bread of Life,

- thirsted on the cross so that I may drink from the fountain of living waters,

- had no place to lay his head so that I may lay my head on his chest and rest forever,

- took my shame so that I may receive his holy Name,

- died so that I can live,

- lost so that I may gain,

- broke the bond with the Father so that I may never lose it forever,

- took my hatred away so that I may have his love within me all the days of my life. *(Thursday, June 4, 2015 at 6:08 A.M. CDT)*

THE BEAUTY MAKER (2)
From my heart to yours—

I said, "Honey, why don't you throw those roses away, they're dry and worthless, they're good for nothing!" She said, "You don't know what I'm going to do with them." I walked away shaking my head and thinking these are good for nothing. Then came back! WOW! She said, two people I love dearly gave them to me on my birthday, and some are over a year old. I thought "No Way!" Isn't that what God does with us?! Let's give each other time, and see what God does! It's called: Amazing Grace in the hands of the Almighty! *(Thursday, June 4, 2015 at 12:40 P.M. CDT)*

THE BEAUTY MAKER (1)
From my heart to yours–

I laughed out loud about the roses. I asked her "How did you keep them so crisp and looking fresh and together?" She said, "I tied them with a rubber band and hung them upside down". Ouch!!! I laughed thinking "Isn't that what God does with us, hold us upside down in life's experiences, and keeps an eye on us until such time that He chooses?" And then......beauty from ashes, a powerful army from dry and disconnected bones (Ezekiel 37). *(Thursday, June 4, 2015 at 2:50 P.M. CDT)*

ETERNAL PERSPECTIVES
From my heart to yours–

Revealing his eternal glory reveals also my infernal sinfulness (Isa. 6), and all at once I recognize in the cross of Christ a union of: - both judgment and mercy, - both grace and truth, - both joy and agony, - both majesty and emptiness, - both heaven and hell, - both everlasting love and separation from God, - both power of sin and power of grace, - both self-control and self-surrender, - both the old and new, - both peace and vengeance, - both demand of debt payment and its satisfaction, - both sinfulness and justification, - both eternal forgiveness and damnation, - both singing of praises and gnashing of teeth, - both the Son of God and Son of Man. - both the Savior and the Sinner. Union forever! Communion like never! Then He said, "It is finished!" He died to forgive all my sin. He rose again so I can stand in the Presence of God. Now, I have all I need in the bright face of Jesus Christ who loved me. The song says: "What grace is this that brought my Savior down, that made Him leave His glorious throne and crown. The one who made the earth, the sky, and sea. Who put the stars in every galaxy! What condescension, oh how can it be! What shame He suffered oh what agony! And then the death He died, for sinners crucified, What grace is this! What grace is this?!" His name is Jesus. He's my Lord and Savior! *(Friday, June 5, 2015 at 12:37 A.M. CDT)*

HOLY SPIRIT ENIGMA
From my heart to yours—

The irony of the Holy Spirit, the wind from heaven, is that when He blows, He brings order instead of chaos to everything in life, in the family, and in the church. He is always right, righteous, and right-on-target. Another irony of the Holy Spirit is that when I submit to Him and His leading, I am set free; and when I decide to take control, I lose and become a slave to a lifestyle that breeds rebellion, discontentment and grinding bondage. Life with Him is when I choose to yield to Him, and obey His call to love Christ with all my heart, my soul, and all my mind. *(Friday, June 5, 2015 at 4:18 P.M. CDT)*

IRONY OF THE SPIRIT (1)
From my heart to yours—

The irony of the Holy Spirit, the wind from heaven, is that when He blows, He brings order instead of chaos to everything in life, in the family, and in the church. He is always right, always righteous, and always right-on-target. It's not about what He does FOR me, or what I do FOR Him, or about "pooling our resources", but about what He does IN me so I will be like Him. *(Friday, June 5, 2015 at 4:32 P.M. CDT)*

IRONY OF THE SPIRIT (2)
From my heart to yours—

Another irony of the Holy Spirit is that when I submit to Him and His leading, I am set free; and when I decide to take control, I lose and become a slave to a lifestyle that breeds rebellion, discontentment and grinding bondage. Life with Him is when I choose to yield to Him, and obey His call to love Christ with all my heart, my soul, and with all of my mind. *(Friday, June 5, 2015 at 4:48 P.M. CDT)*

A CHILD OF THE KING
From my heart to yours—

Becoming a child of the King of kings is indeed a wondrous miracle every time it happens, regardless of time or place. But to think that I can remain a child and expect things to remain as enjoyable as ever is very misleading, and a strong misrepresentation of the Gospel of our Lord and Savior Jesus Christ. That's why Jesus sent us the Promise of the Father, the Holy Spirit Himself". *(Friday, June 5, 2015 at 10:14 P.M. CDT)*

GOD APPROACHABLE
From my heart to yours—

Just because God is beyond human comprehension, does not mean God is unapproachable, for His initiative made "drawing near" possible through the cross of Christ. *(Saturday, June 6, 2015 at 6:08 A.M. CDT)*

GIVING HIM GLORY
From my heart to yours—

When John said, "And the Word became flesh and dwelt among us, and we beheld His glory, the glory as of the only begotten of the Father, full of grace and truth. (John 1:14)", he was not adding value to the glory by saying "as the only begotten of the Father", but describing it as SO exceptional that it had to be from outside ANY human experience. That's why the words were initiated by divine inspiration and not by human perspiration. And to think that this is only the beginning of what true followers have "in Christ"...... Oh! My, my, my! With my whole being, I'm driven to say, "Bless the Lord, oh my soul, and ALL that is within me, Bless His Holy Name." *(Saturday, June 6, 2015 at 6:19 A.M. CDT)*

TRANSCENDENT GLORY
From my heart to yours—

To the true follower of Christ, giving Him glory is not optional or seasonal or temperamental. True glory is not something I give, because I have nothing. Rather, it is something I behold or I reflect. Where it says, "Give Him the glory" or "and they glorified God" happens only by the enablement of the Holy Spirit within. This is why it is comprehensively true to say, "we are all his". The glory of God is independent of me. I don't add to it, or take away from it. Furthermore, whenever glory was evident in human experience, people's heads were to the ground, people were "as dead", people saw their own sin and repentance happened, and people were quiet at times. One thing for sure, true glory always brings about true worship. Sadly, there is false worship, and fake perception of glory. *(Saturday, June 6, 2015 at 6:36 A.M. CDT)*

TRUE GLORY
From my heart to yours–

In any human expression, be it thought, or expression of thought in word or deed, we only need answer the question: "Is Christ receiving all glory?" It is more difficult than we think. Only the Spirit "knows the deep things of God." Hence, the intentions of God are always far beyond human comprehension. Yet, "the secret of the Lord is with them that fear Him." This is where In my heart I feel numb, and in my mind I feel dumb. Still, I'd rather stand at His doorsteps than to live anywhere else. I'm beginning to understand the picture of the deer panting for the water. "*Crown Him with many crowns / the Lamb upon His throne*". (*Saturday, June 6, 2015 at 6:38 A.M. CDT*)

THE SPIRIT GLORIFIES THE SON
From my heart to yours–

A proper view of the Holy Spirit will never overshadow the glory of Christ because the Spirit always glorifies the Son, and not the reverse; and that's only in the Spirit's work in the Church, for in their divine essence, they are equal. Yet, they yield in union, they fellowship in communion, and love abounds in eternal majesty. (*Saturday, June 6, 2015 at 6:42 A.M. CDT*)

My Hiding Place
From my heart to yours—

In summary, man is either hiding FROM God, or hiding IN God. At the crossroads stands the cross of Christ. *(Saturday, June 6, 2015 at 7:13 A.M. CDT)*

Definition, Not An Easy Task
From my heart to yours—

Few months ago, I asked a group of dear friends to help me define the word, "car". Ten minutes later we were still grappling with this difficult task. ... And we think we can easily define: "LOVE"?!!! Then the Word became flesh, tabernacled among us, and we beheld.... ...and now, the rest of the story is taking place. Love one another! *(Saturday, June 6, 2015 at 7:20 A.M. CDT)*

When the Spirit Moves
From my heart to yours—

The Holy Spirit doesn't move when people speak, but people move whenever the Holy Spirit speaks. We don't instruct Him; but He instructs us to listen to Him; then we move in His power and at His direction. How do I know? Because, then, Jesus Christ is glorified every time, the church grows every time, conviction happens every time, the Gospel of Jesus Christ is presented with power, faith is exercised transparently. Disruption of status quo happens, comforting the disturbed happens, there is communion with the Risen Lord, love and mercy abound in fellowship, grace and truth are made manifest. In fact the full character of Christ is on display, so much so that people begin to taste the power of the Spirit, individuals decrease, and Christ increases and is made fully known. That's the power of the Gospel! Who does all this and more? No one but the very powerful Spirit of Christ. What do I do as I serve Him? I worship! Jesus! That's what it's all about. *(Friday, June 12, 2015 at 2:34 P.M. CDT)*

LEARNING TO RUN SCARED
From my heart to yours–

I'm learning to run scared that what I want, happens; Scared that God will let me do what I want for a season; Scared that I get busy for the sake of appearing to others as "spiritual" enough; Scared to do anything in human wisdom. And all along, I am not aware that I lost the art of discerning and practicing the Presence and Fear of God", because only then, worship happens; only then, Christ is glorified; only then, I come to the end of "ME", and begin to discover the bright glory and matchless Name of the Christ. That's when I'm immediately prompted to "take off my shoes" wherever I may be, because the ground is holy and the place is the "house of God". The strange thing is that such place may in fact be the very valley of the shadow of death. *(Friday, June 12, 2015 at 3:45 P.M. CDT)*

MINOR ADJUSTMENTS IN THINKING
From my heart to yours–

Once in a while, I get bothered by the way I think. Usually, it is about time when I need to make some adjustments, and He does some necessary tweaking in the way I think. For "As a man thinks in his heart, so is he." Here are some examples:

(1) The Holy Spirit does not move when we are ready, but when He is. That's called "His will on earth as it is in heaven".

(2) The Holy Spirit does not speak what we wish, because we are never sure when the correct time is. Also, the Spirit hates Russian roulette. That's called His "Freedom of Speech and Practice".

(3) Every single time the Holy Spirit moves He hits His target, He accomplishes His purpose, and He glorifies Christ. We lack such accuracy of the what, why, and when. That's called "Divine Union Expressed".

(4) The Holy Spirit covers all expenses, and it maybe from what's in my pockets. He not only owns that, but He also owns me. I may disagree but that's the least of His concerns. That's called "Sovereignty".

(5) The Holy Spirit is never impressed with anything fleshly; in fact, He hates anything "according to the flesh".

That's called "Singleness of a Pure Mind". *(Friday, June 12, 2015 at 5:07 P.M. CDT)*

~~~

SOVEREIGN DELIGHT
From my heart to yours—

Sovereignty of God is something I get to taste at times, but not devour. Majesty, on the other hand, is something that devours me and I don't get to taste it, but it enables me to worship in Spirit and truth. *(Saturday, June 13, 2015 at 9:07 A.M. CDT)*

~~~

ELIZABETH ELLIOT DIED
From my heart to yours—

Simply, a woman of God who walked with God and today went home to be in His holy Presence forever. After all, we will be forever with the one we love most. Elisabeth Elliot, wife of Jim Elliot, was used mightily among Ecuador's Auca Indians even after her husband was speared to death at age 29. Then she won them over with the only weapon that never fails: God's Love. Everything they wrote, or was written about them, is worth owning, reading, viewing, and/or meditating upon. Who will be the next Elisabeth? (or Jim?). *(Monday, June 15, 2015 at 4:38 P.M. CDT)*

FEW WORDS BUT ETERNAL
From my heart to yours–

"He is no fool who gives what he cannot keep to gain that which he cannot lose." (Jim Elliot, missionary, died at 29)." *(Monday, June 15, 2015 at 6:55 P.M. CDT)*

RELEVANCE AND VANITY
From my heart to yours–

"But if a man lives many years, and rejoices in them all, let him remember the days of darkness, for they will be many. All that is coming is vanity." (Ecclesiastes 11:8) Let me make sure I have it right. In considering life, I see from the start:
- Someone kicking and screaming,
- Clumsy, dirty, and shriveled up
- Waking up at many odd hours,
- Needing medicine to keep me healthy,
- Eating in small amounts,
- Needing a walker to get around,
- Having difficulty walking,
- Needing help with almost anything,
- Having no sense of taste,
- The eyesight is very weak,
- Having difficulty making friends,

- Ignored most of the time,
- Focused on what matters to me,
- Needing social interaction,
- Acquiring few friends who really care,
- Having stitches and scars and needle marks,
- The speech is unintelligible,
- Someone else carries me,
- The thoughts are fragmented or not there,
- Making payments almost all my life,
- Experiencing frustrations, sadness and grief,
- Becoming acquainted with death,
- Tears flow and sometimes for no reason,
- Giving answers when there is no question,
- Beginning to lose or forget things,
- Elated over insignificant things,
- Taking much time to express my thoughts,
- Am told I need meaning in life, and wonder what the "meaning" means,
- Gaining where it matters less, and losing where it matters most,
- Wasting the mind and minding the waist,
- And the list goes on.

I'm not sure if it's around the beginning or nearing the end, but I know everything in between is a mere "dash" or a hyphen at best. I conclude, to make sense, that the real meaning of life (past to future) begins at the cross of Christ, and finds the relevance of its details in Him. He never changes, and enables me to do all things through Him. Yes, His name is Jesus. *(Sunday, June 21, 2015 at 11:01 P.M. CDT)*

HEAVENLY HARMONY
From my heart to yours–

Just because we live in a religious atmosphere of disagreements and problems, we need not transfer the same mindset in our attempt to understand how the Father, Son and Holy Spirit relate to one another. Why? Because they never had any disagreements. Ever! The three-fold basis is: Absolute Love, Yielding Fellowship, and Union that never gives up. And look at how long they've worked together, what they accomplished, and still love one another so completely!!! What amazes me is that they invited us to be part of that lifestyle, shared the divine nature, and gave us the same resources to succeed. It's called: Amazing Grace! His Name is Jesus, Yes, Jesus! *(Tuesday, June 23, 2015 at 10:09 A.M. CDT)*

ARAB, BUT NO SPRING
From my heart to yours–

The Arab world and North Africa in their entirety can learn from Charleston, SC. Forgiveness, unconditional Christ-centered, will make the difference! And no one can come close with a counter offer, ever! (Thank you, John Cook, for sharing this powerful message.) *(Tuesday, June 23, 2015 at 4:16 P.M. CDT)*

CHARLESTON IS NOT A DANCE
From my heart to yours–

The WESTERN world too (North and South America) in its entirety can learn from Charleston, SC. The comment said, "Church ain't a culture thing." I would add, "Nuthin' in the Church is a culture thing".

That's why it's the Church of Jesus Christ of Everyday Saints.

~~~

FORGIVENESS
From my heart to yours—

Forgiveness isn't a culture thing, Love isn't either, Communion isn't, Confession isn't a culture thing, Hope isn't, Peace isn't, Mercy isn't either, Being merciful or Obtaining Mercy isn't a culture thing, Faith isn't, Joy isn't either, Acceptance isn't a culture thing, Purity isn't either, Doing the right thing isn't a culture thing, Meekness isn't a culture thing, Blessedness isn't either, Giving isn't a culture thing, Living isn't either, Safety isn't, Help isn't either, Having a moral compass isn't a culture thing, A living Faith isn't a culture thing, Gentleness isn't, Patience isn't either, Self-control is definitely NOT a culture thing, Actually, Being a super power isn't a culture thing either. And this is only the beginning!!! As a matter of fact, "Unless the Lord guards the city, The watchman stays awake in vain." (Psalms 127:1) All the above, and many more, are only a *"Jesus thing"*. In the cross of Calvary, He put death to death, and He brought life and healing in His wings. His specialty is mending the broken-hearted, and setting the captive free. In Him peace can be a reality between the Arab and Jew, the Russian and American, the North and South Korean, Apartheid will be wiped out from the heart, and the black and white together can be a force for peace to reckon with. Muscles will tire, and love isn't for hire. The cross doesn't have a price tag, and in the blood there is life. That's why "the blood will never lose its power!" Yes, His name can only be Jesus, because He saves people from what they got, and will give them what they aren't coming up with in a million lifetimes. *(Tuesday, June 23, 2015 at 6:56 P.M. CDT)*

PRAYING ALWAYS
From my heart to yours–

I will be traveling early Thursday till Monday night to a conference in Vancouver, Canada. Theme: To Know Him and To Make Him Known! Prayer appreciated on many fronts. *(Wednesday, June 24, 2015 at 1:58 P.M. CDT)*

IS HE ENOUGH?
From my heart to yours–

Was the Holy Spirit enough for Jesus the Son of Man to accomplish the work that "God prepared beforehand that [He] should walk in them"? (Ephesians 2:10) If Yes, which it is, then the same Spirit should be enough for me. Isn't that why Jesus said, "It is better for you that I go. And when I go, I will send him to you." (John 16: 8) The only question left for me to answer is, "Do I believe Him?" The rest is details to reflect what my heart decided in silence. *(Friday, June 26, 2015 at 9:05 A.M. CDT)*

WHY "IT'S ALL ABOUT HIM"?
From my heart to yours–

What does it mean when I say: "It's all about Him"? Here it is, at least in part: Having the will, desire, and inclination to do His will and the right thing is but the first step in His will being done "on earth as it is in heaven". "Obedience" is what makes it real, and enables it to bear fruit. Without an obedient heart, I find myself heading in the direction of being duped into thinking my wishes is what is real, and satan wins because I am unable to bear fruit for

Him. Lastly, my obedience is unfettered only when it is in response to the movement of the Holy Spirit in me. He may speak to my heart through others, but I know I'm not listening to people when its fountain is the Spirit who "knows the deep things of God" and its destination is the glory of my Lord, Jesus Christ who died and rose again. *(Friday, June 26, 2015 at 4:12 P.M. CDT)*

TODAY, BE COUNTED
From my heart to yours—

These are the days for the Church to BE the Church. Prayer for the latter rain is needed! *(Friday, June 26, 2015 at 4:22 P.M. CDT)*

STAGES OF THE HOLY SPIRIT MOVING INTO THE HUMAN HEART
From my heart to yours—

The will and inclination to do that which is good and right in His eyes is but the first seed that the Holy Spirit plants deep in my spirit. It is planted deep enough that of its location I know not but I know it's there. How do I know it's there? I know because the Holy Spirit in His first order of business awakened and quickened my spirit from death to life. The timing of His invasion, I know not. But it was the first invasion that caused life to happen. It was the first invasion of its kind that brings about the exact opposite of death. The force He applied, I know not. But when my soul screamed out the scream of the newborn, I took in his breath for the first time in my earthly life. And now, the transient human existence has been bonded with the eternal and I have eternal life in me. And now I "know" Him, not because of what I did, but because of my response to His prompting and attraction of my soul to the Savior on the cross. Yes, He did say, "when I be lifted up, I will draw all to me." Now I know that I am "drawn", and discovered His love, and I learned of the rudiments of what He did on the cross on my behalf. Now, when he planted in me the desire and bent to do what pleases Him, I realized it and was made glad. However, having the desire to glorify Him is one thing, and remains in the realm of wishful thinking until I learn of the second step that begins right away, namely, the step of obedience at the hearing of His voice when He communes with my spirit. Of its timing, I know not. Of its method, I know not. That is why He desires for me to be always listening, even when I lay me down, for He does not slumber or sleep. I will even awaken and am still listening, and have no complaint because now I love Him. *(Friday, June 26, 2015 at 4:25 P.M. CDT)*

GETTING THE PICTURE
From my heart to yours–

(1) God is committed to achieving His objectives for now and for eternity, not ours.

(2) His objectives include tasks that He prepared for us to carry out and walk in.

(3) We can know and carry out those tasks if we know His good and perfect will.

(4) We can know His good and perfect will if we change our mindset, not if we're perfect.

(5) We can change our mindset when we completely surrender to the power of the Holy Spirit in us.

(6) He can be "in us" only through a personal encounter with Christ, the risen Lord.

(7) We can establish a relationship with Him that begins at the cross only.

That's why Jesus went to the cross. That's why it's all about Him.
(Saturday, June 27, 2015 at 4:13 P.M. CDT)

EXPECTING GOD
From my heart to yours—

Expect Him because He is the God over all the "Un's" –

- The Unexpected
- The Unusual
- The Unbelievable
- The Unconquerable
- The Undesirable
- The Unfathomable
- The Unstoppable
- The Undoable
- The Unacceptable ... and,
- The Unlovable

He makes all things new! *(Saturday, June 27, 2015 at 4:20 P.M. CDT)*

RESURRECTION IS NOT A PROGRAM
From my heart to yours—

Good Sunday Morning Everyone! The good news is that Jesus is Risen, satan is beaten, and the tomb is empty. The day is beautiful, and is definitely worth living for Him. The song also says: "There is coming a day, When no heartaches shall come, No more clouds in the sky, No more tears to dim the eye, All is peace forever more, On that happy golden shore, What a Day glorious day that will be." Now, THAT's Good News! *(Sunday, June 28, 2015 at 9:49 A.M. CDT)*

~~~~~

BEAUTIFUL IN HIS EYES
From my heart to yours–

The Canadian (Vancouver) part of God's family. Not perfect, just beautiful because they are covered by the same precious blood of the Lamb. Enjoy! *(Sunday, June 28, 2015 at 12:44 P.M. CDT)*

~~~~~

APPLE OF HIS EYE
From my heart to yours–

God created everything to be the backdrop to the picture of my relationship with Him, so others will see the One you and I love with all our heart and be attracted to Him. *(Sunday, June 28, 2015 at 1:29 P.M. CDT)*

~~~~~

DEBT OF GRATITUDE
From my heart to yours–

THANK YOU is in order to all who lifted the Vancouver retreat in your prayers. Prayers, Many prayers were lifted to the only One who answers prayer. Prayers were offered frequently and throughout the weekend for the conference itself, for the countries of the Middle East and North Africa, and for various ministries that reach out to people with the love of Christ and meeting specific needs. Prayer was offered for the Holy Spirit to descend upon the place to give joy, wisdom, filling, understanding, and peace to troubled hearts. The worship time with our dear brother Mazen A. was consistently very special. A sweet spirit pervaded the place, and all were rejoicing. My prayer is that He, who began a good work, will continue it in everyone's heart; Also, praying that radical living for Christ will increasingly take place. *(Tuesday, June 30, 2015 at 1:25 A.M. CDT)*

GOD'S HUGE FAMILY
From my heart to yours—

Seeing different portions of the family of God, from different countries, different religious backgrounds, different traditions, ALL meeting to worship and to adore the Lord our God was very encouraging, and a piece of heaven on earth. New brothers and sisters, each with his/her own journey of faith, came expecting God to do something new. They were not disappointed. *(Tuesday, June 30, 2015 at 1:28 A.M. CDT)*

SHOCKING BUT TRUE
From my heart to yours—

In trying to explain the critical difference between knowing good and sound doctrine, and knowing God intimately, A. W. Tozer said this: "If a man have only correct doctrine to offer me, I am sure to slip out at the first intermission to seek the company of someone who has seen for himself how lovely is the face of Him who is the Rose of Sharon and the Lily of the Valley. Such a man can help me, and no one else can." Knowing Him can only happen when He opens my eyes to see. That can best happen moment by moment as He knows there is yearning in my heart. Instantly His Spirit senses the desire of my spirit which He awakened, and He shows me the glory and beauty of His face. Then my spirit is at rest. The best of all of His encounters is when the storm is raging, the night is long till morning, the winds are blowing, and twisting the very fabric of my soul. Then, He comes walking on the waters, and I hear His voice saying, "Fear not". There is no doctrine there; just Him who loves me and who just embraced me through the storm. *(Tuesday, June 30, 2015 at 1:35 A.M. CDT)*

♋︎⁓︎

KALEIDOSCOPE OF GRACE
From my heart to yours—

Looking into the kaleidoscope of God's amazing grace and turning it slightly we see that, though he is fully aware of man's penchant desire and bent to sinning, he made available a provision at the cross to repent and be reconciled to God. No one, but no one, has an alternative or anything to offer. Jesus said, "Come to me all you who are tired and have heavy burdens, and I will give you rest." Others give, but they give heavy burdens. That's why His sweet and precious name is JESUS. *(Tuesday, June 30, 2015 at 8:02 A.M. CDT)*

♋︎⁓︎

HIS LOVE
From my heart to yours—

"Behold what manner of love the Father has bestowed upon us that we should be called the children of God." (1 John 3). The Amazing and Unique Love of God:
- His love is above All loves
- It is different from all loves
- He accepts especially the unlovely
- He gives to us unconditionally
- He gives what is in His nature
- His love is true and authentic
- He showers us with it continually
- He gives us another "identity"
- The identity is inextricably tied to Him

- Since He is true, His love is true too

- His name is Jesus!

His love reaches to the highest mountain, and it flows to the lowest valley! *(Tuesday, June 30, 2015 at 8:24 A.M. CDT)*

HEART AND TREASURES
From my heart to yours–

When a person, (or home, local church, or nation) is married to the world, the world will plan to take over the life of that person completely until internal bleeding of the soul begins, and leads to complications and then death. The ones left behind pay the "past due" burden amount. Cause of death: Misplaced Allegiance. "Love not the world." (1 John 2). *(Wednesday, July 1, 2015 at 11:16 A.M. CDT)*

THE JUDAS KISS
From my heart to yours–

Just because God blesses us, does not mean He approves automatically of the way we live. Pretending cannot last forever. I cannot blame or fault the world for hating me. In fact, I expect the world to hate me and do everything in its power to destroy me. But it is disgusting to see someone who claims to be a "believer" and yet hates his fellow brother, and in the same breath says he loves God. "If someone says, "I love God," and hates his brother, he is a liar; for he who does not love his brother whom he has seen, how can he love God whom he has not seen? (I John 4:20) The antidote: Repent,

Hate the sin, and Be reconciled. *(Wednesday, July 1, 2015 at 11:19 A.M. CDT)*

～⌒～⌒～

A GENTLE REMINDER
From my heart to yours–

We are learning in our extended family to adjust to her fragmented thoughts. However, in one of her "Listen-To-Me" moments, Mom paused while she walked to her room, raised her index finger in my face as if to get my attention (and she did), and said something I can never forget. As a reminder to all who love Jesus Christ from a pure heart and wait for His appearing, I pass to you what she said. She said: "Don't ever forget that all our life, we have been living in the grace of God. And He never left us." She started to lower her hand, paused again, raised her finger slightly again and repeated: "Don't forget that!" After 60-something years, to you, my reader friend, I'm confident in saying: "Regardless of the details, nothing is better than living in and knowing God's amazing grace". The grace of God shocks, arrests, fills, then it sets one free to worship and serve Him, and Him alone. Where all people are concerned, that's where grace is applied. *(Friday, July 3, 2015 at 12:16 P.M. CDT)*

～⌒～⌒～

SECRETS AND GLIMPSES OF GRACE
From my heart to yours–

All my life, grace has been attractive to me. Since God gave us His Son, He has been able to embed His grace in us, and in some more than others. Some of its secrets are buried deep in the heart of a true follower of Christ, deep enough that every time when a crisis called for a sad end or closure of a life event, grace, like a seed, dies again and suddenly brings forth fruit of its kind. And life happens again.

So we have the Word saying, "and grace upon grace" (John 1). Abundant grace, Abounding grace, Beautiful grace. The grace of God is the stem cells of the soul. The factory location is not China, but Calvary. If the heart is broken, grace mends it. If a mind is fractured, grace keeps it together. If a relationship is torn asunder, grace has the capacity to repair and rebuild the fences. If a child has gone astray, grace spreads its wings and flies to the erring child and whispers words of life. And the list goes on and on. It is grace, Yes, the princess of all of God's attributes and it dwells throughout His Kingdom. And He said to His disciples, "the Kingdom of God is near you, and it is within you." Grace, that's how. Its beauty was completely revealed to us in the face of Jesus Christ. That's why "the law was given to Moses, but grace and truth found their full expression in Jesus Christ." And, at that point, even God had nothing else of value to give. *(Friday, July 3, 2015 at 7:13 P.M. CDT)*

GRACE IS SO AMAZING
From my heart to yours–

It is amazing in its:

Uniqueness: it gives a person the resilience never to quit.

Comprehensiveness: it permeates all aspects of life.

Effectiveness: it has its own inherent self-initiating authority to act.

Sovereignty: it has authority over all conditions especially the bad ones.

Diversity: it heals and reconciles; it restores; mediates; and it resurrects from death regardless of the extent of evil. *(Saturday, July 4, 2015 at 12:46 P.M. CDT)*

LEARNING TO SAY "I'M SORRY"
From my heart to yours–

If Mom finds it easily among her fragmented thoughts to say "I'm sorry" for, presumably, giving me a difficult time the previous day, I'm sure it should be easier for us with our mind still intact to not waste time and say, to someone we love, "I'm sorry". It's not because of what one says or does, but because of the one we love. Incidentally, the difficult time she is referring to was not wanting to take her medicine when prompted, or not wanting to cooperate when it's bedtime. Imagine the Horror of that!!! Now, *what's* your excuse (and mine)?!! It's for love's sake! *(Sunday, July 5, 2015 at 11:00 A.M. CDT)*

WORDS WON'T SUFFICE
From my heart to yours–

I can never be tenderly affectionate or intensely passionate about my Lord if He does not have my whole heart and I know it. "Feelings" and "words" have no credit in and of themselves, because loving Him is a matter of the heart. It starts with a beat, continues with a rhythm, and gives every day a new song. Loving Him is a heart condition that dwells in His love and His light. Loving Him properly has sanctity about it that words fail to describe because it takes forever to comprehend. Forever starts now. "This is life eternal, that they may know You and your Son whom you sent." (John 17). *(Monday, July 6, 2015 at 9:57 A.M. CDT)*

SPEAKING IN TONGUES - SHHHHHH
From my heart to yours–

For anyone interested in speaking in tongues, I feel reasonable by asking, "What are you doing with the one you have? Are you using it to "tell of the mercies of the Lord" intelligibly? Are you talking to Him about them before you talk to them about Him? We know that "the tongue is like fire". It appears, sad to say, that the busiest group of people for quite some time is the fire department. There may be hybrid cars for people, but there is no such thing as a hybrid faith acceptable to God. Faith and Obedience are twins. The world is dying to hear about one and to see the other consistently. The church has become the laughing stock of society, and has been dismissed as so dysfunctional that they can leave us alone to our downhill spiral and endless games we play. Nowhere in Scripture has it talked about "pleasing people", but even Jesus on earth had a single-minded passion to please the Father. And the Father approved! "Without faith it is impossible to please Him." *(Thursday, July 9, 2015 at 2:23 A.M. CDT)*

MY CROSS
From my heart to yours–

The cross Jesus called me (and each of His followers) to carry is not smooth or polished or gold-plated, but is big enough to be crucified on it so that I die with Him and rise again to a new life in Him. The question remaining is: Do I believe Him that He will never leave me or forsake me? *(Thursday, July 9, 2015 at 3:04 A.M. CDT)*

WHAT HAPPENS WHEN
From my heart to yours–

When a person is truly "saved", he meets the risen Lord. No one else can forgive sin. The rest of the salvation talk is just that - Talk! - When a person truly "prays", he meets the Holy Spirit. No one else can bear an acceptable witness. - When a person truly "intercedes", he goes through a fiery furnace because he takes the place of the one he is praying for. Nothing else suffices. - When a person truly "meets the Holy Spirit", he becomes the "temple of God" and the dwelling place of the Most High. "Holy" is the cry of the Angels. - When a person asks to see the glory of God, he is left in horror at his sin which nailed the Savior to the cross. Then, worship happens!
(Friday, July 10, 2015 at 3:32 P.M. CDT)

NOT EVEN REASONABLE
From my heart to yours–

Is it really reasonable ... that When we pray, (thinking that that means "I talk, He listens, and obeys"), I'm comfortable saying first a few words of "how good he is to 'us'", (whoever 'us' is), then we launch into handing him a list of what basically seems to be instructions, from us to him, and suggestions of what seems to be some good ideas for him to do, especially since he is so 'good' and such a 'super power', ... and on the other side of the coin, when he wants to say something 'personal' to ME in return, or when he already gave me a love letter to read, he glances at ME to see if I'm even listening, he realizes he is talking to himself because I've already exited through the nearest door, or have taken a 'leave of absence' or suddenly developed problems in MY 'inner ear' and ignore him completely, and what's worse is when I come back to talk to him I expect him to be present and responsive to my wishes and I start all over again, without any decent interest in just "sitting still and knowing that he is GOD"? By the way, in English grammar, this above statement (errrr question) is called a "run-on sentence", and I'm guilty as charged. I'm sure Shakespeare is rolling in his grave by now. But, Is it even reasonable? Am I the only one who behaves like that at times? What can be done about it? What are 'we' going to do about it? ... No, no, what am 'I' going to do about it? May I call it: "spiritual dementia"? Meaning, "I'm somewhere off in left field babbling my heart away, and even if I'm wrong, I expect him to know my mind and do what I say? God help!! Prayer: the longing of an empty heart for God, the God who promised to fill it with his glory, and taught us to call Him "Father". *(Saturday, July 11, 2015 at 1:49 A.M. CDT)*

THE WORLD HAS US BEAT
From my heart to yours—

We pretend to be Christians all day long, but the world with all its elements makes no qualms about being determined and takes every step to destroy anything that has to do with Christ, with the cross, with the church, with any family, and with the very soul of man. Just look around! And we cry looking for our pacifier when the spiritual crib stops rocking back and forth. Love not the world!! (1 John 2) *(Saturday, July 11, 2015 at 3:21 A.M. CDT)*

BIG DIFFERENCE
From my heart to yours—

When people cry out to God, they take hold of him. When revival comes, God takes hold of people and doesn't let go. When God's people pray, God listens. But when God speaks, people change. When God's people pray, they step into His presence. But when God moves, His holiness consumes everything in its way. Peter said in his letter, What manner of people should you be"? I had to pull over, and feast my eyes on these wonders from the God of wonders. *(July 18, 2015, 1:30 A.M.)*

WALKING IN THE SPIRIT
From my heart to yours—

Discovering treasures happens one step at a time. So is "walking in the Spirit". Here are some thoughts:

1. Keep trivial things just that, trivial. And only the Spirit leads and grants discernment daily.
2. Live a very disciplined life and judge my heart before the Lord, so I don't have time to judge others and leave them to Him who IS the Judge of all things.
3. Discern what are distractions to God's purposes for me (Eph. 2:10), and avoid them so one would do Only His desire in the life and live before Him.
4. Not everyone who asks is interested in knowing, but in covering their sense of inadequacy or to justify their own actions that they are not willing to give up.
5. Live as an open book before Him knowing that the heart is deceitful above all things. So I don't trust even my own heart, and choose to break down before Him in complete abandon.

I practice "complete surrender" in all things because He knows my heart, and I asked Him to help me not to waste whatever time I have left, but use it to His glory alone. *(July 18, 2015, 12:32 A.M.)*

ONE ANOTHER
From my heart to yours—

After a day of time well-spent with pastors, church leaders, and those who wanted to just come and worship, I learned in human relations that:

1. It's better to be close than to be distant
2. It's better to listen than to talk
3. It's better to love with difficulty than to be pretend with ease
4. It's better to look into someone's eyes than to imagine the person on social media screen
5. It's better to take risk that pleases God than to be stagnant thinking it's contentment
6. It's better to give than to receive
7. It's better to serve with discernment than to wait while giving excuses
8. It's better to go than to do nothing
9. It's better to go expecting God to surprise me than to stay in my comfort zone
10. Pastors and church leaders need prayer most
11. Unless there is anointing, forget it. When I speak, only confusion is expressed.
12. It's better to pray than to preach because in preaching I speak to people but in praying I speak with God
13. When I am too tired, but I need to keep going, I pray and He breathed into me enough of His Spirit to finish the task
14. God respects my schedule and agenda, but is never bound by it. He always brings about something better. I just have to trust Him on that one. He's God!

"Weeping may endure for a night, but joy comes in the morning." (Ps 30). Now, it's time to go home! *(Thursday, July 23, 2015 at 11:54 P.M. CDT)*

AN OFFERING CALLED "SINGING"
From my heart to yours—

As much as I love singing, I do have concerns of late. Here are some thoughts: - Singing is better in response to Conviction of the Holy Spirit and Contrition of the human heart; - Singing is better if submitted to the singular authority of the Word and not to the emotional attachment or personality; - Singing is better when its soundness is driven not by harmony of instruments but by harmony of the heart to God; - Singing is better when its motivation is not popularity of singers but singularity of the Savior; - Singing is better when born in agony and crisis, not in the comforts of life. - Singing does not bring heaven to earth; prayer does. - Singing, to be balanced, must appeal to the mind and heart. Music alone lacks the appeal to the mind, and can easily confuse and mislead the heart. *(Thursday, July 23, 2015 at 10:54 P.M. CDT)*

GOD REACHING TO MAN
From my heart to yours—

Sovereignty means no one knows truth unless it is revealed; No one can unless he is enabled; and No one moves unless he is authorized. When sovereignty meets with love, Christ happens; and when Christ happens, every time, life happens. Revelation always moves from and never toward sovereignty. Sovereignty demands worship and obedience. But for the follower of Christ to obey, Christ dwells in him sovereignly through His Spirit, and becomes the life source within. Then, obedience happens, "*As many as received Him, to them gave He power* (δυναμις – "dunamis" - inherent power) *to become the children* (newborns) *of God, to those who believe in His name.*" Nothing on earth can change a person to become a child of God except by the power of God. Neither can anything bring the dead to life except the very Spirit of God. Then Calvary happened! Counterfeit exists -- (for sovereignty, power, obedience, life, children of God, Order of things, Holy Spirit). Even Christ has an "anti-Christ", i.e., someone who not only opposes him but intensely desires to take His place. But, sovereignty has the final word. "*For He holds everything in the power of His word.*"

His name is Jesus. *(Sunday, July 26, 2015 at 3:52 P.M. CDT)*

WHY PRAY?
From my heart to yours–

"Pray for one another", because:

- Prayer is always precious

- Prayer is always needed

- Prayer is always lacking

- Prayer is what moves heaven

- Prayer is what everyone can do

- Prayer was the lifeline to heaven

- Prayer was the lifestyle of Jesus

You and I want to be like Him, right? *(Monday, July 27, 2015 at 6:38 A.M. CDT)*

WHY A LIFESTYLE OF PRAYER
From my heart to yours–

This is a glimpse into the prayer life of Jesus. My prayer is that you and I get serious, if we're not already, and just begin. Jesus said, "I pray for them". Be like Him and pray...

- For those who serve the physical and spiritual needs,

- For those who follow Him now and in the future,

- For those who have a major undertaking and don't know yet,

- For those who will fail that they hold on to Him,

- For those who have doubts to believe,

- For those who betray to be less and less,

- For those who are hot-headed to come under the Spirit's control,

- For those who are afraid to know that Jesus is near and will never leave,

- For those who are frustrated to rest in His providence and sovereign grace,

- For those who are blessed in ministry not to be impressed by own accomplishments but only by the fact that their names are written in the Book of Life.

He prayed. What's your excuse? *(Monday, July 27, 2015 at 6:39 A.M. CDT)*

WHY PRAY LIKE JESUS?
From my heart to yours–

In all things, we must look to Jesus, for He revealed and showed us how life in the Spirit ought to be. Here is how:

(1) He became man so we can understand

(2) He paid the redemption price so we don't have to

(3) He prayed without ceasing so we pray without ceasing

(4) He prayed in all situations so we do the same

(5) He prayed when happy so that He continues that lifestyle when sad and depressed and bruised

(6) He prayed alone, everywhere, and constantly so we do the same

(7) He prayed always toward the Father without an intermediary so that we pray to the Father through the Son without a second level of intermediary

(8) He prayed on the mountain and in the valley so we do the same

(9) He prayed longing for the Father and His prayer was answered so that we long for Him and not for what we can get from Him

(10) He prayed filled with faith and confident expectation because only the Father knew the Son, so that we can do the same because only He knows us like none other . . . and many more reasons.

He is the only One who answers prayer. I'm not sure if he does not answer that I want anyone else to answer! *(Monday, July 27, 2015 at 6:39 A.M. CDT)*

I CANNOT PRAY LIKE HIM IF
From my heart to yours—

I cannot pray like Him if:

(1) If I'm not like Him

(2) If I'm ashamed of Him

(3) If I don't follow Him

(4) If I don't love Him

(5) If I am not willing to lay my life for Him as He did for me

(6) If I don't have the same passion for Him as He did for me

(7) If I am not surrendered to Him as He was to the Father

(Wednesday, July 29, 2015 at 10:47 A.M. CDT)

I CANNOT PRAY TO HIM EVERY DAY IF
From my heart to yours

I cannot pray TO Him every day if:

(1) If I have divided allegiance

(2) If I have plan "B"

(3) If I don't love Him with my whole heart

(4) If He's not my Lord who died for me

(5) If I don't long for Him as He did to His Father

(6) If I don't spend time with Him

(7) If I am not willing to change for His sake alone. *(Wednesday, July 29, 2015 at 10:52 A.M. CDT)*

I CANNOT PRAY "WITHOUT CEASING" IF
From my heart to yours–

I cannot pray "without ceasing" if:

(1) If I am not detached from the world without ceasing also

(2) If I am not desperate for Him

(3) If I am not willing to give up all for Him

(4) If I am not in the Spirit with Him

(5) If I am not planning to be with Him forever

(6) If I am not aware of the cost

(7) If I not waiting for an answer

(Wednesday, July 29, 2015 at 11:01 A.M. CDT)

～～～

LIFE "ACCORDING"
From my heart to yours–

The difference between living "according to the flesh" and "living according to the Spirit" is like the difference between addiction and marriage. Marriage is life to life; addiction is death to death. Jesus: "I have come that they might have life, and have it more abundantly." He told me the "what" and the "why". What's my excuse not to respond?!! *(Thursday, July 30, 2015 at 7:21 A.M. CDT)*

～～～

A LIVING SACRIFICE
From my heart to yours–

If God does not change me, He will never use me to change the world. If He was filled with the Holy Spirit to become Incarnate and emptied Himself (Phil 2), surely He desires for me to become like Him by emptying myself so I would be filled by the same Spirit. The rest is mere details. Eph. 5:18 "Be continually filled with the Holy Spirit". John 3:34 "God does not give his Spirit using a measuring cup". Jesus presented Himself a "living sacrifice". We want to be like Him, right? (Romans 12:1-2) That's why it's all about Him! *(Thursday, July 30, 2015 at 9:10 P.M. CDT)*

～～～

SOMEWHAT STRANGE
From my heart to yours–

I find it somewhat strange: The world says "Find yourself", and people spend their entire life looking for their "identity". Some even claim that they found it. Then Jesus says, if anyone wants to be my disciple, he must "deny himself". No wonder the world hates Him. *(Saturday, August 1, 2015 at 12:14 A.M. CDT)*

Intercessory prayer happens when one speaks until He runs out of words, and there is still fire within. He curls up like a baby in His presence and waits and cries for the night is long. *(Saturday, August 1, 2015 at 9:59 P.M. CDT)*

WORSHIP BEFORE GOD
From my heart to yours–

The one who truly desires to worship, does not only offer sacrifices, but ultimately becomes the sacrifice himself. The follower lives as Christ did by the same Spirit who accompanied Him as He walked during His earthly life "according to the Spirit", from birth until He entered the Holy of Holies on our behalf. We desire to be like Him, right?!! We cannot enter the Holy Presence of God except (1) we *either* go to the cross first to pay for sin; *or,* (2) go through the One who was crucified on our behalf and become one with Him there. *(Sunday, August 2, 2015 at 12:48 P.M. CDT)*

THE GREAT CHASE
From my heart to yours–

The Chase is on between God and Man. Here is how:

- New Man in pursuit of God is sanctifying and satisfying w/ a new sense of awe

- Lost Man in pursuit of God is frustrating and unsatisfying w/ a sense of disturbing fear

- God in pursuit of a new man is the making of a calling and holy living

- God in pursuit of a lost man is irresistible and disturbing day and night, for a season.

If man surrenders, he wins. How ironic! *(Monday, August 3, 2015 at 5:14 A.M. CDT)*

THE PERPETUAL CURRICULUM
From my heart to yours–

The twelve themes which formed the perfect curriculum of the early Church and caused her to succeed in spreading throughout the world in the first century were:

(1) The Name,

(2) The Way,

(3) The Gospel,

(4) The Risen Lord,

(5) The Disciples,

(6) The Holy Spirit,

(7) The Story,

(8) The Fellowship,

(9) The Blood,

(10) The Lord's Table.

What kept that Church breathing in a world that sought to snuff the very life out of her was:

(11) Prayer, and,

(12) Suffering The reason the church today is ineffective, lackadaisical, and stymied is that we are committed to everything else, and sleeping with the enemy.

Going back may be the first step forward. *(Tuesday, August 11, 2015 at 9:18 A.M. CDT)*

~~~~~~

CHRISTIANITY IDENTIFIED
From my heart to yours–

Christianity that does not tell the story of The Crucified Christ and The Risen Lord is a pernicious heresy of the worst order. Here is why.

(1) It becomes anemic, comatose, and gradually lifeless; and seeks to sustain itself by artificial means and traditions

(2) It deviates from the path that Christ Himself set, which renders the warped product a proverbial "crime against humanity" of a different kind

(3) It impacts countless generations in the most perverse direction, bearing bitter fruit, and breeding a suffocating mindset. *(Tuesday, August 11, 2015 at 9:33 A.M. CDT)*

~~~~~~

A MOM MOMENT
From my heart to yours–

I said, "Remember when your Mom (my Tata Saada) lived with us the last few months of her life?" Mom: "Yes I do." John: "Remember every day when she opened the window by her bedside, she saw the mountains and she recited the verse: "I lift up my ..."" remember?" Mom: "*I lift up my eyes to the mountains, where does my help come from*". That was in 1969, (46 years ago).

My prayer for you today, dear reader, is that (1) you know He is lifted high, (2) you lift up your eyes toward Him regardless of your situation, (3) you know there is help like none other, (4) you have an open heart to receive His gift because all are good, and that (5) you express your gratitude, for God's mercies endure forever. *(Tuesday, August 11, 2015 at 10:51 A.M. CDT)*

LIFE UPSIDE DOWN
From my heart to yours–

After 3 weeks, Mom's birthday roses, still beautiful. Dried upside down. Stayed together. So is life, even when things are upside down. Here's the promise: The peace of God that passes all understanding shall keep (build a fortress and hedge around you) your heart and mind in Christ Jesus. Do you believe? *(Tuesday, August 11, 2015 at 11:49 A.M. CDT)*

CHRIST - THE HEART OF THE CHURCH
From my heart to yours—

Why were the twelve themes the perfect curriculum of the early Church? (And their absence is the reason for today's church's miserable failure.) Here are some details:

(1) The Name: gave identity, affinity, power, reason

(2) The Way: gave foundation, direction, confirmation, and uniqueness of the Master

(3) The Gospel: gave unity of mind and heart, basis, message, argument, power to speak

(4) The Risen Lord: gave the reason to live the resurrection life, and die to be with Him forever

(5) The Disciples: gave community, harmony, similarity, humility, continuity

(6) The Holy Spirit: gave power, life, government, rightness, filling, eternality, and guidance into all truth

(7) The Story: gave a beginning, continuity, reality, familiarity, and powerful end

(8) The Fellowship: gave union with Christ who is at its heart, communion,

(9) The Blood: gave life, freedom, release from guilt, richness

(10) The Lord's Table: gave holy and uninterrupted reminder of fellowship with the risen Lord, and oneness of being and nature.

What kept that Church breathing was:

(11) Prayer: gave entrance, Presence, fire, trust, urgency, protection, purification

(12) Suffering: gave purity, readiness, character, training, hope, change, faith, and fellowship with the Lord Himself.

And, this is only the beginning. Isn't He worthy?!! *(Tuesday, August 11, 2015 at 8:03 P.M. CDT)*

SURVIVAL KIT
From my heart to yours—

Abraham was content with a "tent" and an "altar". They kept:

(1) His heart yearning and steady,

(2) His mind focused and intentional,

(3) His actions ordered of the Lord. Sinned?

Yes. Grace Through and Through.

The rest are details. That's the recipe for an "intimate friend of God". My prayer for you today, dear reader, is that you will be filled with all that God has in store for you through Christ, so much so, that the clutter of the world will be crowded out of your heart. "Above all things, keep your heart with diligence, for out of it flow all matters of life." (Proverbs 4) *(Wednesday, August 12, 2015 at 8:32 A.M. CDT)*

HAVING THE EYES OF JESUS
From my heart to yours—

Whenever Jesus spoke of "the least of these", He was saying:

(1) The "least" are equal in my sight to the "greatest", Always!

(2) "Least" and "greatest" are human, not divine classifications. Drop it!

(3) We are called to serve the least first, because it is counter-culture

(4) We are specifically not called to serve the "greatest" because there is no such thing in the family of God. We are all brothers and sisters.

(5) The true value of "the least" is deep within, so don't look at the outside

(6) The so-called "greatest" are more likely to act like they are "the greatest". Leave that to Mohammad Ali Clay who claimed "I am the greatest". *(Thursday, August 13, 2015 at 8:27 A.M. CDT)*

WHAT IS NEXT?
From my heart to yours–

When the Holy Spirit truly comes into my life, the first thing He does is bring the Savior's love in so I would love everyone, especially the outcasts. *(Monday, August 17, 2015 at 6:49 A.M. CDT)*

LIFE IN THE SPIRIT
From my heart to yours–

1. If I pray that the Holy Spirit meet someone's need, I should expect Him to use MY resources to meet that need, not someone else's. (Monday, August 17, 2015 at 6:50 A.M. CDT)

2. The uniqueness of a mother's love is that she carried the one she loves in her womb for a period of time first. But God graciously gives all, including men, the capacity to show His amazing love if we carry the one He wants to love through us without us choosing to abort, preferring our own comfort zone instead. *(Monday, August 17, 2015 at 6:59 A.M. CDT)*

3. I cannot remotely imagine the love of the Savior toward a lost soul if I don't allow Him to pour that love through me first. *(Monday, August 17, 2015 at 7:00 A.M. CDT)*

4. When the Holy Spirit pours the Savior's love through me to an outcast on the street, and the outcast responds to that love, then I can easily worship with them anywhere. *(Monday, August 17, 2015 at 7:05 A.M. CDT)*

5. If the Holy Spirit succeeds in getting me to love one outcast, then I can easily love many; and like my Savior, I can love all. Then my Lord is glorified through and through. *(Monday, August 17, 2015 at 7:12 A.M. CDT)*

6. I better be careful what I ask for from the Holy Spirit because He just might give it, and by so doing will test how genuine my surrender to Him is. *(Tuesday, August 18, 2015 at 8:04 A.M. CDT)*

7. Asking for "power in prayer" is not asking to have more of God, but asking that God the Holy Spirit would have more of me. *(Tuesday, August 18, 2015 at 8:53 A.M. CDT)*

8. "Prayer", not "telepathy", is how I communicate with the Holy Spirit. And when I speak with Him, I am in the Presence of God instantly. An Awesome Presence like none other. The Eternal God of the universe has allowed me into His Holy Presence, because of His Beloved Son. The main concern is not the answer I desire, but whether I am dressed properly to be in His Presence. Dressed: in holiness, in praise, in transparency, in joy, in longing for my Lord, in humility before Him who defined humility. Then, the answer to my prayer will be His desire, and I'm content and thankful. Preparing me for the Presence is what the Holy Spirit alone does. *(Tuesday, August 18, 2015 at 8:11 A.M. CDT)*

9. "Waiting" is not measured with "Time" but with heartbeats. "Be still and know that I am God." The question is: Do I believe?" Shhhh. *(Tuesday, August 18, 2015 at 8:15 A.M. CDT)*

10. The answer to my prayer costs, not Him, but me, because it is intended to transform, not Him, but me to become, not what I wish because I died, but become in His image more, because I am alive in Him forever. *(Tuesday, August 18, 2015 at 8:19 A.M. CDT)*

FORGIVENESS DEFINED
From my heart to yours

When I was forgiven at the cross, Christ said, in effect, "I'm going to do something that satan cannot hold against you ever again." And He paid all my debts, for love's sake. Now all I have is: Him, and that's all I need. The question is: "Do I believe?" And that's another reason why I love Him. *(Tuesday, August 18, 2015 at 8:24 A.M. CDT)*

*When I am spiritually concerned, as I meet someone's material needs, then I am investing not in time but for eternity. Otherwise, I'm just giving "bread" so I would feel good. Jesus did not come "**feeling**" but He came "**healing**".* (Tuesday, August 18, 2015 at 8:33 A.M. CDT)

LIFTING JESUS
From my heart to yours–

When I lift up Christ alone, two things happen: (1) the Holy Spirit glorifies Him in and through me, and, (2) all else takes its proper place relative to Him, and becomes "less". That's called, not the "correct view of things", but, "the right view of Christ". *(Tuesday, August 18, 2015 at 8:37 A.M. CDT)*

~~~

NOT LIFTING JESUS
From my heart to yours—

When I do NOT lift up Christ alone, two things happen: (1) The Holy Spirit is grieved because of me, and, (2) all else is in chaos relative to Christ, and He becomes "negotiable". That's called, "politically and socially correct view of things", and anything BUT, "the right view of Christ". I can argue to the opposite all I want, and it's added to the chaos that I created. This is why the Spirit of God "hovered over the chaos" to create something beautiful. *(Tuesday, August 18, 2015 at 3:14 P.M. CDT)*

~~~

IN OPPOSITION
From my heart to yours—

Opposing the idea of "complete surrender to the Holy Spirit" is precisely what is meant by "resisting the Holy Spirit". All my life of resistance renders me ineffective, confused, and of no use to Him. Even *that* is an expression of His grace, not toward me, but toward those who might come under my influence and become resistant to the Spirit, like me. The sad part of the picture is that every time I open my mouth of resistance, I have the bad breath of opposing the will of the Spirit in me. Now, That's Sad! *(Tuesday, August 18, 2015 at 8:45 A.M. CDT)*

~~~

Asking for "power in prayer" is not asking to have more of God, but asking that God the Holy Spirit would have more of me. (Tuesday, August 18, 2015 at 8:53 A.M. CDT)

❧

BEING LED
From my heart to yours–

We and Jonathan have been praying for a while how he can be serving the Lord and filling his time. Through a friend, he is now helping as a volunteer at a food distribution ministry. About 100 families come to receive bags of different items. But all those who come have a member of the "prayer warrior teams" pray with them before they leave. That's where Jonathan loves to be. One of the helpers is a 102-year old lady (picture) - today is her birthday :) - who loves him dearly, and looks forward to seeing him every time. This morning, he took several Bibles in Spanish to give to visitors, and was like a horse at the starting gate :). It is a true joy to be on the giving side of things. *(Tuesday, August 18, 2015 at 10:40 A.M. CDT)*

❧

BREATHING CHRIST
From my heart to yours–

Anyone can begin his life in Christ by "receiving Christ the Lord, the Unspeakable Gift". This is not changing my "doing", but changing my "being"; not changing my "actions" but changing my "nature". That's what only the Holy Spirit is able to accomplish completely. But the true baby never stays a baby... The True follower of Jesus Christ moves forward, in principle, by "complete surrender to the governance of the Holy Spirit", who alone can open the follower's eyes to see the Glorious Savior he received at second birth. It's a new lifestyle, a new day, a new relationship. "All that received Him, to them gave He power to become to children of God." "All who are led by the Spirit, they are the maturing sons of God." *(Wednesday, August 19, 2015 at 8:47 A.M. CDT)*

SNAPSHOTS AND GLIMPSES
From my heart to yours—

Don't expect "successful" formulas to replace personal transformation. It doesn't even come close. That's the work of the Holy Spirit alone. *(Saturday, August 22, 2015 at 11:46 P.M. CDT)*

HIS GIFTS
From my heart to yours—

IF the gift(s) of the Holy Spirit, according to His Word, were given to every believer and true follower of Christ, I must ask:

- Why don't leaders of evangelical and traditional churches open their church doors much more?

- Why don't they give the Spirit of the living God the opportunity to invade their stony altars and empty pews and shaken hearts and extract the fears deep within each soul?

- Why don't they allow true members of the "Body", the Church, to breathe the fresh air of the Holy Spirit, and bless all churches and memberships, if indeed they are alive in Christ? *(Sunday, August 23, 2015 at 5:14 A.M. CDT)*

～～～

DAILY EXERCISE
From my heart to yours

Breathing the Spirit of Christ IN, enables true followers to speak Christ Out to others, without exception. *(Sunday, August 23, 2015 at 5:16 A.M. CDT)*

～～～

PART OF A PRAYER LIFESTYLE
From my heart to yours–

To-date, I am yet to be turned down when I ask someone not expecting, "How can I pray for you?" It's not I who is speaking to the person but it's the Spirit speaking to me. It's not a question of "speaking", but of "listening". Practicing obedience to the Spirit of Christ is practicing Christ. *(Sunday, August 23, 2015 at 5:20 A.M. CDT)*

～～～

SEEING HIS GLORY
From my heart to yours–

If I ask to see the glory of God, I must be prepared to be burned by the holiness of God. The Holy Spirit of God can do both. Put differently, I cannot glorify God if I'm not holy. The only One who can make me "holy" is the Holy Spirit. Holiness is the path into His Presence. Surrender + Obedience = Holy life. Jesus surrendered, Jesus obeyed unto death, Jesus is holy. "Holiness" is not a denomination by man, but the domination of the Holy Spirit in man. You want to be like Jesus, right?!! "Pursue holiness without which no one is able to see God." Hebrews 12:14 *(Sunday, August 23, 2015 at 5:39 A.M. CDT)*

HOLY LIVING
From my heart to yours–

Holy living is living wholly for Jesus Christ, because "true" religion that is truly from God is first "pure", that is, unadulterated, clean. (James 1:27) Put differently, which glass of water you would be more inclined to drink: one that's half-filled with poison, or one that has only a drop of poison?!! *(Sunday, August 23, 2015 at 5:44 A.M. CDT)*

He will answer, in His time. The cost may be heavy. For love's sake! "God is able to do exceedingly abundantly more than we ask or think." "Knock and it shall be opened unto you." It's His promise, not mine. Do you believe Him?! *(Sunday, August 23, 2015 at 9:25 A.M. CDT)*

FAITHFUL AND FAITH-FULL
From my heart to yours–

Faithful praying is faith-full praying. It is made known only through the Throne of grace, simply because the Father knows what you and I need. Persistent praying is not insisting on what I want, but it is knowing that I am prostrate before the Throne of God asking in the Name of Jesus. My eyes - always toward Him. *(Tuesday, August 25, 2015 at 5:20 A.M. CDT)*

Being "radical" means I have declared, not what I shall do, but who owns me for the rest of my life. The rest is simply details. *(Tuesday, August 25, 2015 at 5:29 A.M. CDT)*

LONGING
From my heart to yours

I'm getting in the distinct habit of looking up more often and, that, for a couple of reasons: - The King is coming! - I can't wait to see Him!! Longing for that day!!! *(Friday, August 28, 2015 at 6:57 A.M. CDT)*

TO BE A TRUE FOLLOWER OF CHRIST
From my heart to yours–

Some questions I suggest this morning to a true follower of Jesus Christ:

(1) Is there someone who is a non-believer, and you really care about them and want to see them saved?

(2) How serious are you?

(3) Are you willing for the Spirit of God to change you enough to reach them?

(4) Are you willing to change, knowing that He may use someone else, not you, to reach your dear one?

(5) Are you willing to pray without ceasing for them?

If you answered "No" to any of the above, then forget it. If you answered "Yes" to all, here is what you can do (if you can):

(1) Write their name(s) down on a piece of paper and carry it in your pocketbook or purse

(2) Let it be easily accessible, and *never* get rid of it.

(3) Every time you see or touch that paper, plead with God and pray for them like their life depended on you. It just might.

(4) Wait on the Lord!! Wait, until you're numb about earthly ways and thinking.

SALVATION IN A NUTSHELL
From my heart to yours–

If someone is wondering: what exactly is "Salvation"? You may want to think of it like this:

- It's created and delivered in heaven at designer's expense;

- 100% guaranteed to work without any fine print;

- It's 100% personal, non-refundable, non-customizable, non-transferable;

- Cannot be loaned or borrowed, never gets old or ruins;

- Will never have recalls;

- Doesn't discriminate by age, color, race, religion, national origin, gender, or sexual orientation;

- Minorities and women encouraged to receive it;

- One size fits all because His love reaches to the highest mountain and flows to the lowest valley;

- It's not seasonal and is not for sale;

- No advertising or special coupon needed;

- You don't need to "Google" it because it's at Calvary;

- The URL is "www.U-R-Loved.byHim";

- You don't need a super star or a movie star to tell you about it because they may likely become fallen star;

- It is backward and forward compatible automatically;

- It wasn't the result of some research and development department, or clinical trials on monkeys;

- No need for co-signor or co-sponsor;

- Has no spiffs ever;

- Has no side effects except one which is a life changed into His likeness;

- It is PAID IN FULL IN ADVANCE because mankind was in total foreclosure;

- The forecast was definitely NOT good;

- Wall Street was up the wall hedging their bets, and economists did not find it in their charts and psychologists were going nuts trying to replace it with behavior modification;

- The sociologists suggested better self-esteem but that theory quickly ran out of steam;

- No killing is needed to attain it, or a sacred place to stain it;

- It is not affiliated with any prayer cloth or cheese cloth;

- It's not to be taken (or stolen or bought or bartered or negotiated) because it's a gift;

- It is not financed because the debt is too big and the applicant (you or me) is already bankrupt;

- Chapter 7 and Chapter 13 bankruptcy do not apply because we were beyond protection from God's wrath and not fit for re-structuring;

- It's never been in draft mode or beta testing;

- It's not a la carte;

- It's all or none because it cost the blood of the Father's Son;

- It has no denominational pull or push;

- It's not in a piece of wood or at a place to visit if you could.

Well, you may ask, "So, What is it then?" Here are some thoughts about the answer: Salvation is:

- A cry of faith from the bottom of the human heart,

- A cry that says by faith 'God, I need your kind of faith to believe what you did on Calvary's cross for me; and bear with what I'm about to say, but would you, dear God, for the life of me, have my heart and life in exchange for the life you gave to me on the cross? Would you, God? And I have no guarantees of my own because I have failed so much, but I have your promise to hold on to that you, God, have covered my debt completely and will forgive me for the asking with all my heart, will accept me, will make me whole again, will breathe in me your Spirit of life, will make me your child, will give me your name, will grant me to live again, to love you again, to serve you gladly and to worship you forever. Will you have me, Lord, as I am?"

Then, listen, for He was heard saying all along: "Come unto me all you who are heavy-laden and I will give you rest". Would you receive Him as Savior?!

This is where you and I say, if we accept Him, "Thank you, Lord. I accept by faith what you've done. Thank you for taking all my sins away. Thank you for covering me with your blood and making me clean. Lead me every day as you promised. My desire is to live for you, and to do your will in my life even if it cost me what it cost your Son Jesus." *(Friday, August 28, 2015 at 10:35 P.M. CDT)*

A GOOD MULE
From my heart to yours–

It's ironic that a mule never chooses the field where he is to plow, and is useless without being in a field, somewhere. Please note: - He has to be owned first - He has to be led to a field daily - He always wears a yoke for discipline - He is always led down a preset path - His purpose is to prepare the ground - He always takes part in the spread of seed - He tires at the end of his day - He gets to eat his daily portion while he works - He never knows the full plan for His day - He practices obedience to His owner - He may not get to see the harvest - He is rewarded at the end of his day with rest, removal of the yoke, and refreshment in his owner's house. Not bad, even for a mule! *(Monday, August 31, 2015 at 10:46 A.M. CDT)*

NON-SPOTLIGHT WORSHIP
From my heart to yours

Calvary is the beginning of a life of worship that is acceptable to God. Calvary is a place created by design only for sinners. When received, redeemed, and renewed, they normally stay there. They know, no other place accepts them. *(Monday, August 31, 2015 at 10:55 A.M. CDT)*

BLENDING INTO GOD
From my heart to yours

When I read the mind of God expressed in the Scriptures, I find Him allowing my mind to blend into His. He has no problem with that. He is so good He even gave me His Spirit to understand it. How sad that most people are content by choice to receive a modest portion prepared by someone else once per week, on Sunday, when the feast is in front of me in fact day and night. *(Monday, August 31, 2015 at 2:29 P.M. CDT)*

BOOKS, SILENT WINDOWS TO THE SOUL
From my heart to yours

It is said: "Books are the only thing you buy that will make you richer." Reading the Bible makes one even richer, forever. "Let the Word of Christ dwell in you richly." *(Monday, August 31, 2015 at 1:34 P.M. CDT)*

RANDOM THOUGHTS ON WRITING BOOKS
From my heart to yours

1. Writing this book, I found, is like having a silent conversation with God. I discovered how inadequate I am.

2. I felt like a bumblebee which doesn't know that its aerodynamic attributes don't qualify her to fly, but it keeps flying trying to discover the world.

3. I had no intention in this writing to "tell" anyone what to think or believe, but I did intend to transmit infectiously if possible the passionate desire to simply think, and reconsider what we assume falsely at times.

4. A plot speaks of intent and of charting a hidden course left for the reader to unravel. In contrast, I told the reader beforehand, in bite-size, that I'm discovering a path vastly

richer than this world can absorb; hence, the preeminence of Christ.

5. The most difficult task before me during the writing process was leaving everything behind and declaring my heart's bankruptcy before Him who died on the cross for me, and captured my heart.

6. This book is no ocean wide, but is in fact trickles among rocks and muddy thinking, in desperate longing to find the ocean.

7. While I was writing, I wanted to speak to someone and make him my audience. At first I discovered I may be talking to myself. Then I learned that my Father wrapped His arms around me to help me unravel my heart before Him, then He assembled my thoughts in a way that only He can. And I was made glad, not because I wrote, but because He loved me so.

8. In writing, I learned that I was turning the pages of my soul, and discovered they were quite wrinkled. *(Sunday, September 6, 2015 at 12:33 A.M. CDT)*

UNIQUENESS OF JESUS
From my heart to yours

I find it very unreasonable and strange that people flock to walk where Jesus walked, but don't want to die where Jesus died. He has no trinkets to sell, but He signed His name with blood on the cover of a book called "The Book of Life". It still holds true that unless the Holy Spirit moves with the shock of new life, convicts of sin, and shows how desperately man needs a Savior, forget it! Patronizing Jesus with a visitor's visa won't work; then back to the same old stuff -- Feeling good, but still dead. *(Sunday, September 6, 2015 at 9:34 P.M. CDT)*

ACCEPTABLE WORSHIPFUL SERVICE
From my heart to yours

I know that I'm serving Christ out of pure love toward Him, regardless of details, if what I do leads me to worship Him alone, and not a growing feeling of obligation that simply makes me feel good for a season. *(Monday, September 7, 2015 at 4:55 A.M. CDT)*

LOVELY CONSTRAINTS
From my heart to yours

"The love of Christ constrains me", means, it will bond me to every other person who loves Christ with a pure heart, and will bind me to deliver the love of a bruised Savior's head to the whole world. *(Monday, September 14, 2015 at 2:44 A.M. CDT)*

PRODDING AT NIGHT
From my heart to yours

When the Spirit prods me to wake up early or in the middle of the night, it is intended to pay attention and prepare myself to be in the holy presence and to worship. *(Monday, September 7, 2015 at 5:00 A.M. CDT)*

When I go to sleep with the Lord on my mind, His Spirit may wake me up during the night just to spend time in His holy presence, for love's sake. *(Monday, September 7, 2015 at 5:03 A.M. CDT)*

LONGING FOR HIM ALONE
From my heart to yours

Longing for Him is a lifestyle, a dedication, uninterrupted and holy. In eternity past, that was His heartbeat toward me, before I came to be, for His holy Presence is the NOW that never changes or is affected by human events. *(Monday, September 7, 2015 at 5:09 A.M. CDT)*

THE CROSS — THE BEGINNING FROM THE END
From my heart to yours

1. To think that He loved me though I was dead in sin makes me wonder why and how can it be. He took the first step that became, over time, a suspended storm on Calvary's cross. Then He wrapped His arms around me and died, and gave me life again. . . For love's sake. Dallas Holmes sang: *"Here we are in your presence Lifting holy hands to You Here we are praising Jesus For the things He's brought us through. I don't have the words to tell You how I feel, I just don't know what I can say I'm not worthy to speak Your Holy Name, Yet You tell me You love me just the same."* *(Monday, September 7, 2015 at 5:22 A.M. CDT)*

2. When Christ died, He paid our debt and the Triune God embedded followers into Him forever. We were not added, but

we were embedded, to be one with Him for the sake of Christ. *(Sunday, September 13, 2015 at 10:06 A.M. CDT)*

❦

HOW FAR HIS LOVE
From my heart to yours

The first news this morning said that "the farthest known galaxy is 13.2 billion years old." The first thought in my mind was of my Lord saying, "Yes, I know. I was there when that came. It was no accident." I worshipped, because suddenly I caught myself in a holy hush. *(Monday, September 7, 2015 at 5:41 A.M. CDT)*

❦

WORSHIP – A CONSUMING PASSION
From my heart to yours

1. True worship creates a longing that will find no rest except at His feet in gratitude - all His, all ours, all holy & true, for love's sake. *(Sunday, September 13, 2015 at 10:05 A.M. CDT)*

2. True Worship begins when we declare our spiritual bankruptcy at the cross and get accepted at the Throne for His Son's sake, Forever. *(Sunday, September 13, 2015 at 10:05 A.M. CDT)*

3. "Hallowed" is not for a place we designate, but for the Name of the God we worship and adore forever, "on earth as it is in heaven." *(Sunday, September 13, 2015 at 10:05 A.M. CDT)*

4. In a seriously fractured world "en toto" (in its totality), I daily pray, "Lord, unify my heart to fear Your Holy Name." That's where worship begins and ends. *(Sunday, September 13, 2015 at 10:06 A.M. CDT)*

5. God's "holy place" is always: Clean, Holy, Ready; All His, always His, alone His, uniquely His; For glory, for Prayer, for Worship, Forever. *(Sunday, September 13, 2015 at 10:06 A.M. CDT)*

6. God's Presence is in His holy place. "Don't you know that you are the temple of God and the Spirit of God dwells in you." We are *His* place of work, and *Ours* to worship. *(Sunday, September 13, 2015 at 10:07 A.M. CDT)*

~~~

SINGLE-MINDEDNESS
From my heart to yours

"*I have but one passion: It is He; it is He alone.*" - Count Zinzendorf

He was the man who, in his own words, had "a trusting relationship with Jesus Christ for nearly 40 years." He was the man whose ships carried the missionaries of God throughout the world during the 100-year Moravian revival of the 1700s. His passion was one: Jesus Christ alone. *(Monday, September 14, 2015 at 1:21 A.M. CDT)*

"*There is no Christianity without Community, the community of those who are passionate about Jesus Christ, and Him alone.*" - Count Zinzendorf *(Monday, September 14, 2015 at 1:32 A.M. CDT)*

"*Missions is simply this: Every heart for Christ is a missionary, every heart without Christ is a mission field.*" - Count Zinzendorf *(Monday, September 14, 2015 at 1:33 A.M. CDT)*

Count Zinzendorf wrote these words in his diary: "*I commune with the Friend of my heart, the ever present Savior, daily ... I am spending a whole hour from six to seven in the morning, as well as in the evening from eight to nine, in prayer*." Here's an example of someone passionate for Jesus Christ. What is your heart passionate for? *(Monday, September 14, 2015 at 2:21 A.M. CDT)*

~~~

SPIRIT-MINDEDNESS
From my heart to yours

There is nothing dry and formal in the fire from the Holy Spirit and the passion for Jesus Christ and His Gospel for a lost world. *(Monday, September 14, 2015 at 2:07 A.M. CDT)*

DUNGEONS UNLIMITED
From my heart to yours

The world may be as dark as a dungeon, as dead as a doornail, and as dry as a bone. But give the Holy Spirit a chance, and darkness will turn to light, deadness turns into life, and dryness turns into a fountain of living water. Praying that the Spirit of the Living God may breathe over the churches of the Middle East and the people of God. Will you join me?! *(Monday, September 14, 2015 at 2:14 A.M. CDT)*

~~~

GIDEON'S 300
From my heart to yours

The Moravian Revival that started in today's Germany and spread throughout the world for 100 years. Fifty years after that, William Carey, the missionary to India (b. 17 August 1761 – d. 9 June 1834), laid the report about the Moravians in front of the church in England and said these historical words: "See what the Moravians have done! Cannot we follow their example and in obedience to our Heavenly Father go out into the world and preach the Gospel to the heathens?" About the small Moravian church, the well-known German historian, Gustav Warneck, (1834-1919), wrote: "This small church in twenty years called into being more missions than the whole Evangelical Church has done in two centuries." That's called the Power of the Outpouring of the Holy Spirit. That's the "Power of God unto Salvation." That's, in summary, the Power of the Gospel of our Lord and Savior Jesus Christ. *(Tuesday, September 15, 2015 at 4:54 A.M. CDT)*